EU COMPETENCE AND POWER

This innovative book identifies and explains the concepts that determine whether the EU may act.

'Competence' is about more than competence alone: there is also power. Competence is the field in which the EU may act; power is the EU institutions' actual authorisation to act in a field of EU competence. Through a rigorous examination of legal disputes that involve the EU treaties, legislation, case law and archival evidence, this book illustrates how competence and power differ and why recognising this distinction leads to a more nuanced and precise analysis of whether the EU may act. This will be of interest to EU law scholars and practitioners, as well as international law specialists.

Volume 140 in the Series Modern Studies in European Law

Modern Studies in European Law

Recent titles in this series:

The European Convention on Human Rights and Private Law: Comparative Perspectives from South-Eastern Europe
Edited by Mateja Durovic and Cristina Poncibò

Judging Composite Decision-Making: The Transformation of European Administrative Law
Filipe Brito Bastos

EU Diplomacy in Multilateral Fora
Edited by Christine Kaddous and Frank Hoffmeister

The Market Citizenship Illusion: Free Movement Rights for Atypical Workers
Alice Welsh

Actors and Roles in EU Disability Law
Edited by Delia Ferri and Eva S Krolla

The Impact of War (in Ukraine) on the EU
Edited by Inge Govaere, Sacha Garben and Eleanor Spaventa

The European Judiciary: A Community of Law and a Community of Judges
Edited by Alejandro Saiz Arnaiz and Joan Solanes Mullor

Dissensus over Liberal Democracy: Insights from European Judges
Edited by Ramona Coman, Viktor Kazai, Leonardo Puleo and Andrew Bradley

Structural Principles of EU Law
Marcus Klamert

Environmental NGOs and Access to Justice before the CJEU
Mario Pagano

Dealing with Rule of Law Crises in the European Union: Challenges from a Comparative Federalism Perspective
Niels F Kirst

EU Citizenship and Responsibility: The Evolving Roles of the Union, the Individual, and the Member States
Maria Haag

EU Cities Facilitating the Commons: Building Blocks of European Constitutional Law for Local Democracy
Chiara Salati

EU Competence and Power
Hannah Bogaert

For the complete list of titles in this series see www.bloomsbury.com/uk/series/modern-studies-in-european-law/

EU Competence and Power

Hannah Bogaert

•HART•
OXFORD • LONDON • NEW YORK • NEW DELHI • SYDNEY

HART PUBLISHING

Bloomsbury Publishing Plc

Kemp House, Chawley Park, Cumnor Hill, Oxford, OX2 9PH, UK

1385 Broadway, New York, NY 10018, USA

Bloomsbury Publishing Ireland Limited, 29 Earlsfort Terrace, Dublin 2, D02 AY28, Ireland

HART PUBLISHING, the Hart/Stag logo, BLOOMSBURY and the Diana logo are trademarks of Bloomsbury Publishing Plc

First published in Great Britain 2026

A catalogue record for this book is available from the British Library.

A catalogue record for this book is available from the Library of Congress.

ISBN: HB: 978-1-50999-090-0
ePDF: 978-1-50999-092-4
ePub: 978-1-50999-091-7

Typeset by Compuscript Ltd, Shannon

For product safety related questions contact productsafety@bloomsbury.com

To find out more about our authors and books visit www.hartpublishing.co.uk. Here you will find extracts, author information, details of forthcoming events and the option to sign up for our newsletters.

ACKNOWLEDGEMENTS

This book is based on my doctoral thesis. I am especially grateful to my wonderful supervisor at Oxford, Professor Liz Fisher, for her enthusiastic guidance and encouragement.

Professors Stefan Enchelmaier and Ulla Neergaard examined the thesis and provided invaluable feedback on how to turn it into a book. Sinead Moloney, Verity Stuart, Alan O'Dowd, Sasha Jawed, and the team at Hart Publishing made the publication process a pleasure. Their constructive comments and confidence in the project were a great help. Many thanks as well to my colleagues at Freshfields for supporting the book project and for sharing my excitement about EU ('competence') law, and especially to the partners and HR team who gave me time to write.

My thanks also go to all other persons, whether individually mentioned in these acknowledgements or not, who supported me during my legal studies and in writing this book. They include Professor Inge Govaere, who introduced me to EU law, and Professor Steve Weatherill, who inspired me to think about 'competence'. I was very lucky to also have Professors Paul Craig and Alison Young as EU law tutors. Professors Dirk Heirbaut and Frederik Dhondt motivated me to write a doctoral thesis. Rita Liudvinaviciute, Andreas Norberg, Michael Moore, and Eva Karlsson of the Council Legal Service first showed me EU law in practice. I am also grateful to the Oxford EU Law Discussion Group and, of course, to my friends Ekati, Liana, and the Gent group.

The doctorate and the book would not have been possible without access to legal resources. The librarians at the Bodleian Law Library and the Hertford College Library were always incredibly helpful. The team at the Library of the Max Planck Institute for Comparative Public Law and International Law in Heidelberg kindly welcomed me as a visitor. The transparency units of the Commission, the Parliament, and (especially) the Council dealt with regular access-to-documents requests and unveiled documents that made the research much more interesting.

Finally, a big thank you to my parents, my brothers, and to Piotr.

Hannah Bogaert
November 2025

TABLE OF CONTENTS

PART 2
DESCRIPTIVE

PART 3
EVALUATIVE

TABLE OF ABBREVIATIONS

<u>Union and Community Treaties</u>

TECSC	Treaty establishing the European Coal and Steel Community [1956]
TEEC	Treaty establishing the European Economic Community [1957]
SEA	Single European Act [1986] OJ L169
TEC (Maastricht)	Treaty establishing the European Community [1992] OJ C224
TEC (Amsterdam)	Treaty establishing the European Community [1997] OJ C340
TEC (Nice)	Treaty establishing the European Community [2002] OJ C325
TEU (Maastricht)	Treaty on European Union [1992] OJ C191
TEU (Amsterdam)	Treaty on European Union [1997] OJ C340
TEU (Nice)	Treaty on European Union [2002] OJ C325
TEU (Lisbon)	Treaty on European Union [2012] OJ C326
TFEU	Treaty on the Functioning of the European Union [2012] OJ C326
Charter	Charter of Fundamental Rights of the European Union [2012] OJ C326

<u>Union and Community Entities</u>

CFI	Court of First Instance
CJEU	Court of Justice of the European Union
ECB	European Central Bank
ECJ	European Court of Justice
EC	European Community
ECSC	European Coal and Steel Community

EEC	European Economic Community
EU	European Union

Other Union and Community abbreviations

CAP	Common agricultural policy
CCP	Common commercial policy
CFSP	Common foreign and security policy
EAP	Environmental Action Plan
ECI	European Citizens' Initiative
EPC	European political co-operation
JHA	Justice and home affairs
PSPP	Public sector (asset) purchase programme
SSM	Single Supervisory Mechanism

Member State Abbreviations

Benelux	Belgium, the Netherlands, and Luxembourg
BverfG	Bundesverfassungsgericht

International Abbreviations

ECHR	Convention for the Protection of Human Rights and Fundamental Freedoms
GATS	General Agreement on Trade in Services
GATT	General Agreement on Tariffs and Trade
ICJ	International Court of Justice
ILO	International Labour Organization
PCIJ	Permanent Court of International Justice
TRIPS	Agreement on Trade-Related Aspects of Intellectual Property Rights
UN	United Nations
US, United States	United States of America
WTO	World Trade Organization

TABLE OF CASES

ECSC, E(E)C, and EU

Judgments and Opinions of the Court of Justice

Judgments of the Court of First Instance and General Court

Advocate General Opinions

International

National

Germany

France

United States

Applications and submissions

EC and EU

Germany

TABLE OF TREATIES AND LEGAL ACTS

ECSC, E(E)C, and EU Laws

Founding Treaties

Regulations

Directives

Decisions

European Conventions

Member State laws

International laws

TABLE OF PREPARATORY DOCUMENTS AND NON-BINDING ACTS

Treaties

Paris

Rome

Single European Act

Maastricht

Amsterdam

Lisbon

Legal acts

Commission

Council

Parliament

European Economic and Social Committee

Other

High Authority

Commission

Council (and Member States)

Parliament

Court

Introduction

'It is essential that the language of the law awakens the same ideas in all men.'[1] Yet in the European Union, a common conceptual understanding of 'competence' does not yet exist. There is no doubt that the EU may only act if, and insofar as, its Member States have authorised it to do so in the Treaties. The principle of conferral constitutes a foundational stone of the EU legal order. It always applied in Community and Union law and is now written down in Articles 5 and 13 TEU.[2] But the meaning of 'competence' itself remains obscure.

Legal scholars tend to direct their focus elsewhere. They explain how the Treaties classify the EU's competences into different categories. They provide detailed discussions on specific Treaty articles. They conduct in-depth analyses of the lawfulness of specific EU acts. They raise concerns that the Union quietly and progressively expands its sphere of action. But they do not present a consistent and shared conceptual understanding of 'competence'. Neither do the EU's institutions. A paradox thus presents itself: 'competence' is crucial, but it does not yet awaken the same ideas in all actors.

PSPP and the Importance of 'Competence' Clarity

A recent legal dispute illustrates why this should change. In the *PSPP* ruling, Germany's Federal Constitutional Court openly set aside a judgment of the Court of Justice of the European Union (CJEU) and replaced it with its own assessment.[3] The dispute at issue concerned the European Central Bank (ECB)'s PSPP government bond-buying programme.[4] In a preliminary reference procedure, the CJEU confirmed that the programme fell within the Union's exclusive monetary policy competence and rejected claims that it violated the principle of proportionality.[5] The Court concluded that the preliminary ruling had 'disclosed no factor of such a kind as to affect the validity' of the decision concerned.[6]

The Constitutional Court disagreed. It found the EU judges' reasoning 'simply not comprehensible', because it diverged without justification from the usual

[1] After Montesquieu, *De l'Esprit des Lois* (Librairie de Firmin Didot, 1862) 490 ('Il est essentiel que les paroles des lois réveillent chez tous les hommes les mêmes idées').
[2] Articles 5(2) and 13(2) TEU (Lisbon).
[3] Cases 2 BvR 859/15 ea [2020] BVerfG.
[4] PSPP stands for public sector (asset) purchase programme.
[5] Case C-493/17 *Weiss and Others* [2018] ECLI:EU:C:2018:1000, paras 70 and 100.
[6] ibid, operative part.

standard of competence review.[7] The EU Court's judgment in *Weiss* was thus 'ultra vires' and the German judges refused to be bound by it.[8] More substantially, they disagreed in several points with the competence and proportionality tests applied by the CJEU. First, the Constitutional Court accused the Court of simply endorsing the ECB's statement of its monetary objectives without paying due regard to the programme's economic effects. Second, it dismissed the CJEU's proportionality test as insufficient, on the ground that it did not include a balance of the programme's monetary benefits with – again – its economic effects.

The impact of the Constitutional Court's own assessment could have been grave. Unless the German Federal Government and Bundestag ensured that the ECB demonstrated the proportionality of its government bond-buying programme, the German Central Bank was prohibited from participating in its implementation.[9] Ultimately, however, that condition was fulfilled.[10]

Much can be said about the Constitutional Court's reasoning. It mentioned the importance of judicial co-operation and mutual respect.[11] Yet it refused to submit a second preliminary reference.[12] It criticised the CJEU for applying an incomplete proportionality test. Yet its own test departed from the EU standard for cases which do not involve fundamental rights or freedoms.[13] It rejected the CJEU's reasoning as 'simply not comprehensible' and methodologically flawed.[14] Yet its own reasoning was inconsistent insofar as it included only economic disadvantages and not advantages in the balancing test.[15] It identified a 'notion that a generous interpretation of the specific competence conferred may, to a certain extent, be compensated by a sound proportionality assessment' in the CJEU's reasoning.[16] Yet the latter did not suggest such a connection.[17]

There was, of course, also the fundamental problem that the Constitutional Court infringed the EU principle of supremacy.[18] It is for the CJEU, and not a national court, to rule on the legality of EU acts. The EU Court's exceptional press statement following the German ruling reminded why. All Member State

[7] Cases 2 BvR 859/15 ea [2020] BVerfG, paras 116, 154, and 163.

[8] ibid, paras 116 and 118.

[9] S Egidy, 'Proportionality and procedure of monetary policy-making' (2021) 19 *International Journal of Constitutional Law* 285, 286.

[10] Fraktionen CDU/CSU, SPD, FDP und BÜNDNIS 90/DIE GRÜNEN, Antrag – 'Urteil des Bundesverfassungsgerichts zum Anleihekaufprogramm PSPP der Europäischen Zentralbank' (2020) BT 19/20621.

[11] Cases 2 BvR 859/15 ea [2020] BVerfG, para 111.

[12] D Sarmiento and JHH Weiler, 'The EU Judiciary After Weiss: Proposing A New Mixed Chamber of the Court of Justice' (Verfassungsblog 2020) verfassungsblog.de/the-eu-judiciary-after-weiss/.

[13] P Eleftheriadis, 'Germany's Failing Court' (Verfassungsblog, 2020) verfassungsblog.de/germanys-failing-court/.

[14] Cases 2 BvR 859/15 ea [2020] BVerfG, paras 116 and 118.

[15] M Maduro, 'Some Preliminary Remarks on the PSPP Decision of the German Constitutional Court' (*Verfassungsblog*, 2020) verfassungsblog.de/some-preliminary-remarks-on-the-pspp-decision-of-the-german-constitutional-court/.

[16] Cases 2 BvR 859/15 ea [2020] BVerfG, para 128.

[17] M Kottmann and R Sangi, 'Gut gemeint, nicht gut gemacht' (*Verfassungsblog*, 2020) verfassungsblog.de/gut-gemeint-nicht-gut-gemacht/.

[18] Case 6/64 *Costa v E.N.E.L* [1964] ECR-00585 ECLI:EU:C:1964:66, 593.

authorities, including national courts, must ensure the full effect of EU law. 'That is the only way of ensuring the equality of Member States in the Union they created.'[19] By setting aside a CJEU judgment, the Constitutional Court committed a serious violation of EU law.

Yet it would be wrong to dismiss the Constitutional Court's judgment altogether. Central in its analysis stands the principle of conferral.[20] The EU may only act if the Member States have authorised it to do so in the Treaties. But these Member States may not decide whether the Union observes the limits of the authorisation. The CJEU adjudicates on the legality of EU acts, and national courts must respect its rulings. This requires trust. It also requires clear and precise legal reasoning. In the German judges' view, this requirement was not met.

That the concrete standards imposed by the Constitutional Court appear unsound misses the point. The judges were right about the importance of clear and precise legal reasoning as such. While certainly not flawless, EU judgments tend to be well thought through.[21] There is, however, room for improvement. Especially for competence, the Court's approach is not yet always as '*calculable*' and transparent as it should be.[22] Indeed, *Tobacco Advertising I* confirmed that 'competence' has limits,[23] and it is settled case law that the choice of legal basis 'must rest on objective factors', including 'the aim and the content of the measure'.[24] But this remains rather vague. It also ignores the Treaties' conceptual nuances. More guidance on the meaning of 'competence' is desirable.

Rediscovering the Concepts of 'Competence'

The good news is that there is no legal vacuum here. What is generally referred to as 'competence', today, is only part of the story. Two main concepts exist, and both matter. The Treaties mention competence, but also power. Competence tells us in what fields the Union may act. These fields cover a certain subject matter and a certain range of objectives. Acting within a given subject matter and a given range of objectives means acting within a field of competence.

Competence does not actually authorise the Union to act. To act, it needs power. Constantinesco drew the attention to the distinction between competence

[19] CJEU, 58/20, Press release following the judgment of the German Constitutional Court of 5 May 2020.

[20] The Constitutional Court's discussion of proportionality itself goes beyond the scope of this book.

[21] K Lenaerts, 'How the ECJ Thinks: A Study on Judicial Legitimacy' (2013) 36 *Fordham International Law Journal* 1302, 1351. For a more critical approach, see, eg G Conway, *The Limits of Legal Reasoning and the European Court of Justice* (CUP, 2012).

[22] 'Calculable' after J Waldron, 'The Rule of Law and the Importance of Procedure' in JE Fleming (ed), *Getting to the Rule of Law* (NYU Press, 2011) 4.

[23] Case C-376/98 *Germany v Parliament and Council* [2000] ECR I-08419 ECLI:EU:C:2000:544.

[24] See, eg Case 45/86 *Commission v Council* [1987] ECR-01493 ECLI:EU:C:1987:163, para 11 and Case C-157/21 *Poland v Parliament and Council* [2022] ECLI:EU:C:2022:98, 121.

and power, in his 1974 doctoral thesis.[25] He elegantly noted: 'Competence without power is ineffective' – 'Power without competence is unlawful'.[26] Power is conferred upon specific EU institutions. Within a certain field of competence, it determines which institution may adopt, by which procedure, which type of legal act with which kind of content, to pursue the objective(s) of that competence. These, in summary, are the concepts of 'competence'.

At this point, a terminological point should be stressed. 'Competence' is generally used to designate the Union's authority to act. In this book, it has a narrower meaning. It is the field in which the Union may act by exercising power. Using the same term for distinct meanings would cause confusion. For that reason, this book uses quotation marks for 'competence' in the wide, generally used, sense. Competence without quotation marks is used for the narrower-field sense.

Admittedly, the distinction between competence and power is currently not perfect. The EU Treaties use both concepts, but do not explain or define them. Moreover, they do not apply the distinction consistently.[27] Neither do the EU institutions and the Member States. Chapter two of this book explains this in more detail. These inconsistencies explain why many legal scholars prefer to treat competence and power as synonymous.[28]

Nonetheless, distinguishing between competence and power has clear merits. First, it introduces a clear, shared conceptual language that facilitates the important dialogue on what the EU may do. Montesquieu emphasised the importance of a common understanding of legal language.[29] Yet the concepts of 'competence' remain obscure today. Second, it contributes to a more precise and nuanced legal analysis. 'Competence' is a rather vague notion. It ignores the wide range of reasons why the principle of conferral may be infringed. The competence–power distinction explicitly recognises these nuances. It makes it possible to analyse with greater nuance and precision whether a certain measure may be adopted, how, and by whom.

Scholarly Context and Approach

Constantinesco famously described the distinct concepts of competence and power in his 1974 doctoral thesis.[30] Fifty years later, legal scholars tend to use

[25] V Constantinesco, 'Compétences et pouvoirs dans les communautés européennes' (Doctoral thesis, Université de Nancy 1974) 82–83.

[26] ibid, 83.

[27] See, eg the contrast between Articles 5(2), 13(2), and 40 TEU (Lisbon), on the one hand (consistent), and Articles 14 and 19 TFEU and Article 51 of the Charter, on the other hand (inconsistent).

[28] See, eg A von Bogdandy and J Bast, 'The Federal Order of Competences' in A von Bogdandy and J Bast (eds), *Principles of European Constitutional Law* (Hart Publishing, 2010) 278; P Craig and G De Búrca, *EU Law: Text, Cases and Materials* (OUP, 2008) 82; T Tridimas and P Eeckhout, 'The External Competence of the Community and the Case-Law of the Court of Justice: Principle versus Pragmatism' (1994) 14 *Yearbook of European Law* 143, 144.

[29] Montesquieu (n 1), 490.

[30] Constantinesco (n 25), 82–83.

competence and power interchangeably. Of course, the literature reflects that 'competence' encompasses both the fields in which the EU may act and the concrete action it may take within these fields. Schütze, for instance, writes about three aspects of 'legal power': competence as the material field in which the EU may legislate, the instruments adopted by specific EU institutions within that field, and the procedures to adopt them.[31] Similarly, von Bogdandy and Bast identify 'horizontal' and 'vertical' competences.[32] The former reflect the fields of EU versus Member State action; the latter tell us which institutions may act and how. And a range of works specifically focus on the categories of EU competence,[33] on specific competences,[34] or on questions of power within them.[35] However, the conceptual distinction between competence and power itself is rarely explicitly addressed.

There are exceptions.[36] Gil Ibáñez distinguishes between competence and power to more accurately identify how the Commission and national administrative authorities supervise and enforce EU law.[37] To illustrate the distinction's relevance, he points out that Article 235 TEC's flexibility clause as interpreted by Opinion 2/94 granted powers, but not competence.[38] Lenaerts and van Ypersele use the distinction to clarify that the EU (institutions) may only exercise power in a field of non-exclusive EU competence if the principle of subsidiarity allows it.[39] Craig finds a 'meaningful difference' between competence and power in the context of the simplified Treaty revision procedure.[40] These scholars distinguish

[31] R Schütze, *European Constitutional Law* (OUP, 2021) 229; R Schütze, 'The European Community's Federal Order of Competences: A Retrospective Analysis' in M Dougan and S Currie (eds), *50 Years of the European Treaties: Looking Back and Thinking Forward* (Hart Publishing, 2009) 65–70.

[32] A von Bogdandy and J Bast, 'The European Union's vertical order of competences: the current law and proposals for its reform' (2002) 39 *Common Market Law Review* 227, 235–36. See also I Hartel, 'Die Zuständigkeiten der Union' in M Niedobitek (ed), *Europarecht Europarecht – Grundlagen und Politiken der Union* (De Gruyter Brill, 2020) 450.

[33] See, eg T Konstadinides, 'The Competences of the Union' in R Schütze and T Tridimas (eds), *Oxford Principles Of European Union Law: The European Union Legal Order: Volume I* (OUP, 2018) 191–220.

[34] See, eg pt II in S Garben and I Govaere (eds), *The Division of Competences between the EU and the Member States: Reflections on the Past, the Present and the Future* (Hart Publishing, 2017).

[35] See, eg C Ecke, P Leino-Sandberg, and AW Ghavanini (eds), *The Dynamics of Powers in the European Union* (Hart Publishing, 2024).

[36] For other examples than those mentioned in this paragraph, see eg O Beaud, 'The Allocation of Competences in a Federation – A General Introduction' in L Azoulai, *The Question of Competence in the European Union* (OUP, 2014) 36; NA Neuwahl, 'Joint Participation in International Treaties and the Exercise of Power by the EEC and its Member States: Mixed Agreements' (1991) 28 *Common Market Law Review* 717, 718. In an international law context, see P Klein, 'Les Compétences et Pouvoirs de l'Organisation Internationale' in E Lagrange and J-M Sorel (eds), *Droit des Organisations Internationales* (LGDJ, 2013) 715–16.

[37] A Gil Ibáñez, *The Administrative Supervision and Enforcement of EC Law: Powers, Procedures and Limits* (Hart Publishing, 1999) 45–70.

[38] ibid, 51; Opinion 2/94 *Adhésion de la Communauté à la CEDH* [1996] ECR I-01759 ECLI:EU:C:1996:140.

[39] K Lenaerts and P van Ypersele, 'Le principe de subsidiarite et son contexte: étude de l'article 3b du traité CE' (1994) 1–2 *Cahiers de Droit Européen* 3, 11–13.

[40] P Craig, 'The European Union Act 2011: Locks, Limits and Legality' (2011) 48 *Common Market Law Review* 1915, 1925. See also Ch 2.

between competence and power precisely because the distinction brings nuance and precision.

This book follows their example. But rather than using the distinction between competence and power as an aspect of the broader analysis, it makes that distinction the central topic. In doing so, it also offers a more constructive 'competence' narrative. Today, a recurrent theme in the 'competence' literature is the notion of 'competence creep'.[41] It raises concerns that the Union quietly and progressively expands its sphere of action outside the boundaries set in the Treaties. Underlying these concerns seems to be an assumption that there is no detailed set of legal rules behind EU 'competence'; 'competence' can expand by stealth, because it lacks clear boundaries. This book is different. It argues that EU 'competence' does not lack legal detail. The problem is that the conceptual framework that ensures such detail has been forgotten.

In that context, it should be emphasised that this book does not aim to add new conceptual nuance to the Union's existing system of 'competence'. It rather aims to show that those nuances already exist in the system as it is. What is competence and what is power does not follow from legal theory, but from a careful reading of the Treaties, the legislation, and the case law of the EU Courts interpreting them. To reflect this, the book rediscovers the concepts of 'competence' through a selection of legal disputes. Each legal dispute offers a concrete example of a real 'competence' question.

The analysis is not limited to the final texts alone. It is also the result of extensive archive work. The preparatory documents of the Treaties and Community and Union legislation reveal that real legal conversations on 'competence' took place between the institutions and between the drafters of the Treaties. They show the foundations of the concepts of 'competence'. Analysing these preparatory documents was thus an important element of this book. Often, a search in the Commission, Parliament, and Council's electronic archives sufficed to obtain them. However, the electronic archives are not complete. Visits to the physical Commission and Council archives, and a long list of access-to-documents requests, led to files which were not yet included in the online databases or publicly available.

In addition to some of the more recent legal disputes, this book also addresses some of the oldest and most well-known. Since most exceptions to access to EU documents may only apply for 30 years, the richest archival material was available for these older legal disputes.[42] Revisiting them is also important. It shows that the

[41] See, eg S Garben, 'Restating the Problem of Competence Creep, Tackling Harmonisation by Stealth and Reinstating the Legislator' in S Garben and I Govaere (eds) (n 34) 300; S Weatherill, 'The Competence Catalogue in the Treaty Establishing a Constitution and the Treaty of Lisbon: Improvement, but at a Cost' in NW Barber, M Cahill, and R Ekins (eds), *The Rise and Fall of the European Constitution* (Hart Publishing, 2019) 109.

[42] Regulation (EC) No 1049/2001 of the European Parliament and of the Council of 30 May 2001 regarding public access to European Parliament, Council and Commission documents, OJ L145.

concepts of 'competence' always existed in Community and Union law. Moreover, by retelling classic legal disputes through the lens of the concepts of 'competence', these classic legal disputes gain clarity. This illustrates why the concepts of 'competence' matter.

There is also a more fundamental point. This book does not only aim to show that the EU system of 'competence' includes significant conceptual nuance. It also aims to show that a system of 'competence' always existed under Community and Union law. Even long before the principle of conferral of competence entered the Treaties, the different European Communities were based on legal rules and principles. This included the principle of conferral. From the start of the European project, 'competence' mattered. By revisiting historical legal disputes, this book remembers that important fact.

Structure of the Book

The analysis begins with a prologue. With a single chapter (chapter one), Part 1 returns to the European Coal and Steel Community (ECSC). Whether the EU may act can only be properly understood when competence is distinguished from power. But this distinction and its importance only fully become clear through an analysis of concrete case studies. Where to start is thus a delicate question. The prologue seeks to lessen the confusion with a view of the past. Studying the ECSC does not only show that questions of 'competence' always existed in Union and Community law. It also provides an opportunity to illustrate the competence–power distinction before embarking on the real journey.

Part 2 is descriptive. It consists of a short overview chapter and three main chapters. The short overview chapter (chapter two) sets out the concepts of 'competence'. The two main chapters explain, respectively, competence and power. The first of these chapters (chapter three) covers competence. Competence relates to the fields in which the Union may act. It has a subject matter and an objectives dimension. Through a set of real legal disputes which raise competence issues in the fields of the internal market, the common commercial policy (CCP), and the EU budget, this chapter clarifies each dimension. A set of proposals on the free movement of non-economically active persons (subject matter), and the *Tobacco Advertising* saga (objectives), illustrate the internal market competence's dimensions.[43] *Opinion 1/94* on trade in services (subject matter) and *Chernobyl*,

[43] See in particular Commission, Proposal for a Council Directive on a right of residence for nationals of Member States in the territory of another Member State COM(79)215; and Directive 98/43/EC of the European Parliament and of the Council of 6 July 1998 on the approximation of the laws, regulations and administrative provisions of the Member States relating to the advertising and sponsorship of tobacco products, OJ L213.

Opinion 2/100, and *Commission v Council*, on health and environmental objectives, do the same for the CCP.[44]

Once a competence exists, the question of power arises. That is the focus of the next chapter (chapter four). Power is the actual authorisation to act. It is granted to specific EU institutions. Power tells us which institutions, through which voting majorities, may adopt which types of legal acts entailing which instruments, to pursue a certain competence objective. This chapter explains these power dimensions and modalities. Again, it uses legal disputes in the fields of the CCP and the internal market. The Union trade mark, Community design, and unitary patent illustrate power's instruments dimension.[45] The creation of an EU-wide intellectual property right contrasted with the harmonisation of national intellectual property rights. In passing, these legal disputes also explain the power dimension of the type of legal act and the power modality of the voting majority. *Geneva Act* also addresses the power modality of which institution(s) may act.[46] In this legal dispute, the Council had amended a Commission proposal so significantly that it violated the Commission's power of initiative. Thus, Part 2 describes the concepts of 'competence'.

Part 3 applies a different approach; it is evaluative. After the concepts' description, it is time to set out their benefits. To do so, the two chapters of this part analyse two recent legal disputes. In these legal disputes, the 'competence' debates fail to convince. This part argues that the distinction between competence, power, and their respective dimensions (and modalities) would contribute to a better result.

The first chapter (chapter five) addresses a recent amendment to the Posted Workers Directive.[47] This Directive was adopted as an internal market measure, under the internal market competence. More specifically, the EU legislator invoked a free-movement-of-services rationale for its adoption. Yet whether the Posted Workers Directive actually promotes the internal market seems questionable. Even more questionable are the Court's reasons to uphold it.[48] In its identification of the Directive's objectives, it conflated the Treaty's horizontal objectives with those of the internal market competence itself. In other words, the CJEU erred in its analysis of competence's objectives dimension.

[44] Opinion 1/94 *Accords annexés à l'accord OMC* [1994] ECR I-5267 ECLI:EU:C:1994:384; Case C-62/88 *Greece v Council* [1990] ECR I-01527 ECLI:EU:C:1990:153; Opinion 2/00 *Protocole de Cartagena sur la prévention des risques biotechnologiques* [2001] ECR I-09713 ECLI:EU:C:2001:664; Case C-94/03 *Commission v Council* [2006] ECR I-00001 ECLI:EU:C:2006:2.

[45] Council Regulation (EC) No 40/94 of 20 December 1993 on the Community trade mark, OJ L11; Council Regulation (EC) No 6/2002 of 12 December 2001 on Community designs, OJ L3; Regulation (EU) No 1257/2012 of the European Parliament and of the Council of 17 December 2012 implementing enhanced cooperation in the area of the creation of unitary patent protection, OJ L361.

[46] Judgment in Case C-24/20, *Commission v Council* [2022] ECR ECLI:EU:C:2022:911.

[47] Directive (EU) 2018/957 of the European Parliament and of the Council of 28 June 2018 amending Directive 96/71/EC concerning the posting of workers in the framework of the provision of services, OJ L173.

[48] Case C-620/18 *Hungary v Council and Parliament* [2020] ECLI:EU:C:2020:1001; Case C-626/18 *Poland v Council and Parliament* [2020] ECLI:EU:C:2020:1000.

The second evaluative chapter (chapter six) explores the Commission's recent proposal to ban the import of Russian gas.[49] The ban would be based on the CCP's Article 207 TFEU.[50] However, the Council may also impose import bans in the context of the common foreign and security policy (CFSP). The CFSP route requires Council unanimity; Article 207 does not. To avoid suspicions that the Commission suggested a legal basis based on pragmatic rather than legal grounds, a solid 'competence' analysis is crucial. Yet the Commission failed to properly justify its choice. This chapter points out the flaws in the Commission's reasoning and uses the concepts of 'competence' to show that (with some caveats) Article 207 indeed applies.

The final part, Part 4, brings a note of optimism. It consists of one chapter (chapter seven). As the two chapters of Part 3 demonstrated, the EU institutions do not always apply a satisfactory 'competence' analysis. This Part shows that they, and the drafters of the Treaties, are also capable of improving their 'competence' approach. It discusses the evolution of the flexibility clause and its interpretation, between the Treaties of Rome and Lisbon. Originally, the EEC institutions invoked or confirmed Article 235 as a legal basis without adequate motivation or delimitation. After Maastricht, much changed. The flexibility clause's scope gained precision and the institutions' reasoning improved. The evolution from Article 235 TEEC to Article 352 TFEU is thus an encouraging one. And that is important. The German Constitutional Court illustrated the need for a more nuanced and precise 'competence' reasoning. The final chapter of this book shows that the aspiration is not unrealistic.

Thus, 'competence' is about more than competence alone. Recognising the existence of a wider range of concepts contributes to a more nuanced and precise legal analysis. In a system based on conferral, that is crucial. EU institutions, national entities, and the public in general must be able to apprehend when and how the Union may act. So far, the distinction between competence and power has remained rather implicit. Explicitly addressing this could accommodate at least part of the concerns of the German Constitutional Court. Benefits would also follow at a larger scale. It is time to rediscover the concepts of 'competence'.

[49] Commission, Proposal for a Regulation on phasing out Russian natural gas imports, improving monitoring of potential energy dependencies and amending Regulation (EU) 2017/1938, COM(2025)828 final/2.

[50] To the extent that it concerns the import ban. Other aspects of the proposal would be based on Article 194 instead.

PART 1

Prologue

This book starts with a prologue. It returns to the European Coal and Steel Community. It is essential to remember that the ECSC was founded on a desire for peace. But it is paramount to remember not only that. Perhaps the greatest strength of the Coal and Steel Community was that it pursued its values in a legal system of conferred 'competence'. Questions of competence and power did not emerge over time. From the start of the European project, they occupied the minds of the drafters of the Treaty, as well as the institutions and academics. The following prologue remembers the issues they reflected upon.

1

Coal, Steel, and 'Competence'

Few European Coal and Steel Community actions were more visible in the streets of Europe than the millions invested in the construction of workers' houses.[1] Suitable housing close to the workplace attracted workers. Avoiding uncomfortable and tiring commutes increased their performance.[2] Undoubtedly, the 'European Villages' contributed to productivity and economic expansion.[3] That the ECSC sponsored these housing projects was, therefore, not surprising. But the legal basis it took recourse to might have been.

The ECSC Treaty provision on financing and investment required a direct and primary contribution to increased coal and steel productivity.[4] Not all commentators identified such a contribution in the financing of workers' houses.[5] Perhaps the European Villages required a different foundation. Whether they were built upon the ECSC Treaty,[6] or upon a social desire unfit to justify a departure from that Treaty, has lost much of its importance today. That this question arose, however, is all the more relevant.

This prologue returns to the beginnings of the European project. In 1951, representatives of six European states signed the Paris Treaty that established the European Coal and Steel Community. The ECSC significantly differed from the current European Union.[7] The Coal and Steel Community's sectoral integration became today's internal market. The Council and the Parliament replaced the High Authority as main decision-maker. A preliminary reference procedure opened the Court to all private parties. Despite these differences between the ECSC and the EU, however, the former's foundations remain relevant. Throughout Community

[1] R Poidevin and D Spierenburg, *The History of the High Authority of the European Coal and Steel Community* (Weidenfeld & Nicolson, 1994) 213, 323, 462, and 552; J Goormaghtigh, 'European Coal and Steel Community' (1955) 503 *International Conciliation* 343, 402.

[2] High Authority, The ECSC in the European Community (1961) 22.

[3] 'Launch of works for the building of a European village in Spiesen' (CVCE), www.cvce.eu/en/obj/launch_of_works_for_the_building_of_a_european_village_in_spiesen_1952-en-ab635d8c-ec6e-4028-9a61-f3f03f91a862.html.

[4] Article 54 TECSC.

[5] Opinion in Case 41/59 *Hamborner Bergbau AG and Others v High Authority* [1960] ECR-00989 ECLI:EU:C:1960:42, 530; C Vos, 'De sociale aspecten van de Europese Kolen- en Staalgemeenschap als juridisch vraagstuk' (1957) 4 *Nederlands Tijdschrift voor Internationaal Recht* 37, 37.

[6] Senaat/Sénat (BE), 1951–1952 84, 113.

[7] A Dashwood, 'The Relationship between the Member States and the European Union/European Community' (2004) 41 *Common Market Law Review* 355, 362; Service Juridique de la Haute Autorité, HAEC CEAB1 97, 6.

and Union history, not only did similarities exist between the Treaties, but the Court also continued to build upon them. The roots of Article 352 TFEU, for instance, lie in the ECSC's Article 95. And the *Meroni* doctrine influenced Union law long after the ECSC era.[8]

The ECSC's most important legacy for this book, however, is its legal approach to 'competence'. It is well known that the Maastricht Treaty introduced an explicit expression of the principle of conferral (of competence).[9] But the principle itself existed already in Community law. It applied even before its explicit inclusion in the Treaties. And its origins date back to the ECSC. The European Villages raised questions, because 'competence' always mattered.

Moreover, not only the principle of conferral, but also the distinction between competence and power, date back to the Coal and Steel era. Although the Paris Treaty did not address this distinction in detail, it did use competence and power in their respective senses. The exercise of '*pouvoirs*', '*Befugnisse*' or '*poteri*' contrasted with the field in which the ECSC enjoyed '*compétence*', '*Zuständigkeit*' or '*competenza*'.[10] The Court confirmed this logic in *Gezamenlijke Steenkoolmijnen*.[11] It distinguished between 'fields' of operation and 'means' for their application.[12] The distinction also emerged, to various extents, in the writings of scholars of that time.[13] Clearly, the origins of the concepts of 'competence' lie in the European Coal and Steel Community.

A search for origins is most effective without the wisdom of hindsight. This chapter, therefore, focuses on the ECSC as it was understood in its early days. The Treaty itself, early jurisprudence of the Court, and academic writings of that time constitute the main sources. Two further caveats apply. Much has been written about the exclusive or shared nature of ECSC competence.[14] There is no room or need to do so here. For the same reason, external powers are not touched upon unless this contributes to the internal analysis.

The chapter goes as follows: first, it introduces the ECSC, the principle of conferral, and the concepts of competence and power; second, it examines the

[8] Case 9/56 *Meroni v High Authority* [1958] ECR-00011 ECLI:EU:C:1958:7. For a recent application, see Case C-270/12 *United Kingdom v Parliament and Council* [2014] ECLI:EU:C:2014:18.

[9] Article 3b TEC (Maastricht).

[10] Article 71 TECSC; Article 2(3) Convention. The Dutch version does not differentiate (both '*compétence*' and '*pouvoir*' are referred to as '*bevoegdheid*'). The later English translation uses 'jurisdiction' rather than 'competence' for '*compétence*'.

[11] Case C-30/59 *De Gezamenlijke Steenkoolmijnen in Limburg v High Authority* [1961] ECR-00003 ECLI:EU:C:1961:2.

[12] ibid, para 23.

[13] P Reuter, *La Communauté européenne du charbon et de l'acier* (LGDJ, 1953) 230; R Kovar, *Le pouvoir réglementaire de la Communauté européenne du charbon et de l'acier* (LGDJ, 1964) 2; P Pescatore, *Le droit de l'intégration* (AW Sijthoff, 1972) 26.

[14] See, eg CF Ophüls, 'Staatshoheit und Gemeinschaftshoheit: Wandlungen des Souveränitätsbegriff' in CH Ule (ed), *Recht im Wandel: Beiträge zu Strömungen und Fragen im heutigen Recht: Festschrift hundertfünfzig Jahre Carl Heymanns* (Heymanns Verlag, 1965) 519; M Zuleeg, 'Les répartitions de compétences entre la Communauté et ses Etats membres' in Institut d'études juridiques européennes (ed), *La Communauté et ses Etats membres: Actes du sixième Colloque de l'IEJE sur les Communautés européennes* (Université de Liège, 1973) 27.

principle of conferral in theory. It contrasts the presence of an explicit principle of conferred power with the absence of an explicit principle of conferred competence. A third part turns to the practice of conferral. Through the flexibility clause, it examines what has been conferred upon the Coal and Steel Community. The final part returns to the European Villages.

I. Coal, Steel, and 'Competence'

Whether the European Union may act depends on its 'competence'. And 'competence' consists of competence and power. Competence relates to the field in which the Union may act. Power is the actual basis on which the Union, through its institutions, may act. Conferral means that EU competence and power only exist insofar as they are allocated to the Union by the Member States, in the Treaties. These concepts already existed in the ECSC. This section explains their meaning. It also introduces the ECSC.

A. Competence, Power, and Conferral

States are sovereign. In principle, they enjoy the inherent freedom to pursue all possible objectives in all possible fields.[15] The European Villages raised questions because the ECSC did not enjoy such freedom. The Coal and Steel Community was not a state.[16] It could only act if the Paris Treaty authorised it to do so.[17] This is the principle of conferral.

All ECSC action, therefore, needed an authorisation in the Treaty. Such authorisation took the form of competence and power. Competence is 'the material field within which an authority is entitled to exercise power'.[18] It designates a certain subject matter in which an authority may, subject to specific authorisation, act to

[15] P Gori, *Les clauses de sauvegarde des traités CECA et CEE* (UGA, 1967) 256; P Reuter, *Droit international public* (Presses universitaires de France, 1958) 229; MS Korowicz, 'Some present aspects of sovereignty in international law' (1961) 102 *Collected Courses of the Hague Academy of International Law* 3, 12; P Guggenheim, 'Les principes de droit international public' (1952) 80 *Collected Courses of the Hague Academy of International Law* 1, 98.

[16] R Schuman, 'Préface' in P Reuter, *La Communauté européenne du charbon et de l'acier* (n 13) 7.

[17] P De Visscher, 'La CECA et les Etats Membres' in Centro Italiano di Studi Giuridici (ed), *Actes officiels du Congrès International d'Etudes sur la Communauté Européenne du Charbon et de l'Acier II* (Giuffrè, 1957) 52; Kovar (n 13) 119; Rapport de la Délégation française sur le Traité instituant la CECA (1951), 22; P Pescatore, *L'ordre juridique des Communautés européennes – Etude des sources du droit communautaire* (Presses universitaires de Liège, 1975) 69; M Lagrange, 'La Cour de justice des Communautés européennes du plan Schuman à l'Union européenne' in PH Teitgen (ed), *Mélanges Fernand Dehousse: La construction européenne* (Nathan, 1979) 127.

[18] R Schütze, 'The European Community's Federal Order of Competences – A Retrospective Analysis' in M Dougan and S Currie (eds), *50 Years of the European Treaties: Looking Back and Thinking Forward* (Hart Publishing, 2009) 65.

pursue certain objectives.[19] This specific authorisation to act within a field of competence constitutes power.[20] Both concepts are indissociably linked. 'Competence without power is ineffective. Power without competence is unlawful.'[21] To function, the ECSC needed both.

B. The European Coal and Steel Community

Whether the ECSC could act, therefore, depended on the Paris Treaty. This Treaty introduced a Community founded upon a common market, common objectives, and common institutions.[22] A non-discriminatory common coal and steel market based on free movement and undistorted competition[23] was designed to further objectives such as increased productivity and better living standards.[24] The ECSC Treaty prohibited a number of practices and measures considered incompatible with that common coal and steel market. At the same time, it introduced rules to regulate that market. Competition was to be fair and undistorted, but not unregulated.[25]

The Paris Treaty regulated the common market in significant detail. It was a '*traité-loi*' rather than a '*traité-cadre*'.[26] A '*traité-cadre*' essentially provides a procedural framework for the adoption of material rules;[27] a '*traité-loi*' establishes such rules directly. In a general common market, prescribing the applicable rules in a single Treaty is not feasible. The ECSC, however, only covered coal and steel. This narrow scope enabled the Treaty to go beyond a framework for co-operation. Instead, it established a fairly complete set of rules for the functioning of the market.[28] To operate, it therefore needed little implementing legislation.[29]

[19] O Beaud, 'The Allocation of Competences in a Federation – A General Introduction' in L Azoulai (ed), *The Question of Competence in the European Union* (OUP, 2014) 36.

[20] K Lenaerts, *Le Juge et la Constitution aux Etats-Unis d'Amérique et dans l'ordre juridique européen* (Bruylant, 1988) 529.

[21] V Constantinesco, 'Compétences et pouvoirs dans les communautés européennes: Contribution à l'étude de la nature juridique des Communautés' (Doctoral thesis, Université de Nancy 1974) 83.

[22] Article 1 TECSC; M Kohnstamm, 'The European Coal and Steel Community' (1956) 90 *Collected Courses of the Hague Academy of International Law* 3, 26.

[23] Article 4 TECSC.

[24] Articles 2–3 TECSC.

[25] Reuter, *La Communauté européenne du charbon et de l'acier* (n 13) 142.

[26] P Reuter, *Organisations européennes* (Presses Universitaires de France, 1970) 188; A Tizzano, 'Art. 8' in R Quadri, R Monaco, and A Trabucchi (eds), *Trattato istitutivo della CECA: commentario* (Giuffrè, 1970) 150; M Lagrange, 'L'Europe institutionelle: Réflexions d'un témoin' (1971) 14 *Revue du marché commun* 216, 222; B Beutler, *Die Europäische Gemeinschaft* (Nomos, 1982) 40.

[27] Service Juridique de la Haute Autorité, HAEC CEAB1 115, 9–10.

[28] Service Juridique de la Haute Autorité, HAEC CEAB1 99, 5.

[29] Assemblée Nationale (FR), troisième séance 6 décembre 1951, 8895; Lagrange, 'L'Europe institutionelle' (n 26) 222; RH Lauwaars, *Lawfulness and legal force of Community decisions* (AW Sijthoff, 1973) 6; Opinion in Case C-128/92 *Banks v British Coal* [1993] ECR I-01209 ECLI:EU:C:1993:860, para 26.

The Treaty did, however, need an entity to execute its rules and ensure the attainment of its objectives. This responsibility lay on a High Authority.[30] This institution was the Community's main decision-maker.[31] It was independent,[32] directly engaged with undertakings,[33] and procured its own funds through levies[34] and loans.[35] To fulfil its tasks, the Authority adopted decisions, recommendations, and opinions.[36] Decisions were binding in their entirety; recommendations only as to their aims; and opinions not at all.

The High Authority adopted these instruments to execute a threefold mission.[37] First, it monitored the good functioning of the coal and steel market and its competition rules. It imposed penalties on undertakings[38] and decided on Member State non-compliance with the Treaty.[39] Sometimes, the Treaty rules required further precision. Thus, the High Authority defined prohibited pricing practices and specified the publication requirements for price lists and conditions of sale.[40] Second, the High Authority provided financial assistance and guidance on investments.[41] Third, it directly intervened in the coal and steel market. It fixed maximum and minimum prices and imposed coal and steel production quotas in situations of shortage or decline in demand.[42] A principle of minimum intervention, however, applied.[43] Under normal economic conditions, imposing publication requirements for prices and conditions of sale sufficed.[44]

Despite its predominant role, the High Authority was not an absolute decision-maker. It often needed to consult a Council of Ministers, or even seek its assent.[45] The more politically sensitive the issue, the greater the Council's involvement.[46] In the context of competition, for instance, the High Authority consulted the Council

[30] Article 8 TECSC.

[31] Reuter, *La Communauté européenne du charbon et de l'acier* (n 13) 51; R Vernon, 'The Schuman Plan: Sovereign Powers of the European Coal and Steel Commmunity' (1953) 47 *American Journal of International Law* 183, 195; Kamer der Volksvertegenwoordigers/Chambre des Représentants (BE) 1951–1952 410, 38; Tweede Kamer (NL) 1950–1951 2228(3), 47.

[32] Article 9 TECSC.

[33] Articles 46–48 TECSC.

[34] Article 49 TECSC.

[35] Reuter, *La Communauté européenne du charbon et de l'acier* (n 13) 54; Vernon (n 31) 195.

[36] Article 14 TECSC.

[37] Service Juridique de la Haute Autorité, HAEC CEAB1 85, 2.

[38] Articles 47 and 58 TECSC.

[39] Article 88 TECSC.

[40] Service Juridique de la Haute Autorité, HAEC CEAB1 115, 7; Article 60 TECSC.

[41] G Bebr, 'The European Coal and Steel Community: a political and legal innovation' (1953) 63 *Yale Law Journal* 1, 12; Articles 49–56 TECSC.

[42] Articles 58 and 61 TECSC; Bebr (n 41) 13; CF Ophüls, 'Das Wirtschaftsrecht des Schumanplans' (1951) 4 Neue juristische Wochenschrift 381, 382.

[43] Articles 5 and 57 TECSC.

[44] Bebr (n 41) 382.

[45] B Rittberger, 'Which institutions for post-war Europe? Explaining the institutional design of Europe's first community' (2001) 8 *Journal of European Public Policy* 673, 673.

[46] J de Soto, *La Communauté européenne du charbon et de l'acier* (Presses universitaires de France, 1958) 124.

before defining control of an undertaking.[47] In the more sensitive commercial policy field, the Authority could not recommend the introduction of quantitative restrictions against anti-competitive third-country imports without Council assent.[48] Exceptionally, the Council replaced the Authority as decision-maker.[49] Political control by an Assembly and judicial control by a Court of Justice further counterbalanced the High Authority's independence.[50]

This institutional structure explains why it is more precise to associate power with specific institutions rather than with the ECSC as a whole. The Paris Treaty always specified which particular institution it empowered to act. A single act often required the exercise of several powers. To invest certain funds in research, for instance, the Treaty involved the High Authority (adoption), the Council (assent), and the Consultative Committee (consultation).[51] Only seldomly did the Treaty entrust a certain field to a single institution. The Authority alone enjoyed both competence and power over concerted practices between undertakings.[52] Usually, however, one field of competence included a number of powers for different institutions.[53]

Thus, the Paris Treaty established an ECSC in a legal system built on the principle of conferral of competence and power. It is now time to examine the foundations of this legal system further: that is, first, the theoretical principle of conferral; and second, the concrete system of conferral resulting from it.

II. The Principle of Conferral

The following section takes a closer look at the principle of conferral. It first examines the principle's origins. Second, it studies how the drafters of the Paris Treaty executed it in view of the distinction between competence and power.

A. Origins

On 9 May 1950, French foreign minister Robert Schuman announced an ambitious plan for Europe.[54] France invited the Federal Republic of Germany[55] and other interested states to pool their coal and steel productions under a common authority, whose decisions would bind the participating states. War would not

[47] Article 66 TECSC.
[48] Article 74 TECSC.
[49] Article 72 TECSC.
[50] Articles 20 and 25 TECSC.
[51] Article 55(2)c TECSC.
[52] Article 65 TECSC.
[53] Case 9/56 *Meroni*, 173.
[54] R Schuman, Déclaration du 9 mai 1950.
[55] Hereinafter 'Germany'.

only become unthinkable, but preparing for it would be materially impossible. The Schuman Declaration famously initiated the process that led to the European Union. Germany, the Netherlands, Italy, and the Benelux countries accepted the French invitation to discuss a new community based on the terms of the Declaration.[56] On 18 April 1951, six representatives signed the Paris Treaty; the European Coal and Steel Community was born.

The ECSC would not have existed without Jean Monnet. The French civil servant not only realised the importance of European unity, but also conceived the plan to secure it. While Robert Schuman engaged his political weight for the initiative, Monnet was its technical architect.[57] From the start, Monnet acknowledged the necessity to delimit the tasks and powers of the High Authority.[58] This remained clear throughout the Treaty negotiations. The Authority's powers were to be conferred by, and concretely determined in, the Treaty.[59]

The roots of this principle of conferral lay in international and national law. Treaty-based organisations enjoyed those competences conferred upon them in their foundational Treaties. Public persons only enjoyed the powers vested in them to attain certain aims. This dual context influenced Monnet and the Treaty. Here first surfaces the relevance of the competence–power distinction.

1. *International Law*

The principle of conferral existed in international jurisprudence long before the ECSC negotiations commenced. In 1922, the Council of the League of Nations asked the Permanent Court of International Justice (PCIJ) whether the International Labour Organization (ILO) had competence on the labour conditions of agriculture employees. The Court ruled that this was indeed the case. Importantly, it stated that an international organisation derived its existence and competence from the Treaty establishing it alone.[60]

Five years later, the PCIJ considered the 'jurisdiction' of the European Commission of the Danube.[61] This Commission had extensive powers to implement the Definite Statute of the (maritime) Danube.[62] The PCIJ confirmed that the Commission was not a state, but an international institution with a special

[56] Communiqué commun publié le 3 juin 1950 par les Gouvernements ayant adheres à la proposition française du 9 mai 1950 (1950), CEAB2 14, 1; P Reuter, 'Le Plan Schuman' (1953) 81 *Collected Courses of the Hague Academy of International Law* 521, 524.

[57] P Gerbet, 'La genèse du Plan Schuman: des origines à la déclaration du 9 mai 1950' (1956) 3 *Revue française de science politique* 525, 544.

[58] J Monnet, *Mémoires* (Fayard, 1976) 350.

[59] Rapport sur les travaux poursuivis à Paris par les délégations des six pays du 20 juin au 10 août 1950 (1950) 15.

[60] PCIJ Advisory Opinion No 3 [1922] 53.

[61] PCIJ Advisory Opinion No 14 [1927] 1.

[62] B de Witte, 'The European Union as an international legal experiment' in G De Búrca and JHH Weiler (eds), *The Worlds of European Constitutionalism* (CUP, 2012) 23.

purpose. Therefore, it only had 'the functions bestowed upon it by the Definite Statute with a view to the fulfilment of that purpose'.[63]

International law scholars, too, widely adhered to this principle.[64] Even Seyerstedt, who generally rejected the principle of conferral as contradicted by practice, considered it 'entirely appropriate' when an organisation was empowered to take decisions binding its Member States.[65]

2. *National Law*

National law principles, too, provided an inspiration. At this point, it is useful to nuance the previously made distinction between a state and the ECSC. Perhaps this distinction was drawn somewhat too starkly. Within states, too, questions of 'competence' arise. This is especially so in federal states. They need a system to determine which competences belong to the federal level and which reside with the regional entities. A principle of conferral forms a part of that determination.

Among the founding Member States of the Coal and Steel Community was, indeed, a federal state. Belgium would only be federalised later; the Federal Republic of Germany, however, was federal from the ECSC's very conception. And Article 70 of its Constitution of 1949 reflected a principle of conferral. It stated that 'the Länder shall have the right to legislate insofar as this Basic Law does not confer legislative power on the Federation'.[66] A principle of conferral thus applied. It is likely that it also influenced at least the German delegation to the Paris negotiations. Throughout these negotiations, Germany expressed its preference for a community with a more federal character.[67] A principle of conferral would have constituted an important part of that character.

But the roots of conferral did not only lie in the federalist tradition. In his Opinion in *Algera*, Advocate General Lagrange referred to a 'principle of public law': the '*principe de spécialité*'.[68] This principle was absent in international jurisprudence until it emerged 40 years later in the International Court of Justice (ICJ)'s Advisory Opinion on nuclear weapons.[69] Lauterpacht explained the ICJ's

[63] PCIJ Advisory Opinion No 14 [1927] 64.

[64] CT Oliver, 'Historical development of international law: contemporary problems of treaty law' (1955) 88 *Collected Courses of the Hague Academy of International Law* 419, 485; Korowicz (n 15) 89; G Andrassy, 'La souveraineté et la Société des Nations' (1937) 61 *Collected Courses of the Hague Academy of International Law* 375, 412; Guggenheim (n 15) 97; Reuter, *Droit international public* (n 15) 229.

[65] F Seyerstedt, 'United Nations Forces – Some Legal Problems' (1961) 37 *British Yearbook of International Law* 351, 460.

[66] Article 70(1) of the Grundgesetz für die Bundesrepublik Deutschland (1949).

[67] Rittberger (n 45) 696; A Boerger and M Rasmussen, 'Transforming European Law: The Establishment of the Constitutional Discourse from 1950 to 1993' (2014) 10 *European Constitutional Law Review* 199, 202.

[68] Opinion in Case 7/56 *Algera and Others v Assemblée commune* [1957] ECR-00081 ECLI:EU:C:1957:6, 82.

[69] ICJ Advisory Opinion *Use of Nuclear Weapons* [1996] 16.

introduction of this principle as a French influence.[70] Indeed, under French administrative law, a public person was authorised to act in order to realise a determined aim and only invested with the powers necessary to reach this aim. This was known as the '*principe de spécialité*'.[71]

The *Algera* reference to public law confirms Lauterpacht's theory. Advocate General Lagrange derived the '*spécialité*' terminology from French (and Belgian) law.[72] Throughout the Community, however, administrative action was, at least to a certain extent, susceptible to challenges on the ground that it constituted an exercise of 'competence' for an aim different than that for which it was conferred.[73] Such a head of judicial review presupposed a principle akin to the '*principe de spécialité*'. The content of the principle must, therefore, have been familiar in all Member States.

B. From Plan to Treaty

Since conferral existed in both international and national law, it was an evident default rule for the ECSC as well. There was no need to expressly confirm it. This explained why Monnet's plan did not include an express principle of conferred competence. Yet the Paris Treaty did include such a principle for powers. Dissenting opinions during the Treaty negotiations explain why an explicit conferral of powers to ECSC institutions overshadowed the implicit principle of conferral of competences to the ECSC as a whole.

Monnet deplored the unanimity paralysis experienced in the intergovernmental Council of Europe and Organisation for European Economic Co-operation.[74] Only a supranational High Authority could avoid such paralysis in the ECSC. The Schuman Plan, therefore, did not foresee a court, assembly, or council. This explained why the early documents discussed the attributions of the Authority and not of the Community. But the French proposal did not fully succeed.[75]

The Belgian, Dutch, and Luxembourgian delegations strongly opposed the Authority as an institutional heavyweight.[76] The small Benelux states feared being overpowered in the Authority and campaigned for a more intergovernmental approach. Decision-making needed to be in the hands of government

[70] E Lauterpacht, 'Judicial review of the acts of international organisations' in L Boisson de Chazournes and P Sands (eds), *International Law, the International Court of Justice and Nuclear Weapons* (CUP, 1999) 98.

[71] R Bonnard, *Précis de Droit Administratif* (LGDJ, 1943) 317; L Berthélémy, *Traité élémentaire de droit administratif* (Rousseau, 1910) 643.

[72] A Buttgenbach, *Manuel de droit administratif* (Larcier, 1966) 46.

[73] JM Auby and M Fromont, *Les recours contre les actes administratifs dans les pays de la CEE* (Dalloz, 1971) 102, 173, 251, 317, 360, and 434.

[74] Monnet, *Mémoires* (n 58), 324; P Reuter, 'Juridical and Institutional Aspects of the European Regional Communities' (1961) 26 *Law and Contemporary Problems* 381, 386.

[75] P Lindseth, *Power and Legitimacy: Reconciling Europe and the Nation-State* (OUP, 2011) 98.

[76] Poidevin and Spierenburg (n 1) 11; Rittberger (n 45) 695; Monnet, *Mémoires* (n 58) 381.

representatives as well. This could be ensured by a committee of ministers with blocking majority, veto, or first-instance appeal power.[77] Germany, for its part, viewed the future ECSC from a federal perspective. It argued for a structure based on a classical separation of powers doctrine and insisted on a strong permanent court.[78]

The ECSC's institutional design was thus the compromise result of intensive debates. This explains why the Treaty focused on the principle of conferred powers and only implicitly confirmed the principle of conferred competences.

C. Conferral of Power (and Competence)

> 'None of the institutions can exercise powers other than those conferred upon it by the Treaty, either in relation to the other institutions or in regard to third parties, whether they be States or private persons.'[79]

Although the Court applied the principle of conferral, it never elaborated on the principle's theory.[80] The first Advocate Generals, however, did. Both Maurice Lagrange and Karl Roemer set out the principle of conferral in their opinions. In *Algera*, Advocate General Lagrange unambiguously confirmed the principle of conferral of powers.[81] Advocate General Roemer, too, underlined that the Treaty system was not based on general power for the High Authority. Rather, it contained 'precisely described powers for individual cases'.[82]

Indeed, the Paris Treaty left no doubt that the ECSC institutions only enjoyed conferred powers. References to conferral existed both with regard to the institutions in general and with regard to the individual institutions. Article 3 of the Treaty listed the tasks of the Community institutions 'within the limits of their respective powers'. Article 6 contained a similar statement. Articles 8, 20, and 26 repeated the principle of conferral of powers for, respectively, the Authority, Assembly, and Council.

It would be wrong, however, to think that no corresponding principle for competences existed. Despite the absence of an express Treaty provision, the principle of conferral applied to competence too. It would have been illogical to combine limited powers with unlimited competences. After all, the existence of a power presupposes the existence of a field of competence in which that power

[77] A Boerger-De Smedt, 'Negotiating the Foundations of European Law, 1950–57: The Legal History of the Treaties of Paris and Rome' (2012) 21 *Common European History* 339, 342; Monnet, *Mémoires* (n 58) 383.

[78] Boerger-De Smedt (n 77) 342.

[79] Opinion in Case 7/56 *Algera*, 82. See also Opinion in Case 1/54 *France v High Authority* [1956] ECR-00007 ECLI:EU:C:1954:4, 30.

[80] See, eg Case 10/57 *Aubert & Duval v High Authority* [1958] ECR-00401ECLI:EU:C:1958:13.

[81] Opinion in Case 7/56 *Algera*, 82.

[82] Opinion in Case 41/59 *Hamborner Bergbau*, 531.

may be exercised. 'Competence without power is ineffective.'[83] Moreover, the principle of conferral of competence also followed from the Treaty's general scheme. Part Three listed the fields in which the institutions were empowered to act. This suggested that the ECSC lacked (specific) competence in other fields.

III. The System of Conferral

For competence and power, conferral constitutes both 'raison d'être' and principal limitation.[84] Competence and power exist because they are conferred, and insofar as they are conferred. But the principle of conferral also has its limits. It remains silent on the content of what is conferred. Whether the ECSC enjoyed the most general competence and power, or only the narrowest, was for the drafters of the Treaty to decide. Based on Article 95(1), the predecessor of today's Article 352 TFEU, this section shows that their choice lay somewhere in between.

A. Competence and Power

> In all cases not provided for in this Treaty where it becomes apparent that a decision or recommendation of the High Authority is necessary to attain, within the common market in coal and steel and in accordance with Article 5, one of the objectives of the Community set out in Articles 2, 3 and 4, the decision may be taken or the recommendation made with the unanimous assent of the Council and after the Consultative Committee has been consulted.[85]

So read Article 95(1) TECSC. This residual 'safeguard clause'[86] enabled the High Authority to attain the ECSC's objectives even in cases not provided for by the Treaty. This authorisation, albeit wide, was expressed in the Treaty. It therefore did not contradict the principle of conferral.[87]

Precisely how significant these paragraphs were for the ECSC's 'competence' depended on their meaning. Article 95(1) could merely grant power in an existing field of ECSC competence or could also confer new competences. In both scenarios, it generated a considerable authorisation to act for the Coal and Steel Community; but only in the latter scenario did this wide conferral also affect fields

[83] Constantinesco (n 21) 83.
[84] Assemblée Nationale (FR), Troisième séance 6 décembre 1951, 8895.
[85] Article 95(1) TECSC. See also para 2 on penalties.
[86] Gori, *Les clauses de sauvegarde des traités CECA et CEE* (n 15) 252; Pescatore, *Le droit de l'intégration* (n 13) 41. G Jaenicke, 'Die Europäische Gemeinschaft für Kohle und Stahl (Montan-Union) – Struktur und Funktionen ihrer Organe' (1951) 14 *Zeitschrift für ausländisches öffentliches Recht und Völkerrecht* 727, 748; Case 38/69 *Commission v Italy* [1970] ECR-00047 ECLI:EU:C:1970:11, para 10.
[87] M Lagrange, 'Les pouvoirs de la Haute Autorité et l'application du Traité de Paris' (1961) 79 *Revue du droit public de la science politique* 40, 45; Lenaerts (n 20) 469; Case T-37/97 *Forges de Clabecq SA v Commission* [1999] ECR II-00859 ECLI:EU:T:1999:66, para 136.

of competence which were otherwise left to the Member States. It was, therefore, crucial to establish which type of conferral Article 95(1) achieved.

Some scholars argued that the High Authority could only act under Article 95(1) in fields where Member State competence was limited already.[88] In such fields, the Treaty limited national competence without accompanying transfer of power to the ECSC.[89] This view was consistent with Article 95(1)'s main application in practice. Article 4c prohibited state aid without exemptions. That strict rule proved to be too draconian, especially during coal crises.[90] The Authority, therefore, adopted a state aid code based on Article 95(1).[91] Article 4c already empowered the Authority to sanction unlawful aid.[92] Under Article 95(1), it exercised an additional power to accept certain aid.

Kovar rejected this narrow view.[93] He argued that only expressly reserved Member State competence limited the application of Article 95(1). The Treaty reserved competence to the Member States in three areas: these were the methods for fixing wages and welfare benefits,[94] and most of the transport[95] and commercial[96] policies. Only the first manifestly excluded the application of Article 95(1). National social competence was only subject to the provisions of Article 68 itself. Articles 70 and 71, on the contrary, referred to the Treaty in general. Arguably, Article 95(1) thus applied to transport and commercial policy as well.

Four arguments support Kovar's wider interpretation. The first is teleological. The founding states concluded the Paris Treaty for a period of 50 years.[97] They understood that half a century could be a very long time for a fluctuating economy. Therefore, Article 95(1) allowed the ECSC to adapt to unforeseen circumstances.[98] It only applied to 'cases not provided for in this Treaty'.[99] For a provision intended to offer flexibility, a limitation to powers alone seems too restrictive.

The need for flexibility also explains why Article 95(1) covered both power and competence. In *Netherlands v High Authority*, the intervening undertakings argued that 'cases not provided for in this Treaty' referred to matters which did not

[88] Tizzano (n 26) 150; Vos (n 5) 37.

[89] Reuter, *La Communauté européenne du charbon et de l'acier* (n 13) 96.

[90] B Goldman, *European Commercial Law* (Stevens, 1973) 766; P Gori, 'Art.95(1)–(2)' in R Quadri, R Monaco, and A Trabucchi (eds), *Trattato istitutivo della CECA: commentario* (Giuffrè, 1970) 1340.

[91] Haute Autorité, Décision 3/65 du 17 février 1965 relative au régime communautaire des interventions des États membres en faveur de l'industrie houillère, OJ 31; Case T-239/94 *EISA v Commission* [1997] ECR II-01839 ECLI:EU:T:1997:158, 64.

[92] Articles 4c and 88 TECSC.

[93] Kovar (n 13) 226.

[94] Article 68 TECSC.

[95] Article 70 TECSC.

[96] Article 71 TECSC.

[97] Article 97 TECSC.

[98] Case 9/61 *Netherlands v High Authority* [1962] ECR-00413 ECLI:EU:C:1962:27, 233; Rapport de la Délégation française sur le Traité instituant la CECA (1951) 22; Tweede Kamer (NL) 1950–1951 2228(3), 47.

[99] Article 95(1) TECSC.

come under the Treaty at all.[100] The Court did not have to answer this argument; Article 70 provided competence and power, so Article 95(1) was not applicable. However, it seems unlikely that the Court would have followed the interveners. Such interpretation would have limited Article 95(1) to fields which normally remained national. It would have excluded the less intrusive conferral of additional powers in fields of Community competence.

Second, the Court interpreted Article 95(1) as a means to depart from the Treaty. In *Netherlands v High Authority*, it ruled that '[t]he only object of the first paragraph of Article 95 is to institute special rules for departing from the Treaty with the object of empowering the High Authority to meet an unforeseen situation.'[101] Admittedly, even the narrow interpretation of Article 95(1) departed from the Treaty. Authorising state aid departed from Article 4c and the Treaty's system of free competition.[102] But in its judgment, the Court did not identify a departure, 'since the High Authority has applied the Treaty in circumstances covered by its provisions'.[103] This seems broader than mere exemptions to Treaty prohibitions.

Third, practice confirmed a wider interpretation. The High Authority invoked Article 95(1) to extend Article 47's duty of information to undertakings outside the scope of the Treaty.[104] Normally, these undertakings fell under national competence. In a similar extension, the Authority imposed price publication obligations on distribution undertakings.[105] This third argument should not, of course, be overstated; institutional practice may not necessarily reflect legally sound practice.[106] Still, this example is relevant insofar as it suggests that Article 95(1) was indeed interpreted widely.

Finally, Article 95(1) specified in detail how and under which conditions the High Authority could act. Yet it remained silent on the acquisition of competence. This suggests that a limitation to power did not apply. Admittedly, the absence of an explicit limitation is not always decisive. Article 95(3)–(4) allowed the ECSC institutions to amend the Treaty. Although the Treaty did not say so, the Court ruled that this '*petite révision*'[107] could not change the division of competences between Member States and Community.[108] However, the Court relied on various

[100] Case 9/61 *Netherlands v High Authority*, 219.

[101] ibid.

[102] Opinion in Case 1/54 *France v High Authority*, 30.

[103] Case 9/61 *Netherlands v High Authority*, 233.

[104] Commission Decision No 3002/77/ECSC of 28 December 1977 requiring dealers in iron and steel products to comply with pricing rules, OJ L352.

[105] Commission Decision No 1836/81/ECSC of 3 July 1981 on the obligation of distributive undertakings to publish price lists and conditions of sale and on practices prohibited for these undertakings, OJ L184.

[106] See Case 68/86 *United Kingdom v Council* [1988] ECR-00855 ECLI:EU:C:1988:85, para 24.

[107] de Soto (n 46) 23; Gori, 'Art.95(1)–(2)' (n 90) 1342; K Carstens, 'Die kleine Revision des Vertrages über die Europäische Gemeinschaft für Kohle und Stahl' (1961) 21 *Zeitschrift für ausländisches öffentliches Recht und Völkerrecht* 1, 21.

[108] Opinion 1/59 *Modification article 56 CECA – I* [1959] ECR-00533 ECLI:EU:C:1959:30, 556; Service Juridique de la Haute Autorité, HAEC CEAB1 85, 3. See also Opinion in Case 74/81 *Flender*

explicit restrictions, notably a prohibition to change the institutional division of powers, which Article 95(1) did not include. Moreover, a crucial difference exists between Treaty amendment without Member State involvement and broad conferral by exactly these Member States. Thus, the restriction of Article 95(3)–(4) did not apply by analogy to Article 95(1).

B. Nearly General Functional Competence and Power

Based on Article 95(1), the ECSC could thus pursue its Treaty objectives even in a field which was not specifically conferred upon it. This did not mean that the ECSC enjoyed general 'competence'. General 'competence' implies that the competent entity may undertake any action in any field it desires;[109] The ECSC and its institutions could not do so. But, unless the Treaty explicitly retained a competence to the Member States, these institutions could undertake any action necessary to fulfil their mission.[110]

The Paris Treaty thus conferred a nearly general functional competence and power upon the ECSC. This was the meaning of Advocate General Lagrange's '*principe de spécialité*'.[111] Pescatore wrote that the Treaty was full of teleology.[112] Ipsen identified a fundamental need for objectives *('Zielbedarf')*.[113] Article 95(1) confirmed that, essentially, the ECSC's system of 'competence' was designed to ensure the attainment of its objectives. Except in fields of competence reserved to the Member States, the ECSC could adopt any action necessary to pursue its objectives.

At the same time, it is crucial to understand the limited character of these objectives. The Treaty expressly linked its objectives of economic expansion, employment growth, and raised living standards to the common market.[114] The same applied to the objectives of Article 3 and the prohibitions of Article 4. Article 95(1)'s statement on the necessity to attain Community objectives 'within the common market in coal and steel', therefore, did not lay down additional restrictions.[115] Rather, it confirmed that the ECSC's objectives were tied to the

v Commission [1982] ECR-00395 ECLI:EU:C:1981:279, 412; Gori, *Les clauses de sauvegarde des traités CECA et CEE* (n 15) 255.

[109] Gori, *Les clauses de sauvegarde des traités CECA et CEE* (n 15) 255.

[110] Kovar (n 13) 143.

[111] Ibid, 142; Reuter, *Droit international public* (n 15) 46.

[112] P Pescatore, 'Les objectifs de la Communauté européenne comme principes d'interprétation dans la jurisprudence de la Cour de justice' in W Ganshof van der Meersch (ed), *Miscellanea* (Bruylant, 1972) 325.

[113] J Larik, 'From speciality to a constitutional sense of purpose: on the changing role of the objectives of the European Union' (2014) 63 *International and Comparative Law Quarterly* 935, 937; H Ipsen, *Europäisches Gemeinschaftsrecht* (JCB Mohr, 1972) 995.

[114] Article 2 TECSC.

[115] Article 95(1) TECSC.

common coal and steel market. It was in this market sphere that the flexibility clause necessarily operated.

C. Conferral and Implication

The importance of Article 95(1) becomes clear in connection with the theory of implied powers. Implied powers are powers which are not expressly conferred upon the ECSC in the Treaty. They can be narrow: 'The existence of a given power implies also the existence of any power which is reasonably necessary for the exercise of the former.'[116] They can also be wide: 'The existence of a given objective or function implies the existence of any power reasonably necessary to attain it.'[117] Both constitute techniques of interpretation. The crucial difference is that only the former operates within a framework of explicitly conferred powers.

How the Treaty was to be interpreted depended on a careful balance between two apparently opposite ideas.[118] On the one hand, the need to ensure the Treaty's effectiveness excluded a strict interpretation;[119] on the other hand, limitations to national sovereignty could only be accepted by means of conferral.[120] A narrow theory of implied powers successfully executes this balancing act. It guarantees the '*effet utile*' of the Treaty, but only to the extent that a related express Treaty conferral exists.[121]

This balancing act is where a wide theory of implied powers fails. It applies a technique of interpretation so wide that the principle of conferral is no longer respected. The Paris Treaty conferred powers to act within fields of competence. Its objectives, however, did not *authorise* any action.[122] The principle of conferral, therefore, excluded the wide formulation of implied powers. But the impermissibility of precisely such technique could have adversely affected the ECSC system. Expressly intended objectives would be deprived of any practical meaning without consequences for their attainment.[123]

There lay the crucial significance of Article 95(1). This article was often invoked to reject a wide theory of implied powers; in reality, this rejection followed from the principle of conferral itself. The merit of Article 95(1), however, lay in

[116] T Hartley, *The Foundations of European Community Law* (OUP, 1981) 87.
[117] ibid.
[118] W Riphagen, 'The case law of the European Coal and Steel Community Court of Justice' (1955) 2 *Nederlands Tijdschrift voor Internationaal Recht* 384, 396.
[119] Kovar (n 13) 214.
[120] Reuter, *La Communauté européenne du charbon et de l'acier* (n 13) 100.
[121] Pescatore, *Le droit de l'intégration* (n 13) 43; De Visscher (n 17) 37.
[122] G Olivier, 'Art. 2' in R Quadri, R Monaco, and A Trabucchi (eds), *Trattato istitutivo della CECA: commentario* (Giuffrè, 1970) 56.
[123] ibid; Pescatore, *Le droit de l'intégration* (n 13) 43.

the fact that it prevented the need for such a wide theory. The following section explains the Court's shift from wide to narrow implied powers and the influence of Article 95(1) on this shift.

1. *Implied Powers and the Pursuit of Objectives*

In *Fédéchar*, the Court implicitly introduced a doctrine of implied powers to ECSC law.[124] It applied a rule of interpretation

> generally accepted in both international and national law, according to which the rules laid down by an international treaty or a law presuppose the rules without which that treaty or law would have no meaning or could not be reasonably and usefully applied.[125]

The High Authority's task to approximate Belgian coal prices to common market prices presupposed a power to fix the former. Interestingly, the Court linked the identification of implied powers to ECSC objectives. It used Article 8 as a guiding principle for High Authority power.

This theory of implied powers linked to objectives originated in the United States.[126] Reviewing the legality of the establishment of a federal bank, the US Supreme Court pioneered a definition of implied powers.[127] It linked federal powers to objectives:

> Let the end be legitimate, let it be within the scope of the constitution, and all means which are appropriate, which are plainly adapted to that end, which are not prohibited, but consistent with the letter and spirit of the constitution, are constitutional.[128]

The Permanent Court of International Justice, too, formulated implied powers widely. The question arose whether an International Labour Organization convention could prohibit employers from carrying out a certain work. The PCIJ answered affirmatively. The participating states intended to grant the ILO wide co-operative powers to protect workers.[129] It was 'not conceivable that they intended to prevent the Organization from drawing up and proposing measures essential to the accomplishment of that end'. The employer aspects were necessary to ensure the efficacity of the workers' protection. Crucially, the PCIJ emphasised the accomplishment of the ILO's ends.

Twenty years later, the International Court of Justice (ICJ) applied a slightly narrower theory of implied powers. In *Reparation for Injuries*, the ICJ stated that an international organisation enjoyed express powers and powers 'conferred upon

[124] Lenaerts (n 20) 469.
[125] Case 8/55 *Fédération charbonnière de Belgique v High Authority* [1977] ECR-00291 ECLI:EU:C:1956:11, 299.
[126] Kovar (n 13) 124.
[127] *McCulloch v The State of Maryland* [1819] 17 US, 414.
[128] ibid, 421.
[129] PCIJ Advisory Opinion No 13 [1926] 18.

it by necessary implication as being essential to the performance of its duties'.[130] It thus linked implied powers to duties rather than objectives. This was narrower than the ILO reasoning. It did, however, remain a wide conception of implied powers.

Finally, the ECSC Court did not find inspiration in international law alone.[131] Traces of implied powers also existed in Member State law.[132] Since this theory was quintessentially a federal one, it found some application in Germany. The Federal Constitutional Court accepted implied powers as a necessary presupposition for an express competence.[133]

2. *Limited Implied Powers*

In ECSC law, the wide interpretation of the theory of implied powers did not hold ground. Some scholars rejected the theory altogether.[134] Adopting an act on the basis of implied powers would be to circumvent the stringent procedures set out in Article 95(1). Even the Court seemed to agree at one point. In *Gezamenlijke Steenkoolmijnen*, it found that economic policy remained a national responsibility unless it had been 'expressly placed within the province of the Community'.[135] This approach appeared to depart from *Fédéchar*.

A compromise option prevailed. The Court shifted to a narrower theory of implied powers in two subsequent cases. The Netherlands and Italy contested a decision of the High Authority to require the publication of transport tariffs.[136] The Court ruled that 'writers and case law agree in recognizing that the rules established by a treaty imply the principles without which these rules cannot effectively or reasonably be applied'.[137] It then examined whether the Treaty provided the relevant powers either expressly or by implication; this was not the case. Importantly, the Court ceased to link implied powers to objectives. It thus applied a significant limitation compared with *Fédéchar*.[138]

This compromise was in line with an alternative doctrinal view. A number of scholars rightly argued that Article 95(1) only excluded the widest form of implied

[130] ICJ Advisory Opinion *Reparation for Injuries* [1949] 12.

[131] Case 8/55 *Fédéchar*, 299.

[132] Gori, *Les clauses de sauvegarde des traités CECA et CEE* (n 15) 252.

[133] S Korioth, 'Artikel 30' in T Maunz and G Dürig (eds), *Grundgesetz: Kommentar Band IV* (Beck, 2006) 25–26.

[134] HJ Rabe, *Das Verordnungsrecht der Europäischen Wirtschaftsgemeinschaft* (Kommissionsverlag Appel, 1963) 158; C Grassetti, 'La Communauté et les Entreprises' in Centro Italiano di Studi Giuridici (ed), *Actes officiels du Congrès International d'Etudes sur la Communauté Européenne du Charbon et de l'Acier IV* (Giuffrè, 1957) 18.

[135] Case C-30/59 *Gezamenlijke Steenkoolmijnen*, 23.

[136] Case 20/59 *Italy v High Authority* [1960] ECR-00663 ECLI:EU:C:1960:33; Case 25/59 *Netherlands v High Authority* [1960] ECR-00723 ECLI:EU:C:1960:34.

[137] Case 20/59 *Italy v High Authority*, 336.

[138] The Court could have reached the *Fédéchar* result under a narrower theory of implied powers. It could have anchored the implied powers to an express Treaty provision rather than to the Treaty's objectives. See Lenaerts (n 20) 469.

powers.[139] The Treaty did not imply all powers necessary to achieve its objectives. However, the narrower formulation of implied powers was acceptable. Article 95 did not exclude implied powers which directly related to an expressly conferred power.

Upon closer consideration, this reasoning also explains the Court's statement in *Gezamenlijke Steenkoolmijnen*. Whether economic policy fell within the ECSC's scope was not, after all, a question of an implied power deduced from a specific ECSC power in a specific field of ECSC competence. It was a question of implied *competence*. Unless they had been expressly conferred upon the Community, fields of economic policy remained within the competence of the Member States. The ECSC could not gain competence from its Treaty objectives by implication. Only Article 95(1) could (partially) fill these competence (and power) gaps.

Thus, ECSC legal thinking showed great attention to detail. The Paris Treaty neither introduced vacant objectives nor encouraged recourse to inappropriately wide techniques of interpretation. Instead, it provided the ECSC with a variety of specific competences and powers. But it also presented a solution in case this 'competence' was inadequate;[140] that solution was Article 95(1). And, crucially, it constituted an implementation of the principle of conferral itself.

D. Peace and the Federation of Europe

'*La paix mondiale ne saurait être sauvegardée sans des efforts créateurs à la mesure des dangers qui la menacent.*'[141] The European Coal and Steel Community's legal system of conferred 'competence' contrasted with its aspirational side. The founding fathers ambitiously dreamed of a Europe united in peace. Their aim was a gradually uniting Community. It would be wrong, however, to think that these aspirations resulted in a self-integrating Treaty. Beyond the limits of implication, any expansion of ECSC competence remained a matter for the Member States alone.

Essentially, the ECSC was a peace project. A common coal and steel market enhanced productivity and employment.[142] Economic unification facilitated Germany's postwar integration.[143] However, although convincing, none of these benefits were decisive. The European project predominantly built on a desire

[139] Gori, *Les clauses de sauvegarde des traités CECA et CEE* (n 15) 253; CF Ophüls, 'Uber die Auslegung der Europäischen Gemeinschaftsverträge' in F Greiss and FW Meyer (eds), *Wirtschaft, Gesellschaft und Kultur. Festgabe für Alfred Müller-Armack zur Vollendung seines sechzigsten Lebensjahres* (Duncker & Humblot, 1961) 290.

[140] Lagrange (n 87) 49.

[141] R Schuman, Déclaration du 9 mai 1950 ('World peace cannot be safeguarded without the making of creative efforts [commensurate] to the dangers which threaten it.').

[142] Poidevin and Spierenburg (n 1) 4.

[143] R Schütze, *From International to Federal Market: The Changing Structure of European Law* (OUP, 2017) 94.

for peace.[144] This explained the choice of a *Coal and Steel* Community.[145] Coal and steel were not only principal economic resources; they were war-making resources.[146] To pool them meant to 'dismantle their malefic prestige and turn them, on the contrary, into a promise of peace'.[147]

This desire for peace explained the choice of coal and steel. But it was not fulfilled by coal and steel, at least not essentially. More important than preventing the forging of weapons was forging unity between the people(s) of Europe based on merged interests.[148] This explained why the ECSC was not Monnet's ultimate aim. A true safeguard against bloody conflicts called for further economic and, above all, political integration.[149] A destiny henceforth would replace age-old rivalries and divisions by bloody conflicts.[150] For Monnet, peace lay 'beyond the nation'.[151] The ECSC did not 'build coalitions between States, but a union among people'.[152] Not the common market, but the ever more united Europe resulting from it, was indispensable to preserve peace.[153]

The ECSC was thus a neo-functionalist project.[154] Monnet designed the common coal and steel market as a springboard for European unity.[155] Sectoral integration would inherently and gradually lead to integration in other fields.[156] It also was the political 'commencement of Europe'.[157] This spillover idea was clearly present in the Schuman Declaration. Economic development would only constitute 'a first step in the federation of Europe'.[158] The common market would become 'the leaven from which may grow a wider and deeper community between countries long opposed to one another by sanguinary divisions'.[159]

But where ECSC thinking was dominated by neo-functionalist ideologies,[160] the letter of Treaty was not. Its Preamble did present the ECSC as the 'basis for a broader and deeper Community'.[161] And it did recall Monnet's idea of

[144] W Hallstein, *Die Europäische Gemeinschaft* (Econ Verlag, 1974) 45.
[145] R Schuman, *Pour l'Europe* (Nagel, 1963) 203.
[146] S Weatherill, *EC Law* (Penguin, 1993) 3.
[147] After Monnet, *Mémoires* (n 58) 348.
[148] ibid, 347.
[149] Pescatore, 'Les objectifs de la Communauté européenne comme principes d'interprétation dans la jurisprudence de la Cour de justice' (n 112) 327.
[150] Preamble of the TECSC.
[151] J Monnet, 'A ferment of change' (1963) 1 *Journal of Common Market Studies* 203, 205.
[152] Monnet, *Mémoires* (n 58) 9.
[153] ibid, 353; Kohnstamm (n 22) 11.
[154] EB Haas, The Uniting of Europe: Political, Social, and Economic Forces (SUP, 1958) ch 8.
[155] Poidevin and Spierenburg (n 1) 3.
[156] J Tranholm Mikkelsen, 'Neo-functionalism: Obstinate or Obsolete? A Reappraisal in the Light of the New Dynamism of the EC' (1991) 20 *Journal of International Studies* 1, 6.
[157] Monnet, *Mémoires* (n 58) 460.
[158] R Schuman, Déclaration du 9 mai 1950.
[159] ibid.
[160] P Craig, 'Integration, Democracy, and Legitimacy' in P Craig and G De Búrca (eds), *The Evolution of EU Law* (OUP, 2011) 3; L Lindberg, *The Political Dynamics of European Economic Integration* (UC Berkeley, 1962) 500.
[161] Preamble TECSC.

'elite-led gradualism' with a pivotal directory role for the coal and steel institutions.[162] The Treaty's articles did not, however, empower these institutions to expand their powers. Further integration remained an aim, but the Treaty itself would not attain it; the Member States could. For instance, the '*petite révision*' authorised the ECSC institutions to amend the Treaty, but only on the condition that the divisions of power and competence remained unaltered.[163]

Neo-functionalism may seem sinister. It hints at integration as a pressure, not a sovereign state choice. Monnet's intention was different. He did envisage the European project to 'gradually' and 'irresistibly spread by osmosis'.[164] But further integration would not cease to be a national choice. The success of the first step of integration would convince the Member States of the desirability of the second.[165] This success required the necessary competences and powers to attain it. Rather than facilitating spillover by design, the Treaty, therefore, set up a wide system of 'competence' from the beginning.

IV. The European Villages

It is now time to revisit the European Villages. In this legal question, two legal bases competed with each other. Article 54 authorised ECSC investment and financial aid actions;[166] Article 95(1) offered an alternative. Both an 'improved standard of living' for workers in the coal and steel industries and the 'highest possible level of productivity' were indeed Treaty objectives.[167] Suitable housing not only improved this standard of living but also attracted the workers vital to productivity.[168] Moreover, the Treaty did not reserve the financing of housing to the Member States.

Thus, the European Villages did not raise questions on the existence of competence or power. Under Article 54, the ECSC had competence in the field of investment and financial aid. The connected power allowed financing actions. Under Article 95(1), the ECSC had competence in the fields of its objectives unless the Treaty excluded it. The connected power allowed any decision or recommendation necessary to attain these objectives. If Article 54 could not constitute a legal basis for the European Villages, Article 95(1) did.

The Court never looked into the European Villages. Advocate General Roemer only discussed their legal basis in the margins of a case on the use of levy incomes.[169] In *Netherlands v High Authority*, the choice between specific and

[162] Craig (n 160) 15; Monnet, *Mémoires* (n 58) 204.
[163] Article 95(3)–(4) TECSC.
[164] Monnet, *Mémoires* (n 58) 561.
[165] Monnet, 'A ferment of change' (n 151) 205.
[166] Opinion in Case 41/59 *Hamborner Bergbau*, 531.
[167] Articles 3(e) and 2 TECSC.
[168] High Authority, The ECSC in the European Community (1961) 22.
[169] Opinion in Case 41/59 *Hamborner Bergbau*, 530.

general legal bases did arise.[170] The Netherlands argued that the specific transport provision did not empower the Authority to adopt recommendations. To adopt transport recommendations, it argued, the Authority had to invoke Article 95(1) instead. The Court did not dwell on this argument. It accepted the recourse to Article 70. This excluded the application of the residual Article 95(1). Moreover, *Netherlands v High Authority* remained an exception. Legal basis disputes only fully emerged in European law in the 1970s.[171]

The nature of the ECSC Treaty could explain this. It did not contain a clear list of competences and powers; identifying them could be like solving a jigsaw puzzle.[172] But, once found, understanding them was much more straightforward. The Treaty precisely described the ECSC's competence and powers. This left little scope for legal basis ambiguity. Rather than ruling on the legal basis for a certain measure, the Court ruled on the delimitation between the Treaty's alternative means of action to pursue a certain objective.[173] For instance, the High Authority lawfully pursued the objective of lower prices by defining prohibited practices under Article 60, even though Article 61 specifically conferred a power to set maximum prices.[174]

A second explanation exists. The choice of legal basis mattered because of different power modalities. Sometimes, however, two legal bases operated in a similar procedural context. For the European Villages, both options required Council unanimity. The only difference consisted in the Article 95(1) requirement to consult a Consultative Committee. Such non-binding consultation would not have thoroughly affected the High Authority's power. In practice, the choice of legal basis would, therefore, not have mattered. Yet the discussion occurred. Even at the dawn of the European project, sophisticated legal thinking on competence, power, and conferral existed. Perhaps the greatest legacy of the European Villages was the debate surrounding them.

V. Conclusion

'In the ECSC lies, beneath piles of coal and steel, the pure gold of constitutional questions.'[175] The European Coal and Steel Community was a peace project; but it was more than that. It was a peace project organised in a legal system of conferred

[170] Case 9/61 *Netherlands v High Authority*, 233.

[171] Case 8/73 *Hauptzollamt Bremerhaven v Massey-Ferguson* [1973] ECR-00897 ECLI:EU:C:1973:90; Case 5/73 *Balkan Import Export GmbH v Hauptzollamt Berlin Packhof* [1973] ECR-01091 ECLI:EU:C:1973:109. See also K Bradley, 'Powers and procedures in the EU constitution: legal bases and the court' in P Craig and G De Búrca (eds) (n 160) 90.

[172] Goormaghtigh (n 1) 357.

[173] Riphagen (n 118) 406; Case 6/54 *Netherlands v High Authority* [1955] ECR-00201 ECLI:EU:C:1955:5.

[174] Case 1/54 *France v High Authority* [1956] ECR-00007 ECLI:EU:C:1954:7.

[175] P Pescatore, 'La Cour en tant que juridiction fédérale et constitutionnelle' in Europäische Arbeitstagung (ed), *Dix ans de jurisprudence de la Cour de justice des communautés européennes* (Heymanns, 1965) 522.

'competence'. Questions on 'competence' always existed in Community and Union law. The principle of conferral always applied. So did the distinction between competence and power. There can be no doubt that the roots of Articles 5(2) and 13(2) TEU lie in the provisions and thinking of the ECSC Treaty. Almost 60 years passed between the Treaties of Paris and Lisbon, but the question of competence remains the same and so do many of its answers. It is useful to remember them.

PART 2

Descriptive

So far, this book has used the distinction between competence and power to tell a story. The prologue returned to the European Coal and Steel Community through the lens of competence and power. Although it prominently featured the two concepts and their distinction, its message was more fundamental: the European project always was a legal project; 'competence' always mattered; and so did the distinction between competence and power.

It is now time to shift the focus to the concepts of 'competence' themselves. This Part 2 describes them. It begins with an overview chapter. This chapter brings the necessary clarity to better understand the in-depth analyses. Then, one chapter explains competence, and another explains power. Crucially, these are not theoretical chapters. The aim is not to show what competence and power are in theory; it is to illustrate, through concrete legal disputes, how competence and power operate in practice.

2

The Concepts of 'Competence'

Almost 50 years ago, the Commission presented a report on European union.[1] The report envisaged the European Economic Community's transformation into a European Union.[2] It notably addressed the Union's 'Fields of Competence' and 'Institutional Structure'.[3] Today, its content is not often remembered.[4] There is no need to revisit it for this book either. One passage, however, is crucial. 'It is necessary', said the report, 'to distinguish ... between the "competence of the Union", which will be used to mean the areas in which the Union can act, and the "powers of the Union", meaning the ways and means by which it acts'.[5]

The Commission thus made a conscious language choice. To ensure a more nuanced and precise analysis, it distinguished between a field of competence and the powers to act within that field. But the Commission did more than that. It also highlighted its conceptual language at the start of its report. Montesquieu emphasised that '[i]t is essential that the language of the law awakens the same ideas in all men.'[6] In 1975, the Commission understood this.

This overview chapter serves a similar purpose. It explains the concepts of 'competence'. Central stands the distinction between competence and power. Competence is 'the material field within which an authority is entitled to exercise power'.[7] Power is the actual authorisation to act.[8] The next chapters will examine each concept, and their respective dimensions, in more depth. They will also explain the benefits of this more nuanced conceptual approach to 'competence'. First, however, it is important that the concepts of 'competence' are clear. And that is where this chapter comes in. It gives an overview of the concepts.

[1] Commission, Report on European Union, COM(75)400.

[2] ibid, 5; B de Witte, 'The European Union as an international legal experiment' in G de Búrca and JHH Weiler (eds), *The Worlds of European Constitutionalism* (CUP, 2012) 28–29; J Westhof, 'L'Union de l'Europe Occidentale avant et après l'élargissement des Communautés Européennes' (1975) 23 *Annuaire Européen* 94, 118.

[3] Commission, Report on European Union, COM(75)400, 14 and 27.

[4] de Witte (n 2) 28.

[5] Commission, Report on European Union, COM(75)400, 10.

[6] After Montesquieu, *De l'Esprit des Lois* (Librairie de Firmin Didot, 1862) 490.

[7] R Schütze, 'The European Community's Federal Order of Competences – A Retrospective Analysis' in M Dougan and S Currie (eds), *50 Years of the European Treaties: Looking Back and Thinking Forward* (Hart Publishing, 2009) 65.

[8] ibid, 65.

Thus, the first section explains competence. The second section clarifies power. There is also a third and a fourth section. The fourth section argues that, although some Treaty versions also use a third concept, the dual distinction of competence and power suffices. The fourth section acknowledges that, although it has clear roots in the Treaties and a long history of institutional application, the distinction between competence and power is often ignored. Recognising that is important. This book reflects the law as it is. It does not impose a new theoretical framework, but starts from the legal materials and draws conclusions from them. When these materials do not distinguish between competence and power, the analysis must reflect that. Nonetheless, the concepts of 'competence' remain relevant. The fourth section also explains why.

I. Competence

The first concept of 'competence' is competence. Competence is the field in which the Union may act (if it has power to do so). Its relevance is obvious. Article 5(2) TEU clearly states that 'the Union shall act only within the limits of the competences conferred upon it by the Member States in the Treaties to attain the objectives set out therein'.[9] By contrast, '[c]ompetences not conferred upon the Union in the Treaties remain with the Member States.'[10] Thus, the Union may only act in fields in which it has competence.

To identify and delimitate these fields, two competence dimensions exist. A certain EU measure falls within a certain EU competence if it concerns the subject matter of that competence and pursues its objective(s). Both dimensions are always present. Their limiting force, however, varies. In the common commercial policy, for instance, competence's subject matter dimension plays a much greater role than its objectives dimension. A CCP measure must govern international trade.[11] But it must not necessarily facilitate that trade. The CCP competence's objectives are so wide that they do not really limit its scope.[12] The genuine competence limitation stems from the subject matter dimension. Governing the international exchange of goods and services, or foreign direct investment, suffices.[13]

Of course, this is not always the case. In other fields of competence, the objectives dimension is very important. Take, for instance, the Union's environment competence.[14] Its subject matter is the environment. But Article 191 also imposes

[9] First sentence of Article 5(2) TEU (Lisbon).

[10] Second sentence of Article 5(2) TEU (Lisbon).

[11] Case C-414/11 *Daiichi Sankyo and Sanofi-Aventis Deutschland* [2013] ECLI:EU:C:2013:520, para 51.

[12] Articles 205 TFEU and 21 TEU (Lisbon).

[13] Article 207(1) TFEU.

[14] Article 191 TFEU.

clear objectives.[15] The Union has an environmental competence to protect the environment. Thus, the Single-Use Plastics Directive falls within the EU environment *competence*, because the Directive *aims* to improve the quality of the environment.[16]

One final example completes the picture. The Union is competent in the field of the common agricultural policy (CAP). Again, that field has a subject matter and an objectives dimension. The Treaty clarifies both. Article 38 TFEU defines agricultural products as 'the products of the soil, of stockfarming and of fisheries and products of first-stage processing directly related to these products'.[17] It thus explains the CAP's subject matter scope. Article 39 addresses its objectives. The Union is competent in the field of the common agricultural policy to aim, among others, 'to increase agricultural productivity' and 'to ensure a fair standard of living for the agricultural community'.[18]

Not all competences are the same. In the Treaties, different competence categories exist.[19] There are exclusive Union competences;[20] there are shared Union competences;[21] and there are coordinating, supplementing, or supporting Union competences.[22] Exclusive Union competence means that only the Union may have the power to adopt legally binding measures.[23] Shared Union competence means that both the Union and the Member States (may) have the power to adopt such measures.[24] Supporting Union competence means that the Union may have the power to adopt legally binding measures which do not harmonise the laws or regulations of the Member States.[25] The drafters of the Treaties thus based the main categories of Union competence on power.

II. Power

Power is the authorisation to act in a field of competence. Like competence, it is conferred. Article 13(2) TEU stresses that '[e]ach institution shall act within the limits of the powers conferred on it in the Treaties, and in conformity with the procedures, conditions and objectives set out in them.'[26] Here, a crucial

[15] Article 191(1) TFEU.
[16] Directive (EU) 2019/904 of the European Parliament and of the Council of 5 June 2019 on the reduction of the impact of certain plastic products on the environment, OJ L155.
[17] Article 38(1) TFEU.
[18] Article 39(1)(a)–(b) TFEU.
[19] Article 2 TFEU.
[20] Articles 2(1) and 3 TFEU.
[21] Articles 2(2) and 4 TFEU.
[22] Articles 2(3), 2(5), 5, and 6 TFEU.
[23] Article 2(1) TFEU.
[24] Article 2(2) TFEU.
[25] Article 2(5) TFEU. See also P Craig, *The Lisbon Treaty: Law, Politics and Treaty Reform* (OUP, 2013) 177.
[26] Article 13(2) TEU (Lisbon).

difference between competence and power emerges. Competence is conferred upon the Union as a whole; power, by contrast, belongs to the institutions. Thus, Article 13(2) addresses the individual institutions.

Admittedly, the Treaties do occasionally refer to Union powers. Article 14 TFEU, for instance, refers to the respective *powers* of the Member States and the Union in the context of services of general interest.[27] This must not, however, be overstated. Differences between the Treaty language versions exist. While the German version also refers to '*Befugnisse*', the French and Italian versions use '*compétences*' and '*competenze*'. Moreover, Article 40 TEU removes all doubts. Within a field of Union competence, the institutions exercise power:

> The implementation of the common foreign and security policy shall not affect the application of the procedures and the extent of the powers of the institutions laid down by the Treaties for the exercise of the Union competences referred to in Articles 3 to 6 of the Treaty on the Functioning of the European Union.[28]

Like competence, power has two dimensions: there is the type of legal act and the instrument. The former is straightforward. Albeit not exhaustively, Article 288 TFEU lists which measures the EU (institutions!) may adopt to act within a field of EU competence.[29] Regulations, directives, and decisions are the most important types, as they are legally binding.[30] To know which legal acts the empowered institutions may adopt, it is necessary to look at the corresponding Treaty legal basis. It either specifies the applicable legal acts or generally refers to 'measures'. In the latter case, the choice is for the empowered institutions.[31]

Again, some examples may be helpful. Within the internal market competence, Article 46 empowers the Council and the Parliament to 'issue directives or make regulations setting out the measures required to bring about freedom of movement for workers'.[32] Thus, these institutions adopted both a *Regulation* on the free movement of workers and a *Directive* on the exercise of workers' rights in the context of their free movement.[33] Other types of legal act are not legally possible.

Other internal market powers allow for a wider range of measures. Article 114 TFEU notably refers to approximation 'measures'.[34] In practice, the EU legislator

[27] Article 14 TFEU.

[28] First para of Article 40 TEU (Lisbon).

[29] Article 288 TFEU; S Weatherill, *Cases and Materials on EU Law* (OUP, 2016) 28.

[30] Article 288 TFEU.

[31] Article 296 TFEU. If the Treaty refers to 'measures' in general, the question is whether the Union should adopt a measure rather than whether it may. Even if the Union institutions enjoy a power to adopt a certain measure, the principles of subsidiarity and proportionality may require them to pick an alternative that is less intrusive for the Member States.

[32] Article 46 TFEU.

[33] Regulation (EU) No 492/2011 of the European Parliament and of the Council of 5 April 2011 on freedom of movement for workers within the Union, OJ L141; Directive 2014/54/EU of the European Parliament and of the Council of 16 April 2014 on measures facilitating the exercise of rights conferred on workers in the context of freedom of movement for workers, OJ L128.

[34] Article 114(1) TFEU.

usually opts for directives here.[35] Less often, she also adopts a regulation. This includes, for instance, for the Digital Markets Act that aims to promote the internal market by imposing certain obligations on certain digital platform service providers.[36] But her power extends to other types of legal acts as well. Even an occasional Article 114 decision of the Parliament and the Council therefore exists.[37]

The second power dimension relates to the instrument used. Some literature uses 'instrument' as a synonym for the type of legal act.[38] In this book, and other literature, it has a different meaning. It designates the means through which the acting institutions aim to achieve the objectives of a certain EU competence.[39] The instrument is thus the content of the measure.

Often, the Treaties do not identify exactly how the Union institutions may act. Article 194 TFEU, for instance, empowers the Parliament and the Council to 'establish the measures necessary to achieve the [energy competence's] objectives'.[40] This leaves a wide margin of discretion to choose the appropriate instrument. But other Treaty powers do come with more specific instruments. The public health competence's Article 168(4)(c) TFEU, for example, specifically empowers the EU legislator to set 'high standards of quality and safety for medicinal products and devices for medical use'.[41]

Sometimes, the Treaties also indicate that power does not include a certain instrument. As mentioned above, Article 114 TFEU empowers the EU legislator to *approximate* national laws to promote the internal market. Harmonisation is thus the power instrument. Other Treaty legal bases, by contrast, explicitly exclude harmonisation. This is, of course, the case for supporting competences such as culture or industry.[42] These competences, by definition, exclude harmonising powers.[43]

Power also comes with modalities. These modalities relate to the procedural side. First, there is the modality of which EU institution(s) may act. Articles 114 and 115 TFEU perfectly illustrate this. Both are internal market powers. But the latter empowers the Council to harmonise national laws, while the former identifies the Council and the Parliament as co-legislators.[44] Second, there is the modality of the required voting majority. The same internal market powers

[35] See Member States, Declaration on Article 100A of the EEC Treaty, EC Bulletin Supplement 2/86, 24.

[36] Regulation (EU) 2022/1925 of the European Parliament and of the Council of 14 September 2022 on contestable and fair markets in the digital sector and amending Directives (EU) 2019/1937 and (EU) 2020/1828 (Digital Markets Act), OJ L265.

[37] See, eg Decision (EU) 2017/899 of the European Parliament and of the Council of 17 May 2017 on the use of the 470–790 MHz frequency band in the Union, OJ L138.

[38] P Craig and G De Búrca, *EU Law: Text, Cases, and Materials* (OUP, 2020) 143.

[39] R Schütze, *Foreign Affairs and the EU Constitution – Selected Essays* (CUP, 2014) 250.

[40] Article 194(2) TFEU.

[41] Article 168(4)(c) TFEU.

[42] Articles 167(5) and 173(3) TFEU.

[43] Article 2(5) TFEU.

[44] Articles 114(1) and 115 TFEU.

clarify the point. Article 115 requires unanimity in the Council;[45] for Article 114, a qualified majority suffices.[46]

Thus, to act, the European Union needs 'competence'. 'Competence' consists of competence and power. Competence is the field in which the EU (institutions) may act. Power is the institutions' actual authorisation to act. Competence has two dimensions. To fall within a certain field of competence, a measure must relate to the subject matter of that competence. It must also pursue its objectives. Power, too, has two dimensions. It determines which type of legal act one or more EU institutions may adopt and which instruments they may use. Power modalities govern the procedural side. These, in summary, are the concepts of 'competence'.

III. Competence, Power, and Attributions?

Admittedly, a third 'competence' concept may exist. Another reading of Article 13(2) TEU shows why. In the English translation, this provision refers to the *powers* of the EU's institutions. This confirms the dual competence–power distinction. But not all Treaty language versions are the same. The French, Greek, Italian, Spanish, Romanian, and Portuguese versions use a different concept: they refer to '*attributions*', 'αρμοδιοτήτων', '*attribuzioni*' '*atribuciones*', '*atribuţiilor*' and '*atribuições*', rather than to '*pouvoirs*', 'εξουσίες', '*poteri*', '*poderos*', '*puterile*', and '*poderes*'. And this third concept is not limited to Article 13(2) alone.[47]

Most Treaty language versions do not use a third concept. This approach is preferable. It is not clear whether '*attributions*' have a distinct meaning from the concept of power as explained in this book. Legal experts involved in the draft Constitutional Treaty did emphasise that the French concept of '*attributions*' could only be used at the institutional level, and not for the Union as a whole.[48] As mentioned above, the same applies to power.

If anything, this additional concept merely seems to reflect an idea of powers *within fields of competence*. Article 11 TEU on citizens' initiatives illustrates this.[49] It stipulates that a certain number of citizens may invite the Commission, 'within the framework of its powers, to submit any appropriate proposal on matters where citizens consider that a legal act of the Union is required for the purpose of implementing the Treaties'.[50] The French, Greek, Italian, Spanish, Romanian, and

[45] Article 115 TFEU.

[46] Article 114(1) TFEU.

[47] See, eg Articles 11(4) and 40 TEU.

[48] IGC Secretariat, Editorial and legal comments on the draft Treaty establishing a Constitution for Europe – Basic document CIG 4/03, 59.

[49] See also, eg Article 197 TEEC (referencing the powers/attributions of the Economic and Social Committee's transport section, which was responsible for the field of transport) and Article 15(6) TEU (referencing the powers/attributions of the High Representative of the Union for Foreign Affairs and Security Policy in the field of the common foreign and security policy).

[50] Article 11(4) TEU (Lisbon).

Portuguese versions do not refer to powers, but to a variant of '*attributions*'. This reflects that Article 11 only authorises the Commission to propose a measure that falls under an EU institution's power to act in a field of EU competence.

Nonetheless, the use of '*attributions*' remains regrettable. It is not ideal to apply a concept in a few Treaty language versions, but not in the others. Indeed, not all Treaty language versions distinguish between competence and power either (see Table 1 below). The vast majority, however, do apply the distinction. That is where the much rarer third concept differs. Moreover, its existence does not bring real added value. As Constantinesco's formula so eloquently puts it, power requires competence. The dual concepts of competence and power thus suffice. The following table lists these concepts as they appear in the Union's twenty-four official Treaty language versions.

Table 1 Competence and power in the 24 official EU languages

English	Competence	Power
Bulgarian	компетентност	правомощие
Croatian	*Nadležnost*	*Ovlast*
Czech	*Pravomoc*	
Danish	*Kompetence*	*Beføjelse*
Dutch	*Bevoegdheid*	
Estonian	*Pädevus*	*Volitus*
Finnish	*Toimivalta*	
French	*Compétence*	*Pouvoir*
Gaelic	*Inniúlacht*	*Cumhacht*
German	*Zuständigkeit*	*Befugnis*
Greek	Αρμοδιότητα	Εξουσία
Hungarian	*Hatáskör*	
Italian	*Competenza*	*Potere*
Latvian	*Kompetence*	*Pilnvara*
Lithuanian	*Kompetencija*	*Įgaliojimas*
Maltese	*Kompetenza*	*Setgħa*
Polish	*Kompetencja*	*Uprawnienie*
Portuguese	*Competência*	*Poder*
Romanian	*Competență*	*Putere*
Slovak	*Právomoc*	
Slovenian	*Pristojnost*	*Pooblastilo*
Spanish	*Competencia*	*Poder*
Swedish	*Befogenhet*	

IV. Is Competence Power?

Yet there is a weakness to this approach. The Treaties do not apply the distinction between competence and power consistently.[51] Discrepancies exist both within the same Treaty language version and between the different versions. Moreover, a lack of consistency also presents itself in the thinking of the Member States and the reasoning of the Court. Three examples suffice to illustrate this.

A. The Treaties

Several prominent Treaty provisions reflect the distinction between competence and power. Many of them featured in the previous analysis. There are the two principles of conferral.[52] There are the lists of fields of competence.[53] And there is the clear separation between competence and power in Article 40 TEU. Other Treaty provisions, however, are different. They fail to consistently apply the distinction.

A first example comes from the Charter of Fundamental Rights. Article 51(2) of the Charter states that '[t]his Charter does not establish any new power or task for the Community or the Union, or modify powers and tasks defined by the Treaties.'[54] However, Article 6(1) TEU states that '[t]he provisions of the Charter shall not extend in any way the competences of the Union as defined in the Treaties.'[55] Moreover, other language versions of Article 51 do refer to '*compétences*', '*Zuständigkeiten*', and '*competenze*'. This inconsistency creates uncertainty. Under the versions referring to competence, the Charter may lead to an increase of Union power. Under the versions referring to power, such increase is excluded. In a contribution in the discussions on the Draft Constitutional Treaty, the then Director-General of the Council Legal Service suggested the former.[56]

A second example stems from Article 19(1) TFEU. This provision empowers the Council, '[w]ithout prejudice to the other provisions of the Treaties and within the limits of the powers conferred by them upon the Union', to 'take appropriate action to combat discrimination based on sex, racial or ethnic origin, religion or belief, disability, age or sexual orientation'.[57] Article 19(1) thus authorises the Council to act. It is a Treaty legal basis. Yet it also specifies that the Council may

[51] T Tridimas and P Eeckhout, 'The External Competence of the Community and the Case-Law of the Court of Justice: Principle versus Pragmatism' (1994) 14 *Yearbook of European Law* 143, 144; B Sage-Fuller, F Prinz zur Lippe, and S Ó Conaill, 'Law and Language(s) at the Heart of the European Project: Educating Different Kinds of Lawyers' in M Freeman and F Smith (eds), *Law and Language* (OUP, 2013) 508 fn 75.

[52] Articles 5(2) and 13(2) TEU (Lisbon).

[53] Articles 3–6 TFEU.

[54] Article 51(2) Charter.

[55] Article 6(1) TEU (Lisbon).

[56] European Convention, Working Document 13 of Working group II 'Incorporation of the Charter/accession to the ECHR', CONV 2002–2003, 18.

[57] Article 19(1) TFEU.

only act within its existing powers. This statement is rather puzzling. It either has no meaning at all (Article 19(1) itself grants a power to act) or is contradictory (why need a different power if Article 19(1) provides a legal basis?).

To overcome this conundrum, Article 19(1)'s reference to power is often read to mean competence instead.[58] Within the existing fields of Union competence, this provision then grants an additional power. Other language versions support this interpretation. The French, German, and Italian versions of Article 19(1) refer to '*compétences*', '*Zustandigkeiten*', and '*competenze*', respectively.[59] The preparations of the Lisbon Treaty provide further backing to this interpretation. A lawyer-linguist document clarifies that the legislation concerned may be adopted 'in all domains entering the competences of the Union'.[60]

Even with a reference to competence, however, Article 19(1) remains problematic. Indeed, the provision cannot logically refer to powers. But a limitation to the Union's existing competences is not convincing either. Article 19(1) does more than simply conferring a new power; it also links this power to a new objective. It allows the Council to adopt measures with the *aim* of combating various forms of discrimination. Article 19(1) thus also affects competence's objectives dimension. Within the Treaties' existing subject matter competences, it introduces a non-discrimination objective and a power to pursue that objective. A Council Directive implementing the principle of equal treatment between persons irrespective of racial or ethnic origin thus limits its scope to subject matters such as 'employment' and 'access to and supply of goods and services'.[61] Article 19(1) itself, however, reflects nothing of this 'competence' nuance.

B. The Court

The Court does not consistently distinguish between competence and power. However, even without using the terms competence and power, it has clearly recognised the relevance of their respective meanings. In *Gezamenlijke Steenkoolmijnen*, it contrasted 'fields' of operation with 'means' for their application.[62] And when several Member States challenged a Commission Decision setting up a prior communication and consultation procedure on migration policies in relation to non-member countries, the judges identified two separate questions.[63] First,

[58] P Craig, *EU Administrative Law* (OUP, 2012) 545; M Bell, *Anti-discrimination Law and the European Union* (OUP, 2002) 131.

[59] Article 19(1) TFEU.

[60] Juristes-linguistes, Explications relatives à la Charte des droits fondamentaux, 4630/07, 12 (*'dans tout domaine entrant dans les compétences de l'Union'*).

[61] Article 3(1) of Council Directive 2000/43/EC of 29 June 2000 implementing the principle of equal treatment between persons irrespective of racial or ethnic origin, OJ L180.

[62] Case C-30/59 *Gezamenlijke Steenkoolmijnen* [1961] ECR-00003 ECLI:EU:C:1961:2, 23.

[63] Commission Decision 85/381/EEC of 8 July 1985 setting up a prior communication and consultation procedure on migration policies in relation to non-member countries, OJ L217; Joined Cases 281,

'whether collaboration between Member States in the social field, as provided for in the first paragraph of Article 118, extends to migration policies in relation to non-member countries'.[64] Second, 'whether the arrangement of consultations, a task conferred on the Commission by the second paragraph of Article 118, empowers the latter to issue binding measures'.[65] The first question concerned competence; the second question concerned power.

Yet the main legal basis formula does not reflect the concepts of 'competence'. The Court has repeatedly ruled that the choice of legal basis of a Union measure 'must rest on objective factors that are amenable to judicial review'.[66] These factors include 'the aim and the content of the measure'.[67] A measure's context is also relevant.[68] Clearly, this formula does not hint at a distinction between competence and power. And it certainly does not recognise the further dimensional nuances within each concept. This is significant. If the Court consistently distinguished between competence and power, surely its principal 'competence' formula would reflect this. But that is not the case.

C. The Member States

Finally, the drafters of the Treaties do not always recognise that competence and power are distinct either. The distinction's importance did arise during the preparations for the Constitutional Treaty. In the discussions on the flexibility clause,[69] members of the Belgian delegation to the Convention invoked the distinction to clarify the clause's scope. They emphasised that the scope served to mitigate a lack of Treaty powers, not of competences.[70] The Belgian delegation thus distinguished between competence and power, to clarify what the Union might do.

There is also a counter-example. It concerns Article 48(6) TEU on the simplified Treaty revision procedure. This provision allows the European Council to amend Part III of the TFEU, which sets out the Union's internal policies and actions (or competences and powers). Crucially, such an amendment 'shall not increase the competences conferred on the Union in the Treaties'.[71]

283 and 285/85 *Germany, France, Netherlands, Denmark and United Kingdom v Commission* [1987] ECR-03203 ECLI:EU:C:1987:35, para 2.

[64] Joined Cases 281, 283 and 285/85 *Germany, France, Netherlands, Denmark and United Kingdom v Commission*, para 11.

[65] ibid.

[66] See, eg Case 45/86 *Commission v Council* [1987] ECR-01493 ECLI:EU:C:1987:163, para 11; and Case C-157/21 *Poland v Parliament and Council* [2022] ECLI:EU:C:2022:98, para 121.

[67] Case 45/86 *Commission v Council*, para 11; and Case C-157/21 *Poland v Parliament and Council*, para 121.

[68] Case C-626/15 *Commission v Council (Antarctic MPAs)* [2018] ECLI:EU:C:2018:925, paras 75–76.

[69] Article 352 TFEU. See Chapter 7 for a more detailed discussion on this provision.

[70] L Michel, K De Gucht, E Di Rupo, A Van Lancker, P Chevalier, and M Nagy, Proposition d'amendement à l'Article 16, CONV 2002–2003.

[71] Article 48(6) TEU (Lisbon).

That condition reached Germany's Federal Constitutional Court. In a claim on the compliance of the Lisbon Treaty with the German Basic Law, an applicant argued that Article 48(6) only excluded the attribution of new competences to the Union.[72] New powers, by contrast, remained possible. The German government dismissed this argument. It denied that EU law recognised any distinction between competence and power. The Constitutional Court did not provide an answer and lacked the jurisdiction to do so anyway. In the CJEU, the question never explicitly arose.

At first sight, the applicant's concerns were largely unfounded. Indeed, Article 48(6) TEU does not explicitly exclude the conferral of new powers. But it does limit the simplified revision to Part III of the TFEU.[73] The European Council could not, therefore, introduce harmonisation powers in fields of supporting competence.[74] After all, such an amendment would affect the categories of competence in Part I of the Treaty. Moreover, by virtue of Article 352 TFEU, the Union already enjoys all necessary powers within its existing competences and with respect to the constraints imposed by their categorisation. Since this only excludes harmonisation in a field of supporting competence, new powers cannot enter the Treaty through simplified revision.[75] Either these powers already exist under Article 352 or they unlawfully change the categorisation of competences.

Yet the simplified revision could still have significant power consequences. The previous paragraph only shows that it has little effect on power's instrument dimension. Nothing prevents the European Council from expanding the possible types of legal act within an existing power. Such an amendment would not go beyond Part III. But it would expand the EU institutions' powers. In addition, the European Council could also change power's procedural modalities. Thus, whether Article 48(6) excludes expansions of 'competence' or only of competence does indeed matter. The concepts of 'competence' can bring clarity here.

V. Conclusion

This short chapter gave an overview of the concepts of 'competence'. It explained the concepts of competence and power, and their dimensions (and modalities). None of this is new. The concepts' roots lie in the Treaties. They have long explained the Treaties, the secondary legislation, and the reasoning of the Court. The difficulty is that there are also counter-examples. The Treaties do not consistently

[72] Cases 2 BvE 2/08 ea [2009] BVerfG; F Mayer, Stellungnahme des Deutschen Bundestages in dem Organstreitverfahren 2 BvE 5/08, 134.

[73] See Case C-370/12 *Pringle* [2012] ECLI:EU:C:2012:756, paras 46–70.

[74] P Craig, 'The European Union Act 2011: Locks, Limits and Legality' (2011) 48 *Common Market Law Review* 1915, 1925.

[75] Article 352(3) TFEU.

distinguish between competence and power. Neither do the Union's institutions or the Member States.

Nonetheless, the concepts of 'competence' matter. They bring clear benefits. The current 'competence' debate needs more nuance and precision. And it needs concepts which are generally understood by all actors. Indeed, the existing conceptual distinctions are imperfect. Dismissing them is, therefore, understandable. This book, however, provides a different solution. It brings the concepts forward, explains them, and applies them with consistency.

3

Competence (and Power)

Logically, the 'competence' analysis starts with competence. Without a possible field of action, there can be no concrete authorisation to act either. Power only matters if there is competence. In Constantinesco's words, '[c]ompetence without power is ineffective' and '[p]ower without competence is unlawful'.[1] The details of power are, therefore, examined in the next chapter. This chapter starts with competence. It describes how the notion of competence and its two dimensions appear in concrete legal disputes. Such legal disputes exist in all areas of EU competence. But it is in the area of the internal market that concerns of competence creep often arise. It is, therefore, also in this area that a more nuanced 'competence' analysis is especially helpful.

The case study of non-economically active persons first clarifies the subject matter dimension of the internal market competence. Then, the Tobacco Advertising Directives explain the objectives dimension.[2] Both are important and, especially the latter, well-known legal disputes. They will not, however, produce a comprehensive overview of the EU's internal market competence. That is also not the point. This is not a chapter about the internal market competence. It is a chapter on competence, illustrated through internal market legal disputes.

To further emphasise this point, this chapter includes a second section. It contrasts the internal market example with that of the common commercial policy. Of course, drawing the boundaries of a specific competence and identifying the available powers within it requires an individual assessment. But the distinction between competence and power itself remains the same. The CCP competence, too, comes with a subject matter and an objectives dimension. And within each dimension, questions of power equally arise. The concepts are identical. Only their application differs.

[1] V Constantinesco, 'Compétences et pouvoirs dans les communautés européennes' (Doctoral thesis, Université de Nancy 1974) 83.

[2] Directive 98/43/EC of the European Parliament and of the Council of 6 July 1998 on the approximation of the laws, regulations and administrative provisions of the Member States relating to the advertising and sponsorship of tobacco products, OJ L213.

I. Internal Market

The internal market is seen as the 'crown jewel' of the European Union.[3] It is referred to as 'the most important development of the Community since it was founded'.[4] It is claimed to be 'an indispensable base for increasing the prosperity of the Community as a whole'[5] and, ultimately, an instrument for peace on the European continent. But, and perhaps most of all, the internal market is also a legal concept.[6] How its scope is defined has direct legal consequences. It is the subject matter of an EU competence, and its good functioning is the objective of that competence.

Since the Single European Act,[7] these two competence dimensions clearly follow from the internal market's definition. One paragraph of the current Article 26 TFEU reflects the objectives dimension: 'The Union shall adopt measures with the aim of establishing or ensuring the functioning of the internal market, in accordance with the relevant provisions of the Treaties.'[8] Another reflects the subject matter dimension: 'The internal market shall comprise an area without internal frontiers in which the free movement of goods, persons, services and capital is ensured in accordance with the provisions of the Treaties.'[9] What follows is an exploration of each competence dimension through a real legal dispute.

A. Subject Matter

To fall within a certain field of competence, an EU measure must relate to the subject matter of that competence. Understanding the scope of a competence's subject matter is, therefore, crucial. At first sight, the internal market competence poses no difficulties in that regard; its subject matter is, of course, the internal market.[10] Unlike many other subject matters, the internal market is a defined Treaty concept. It is the 'area without internal frontiers in which the free movement of goods, persons, services and capital is ensured in accordance with the provisions of the Treaties'.[11]

But Article 26 did not always exist. And neither did the internal market itself. Moreover, its eventual creation and definition could not entirely exclude subject matter questions. The case study of non-economically active persons shows why.

[3] A Renda, 'Single Market 2.0: The European Union as a Platform' in S Garben and I Govaere (eds), *The Internal Market 2.0* (Hart Publishing, 2020) 188.
[4] FA Cockfield, *The European Union: Creating the Single Market* (Wiley, 1994) 1.
[5] Commission, White Paper on Completing the Internal Market, COM(85)310, 8.
[6] S Weatherill, *The Internal Market as a Legal Concept* (OUP, 2017) 11.
[7] New Article 8a TEEC (SEA).
[8] Article 26(1) TFEU.
[9] Article 26(2) TFEU.
[10] Article 26 TFEU.
[11] Article 26(2) TFEU.

1. A Preliminary Point: From Common to (Common and) Internal Market

Before examining the place of non-economically active persons in the internal market competence, a preliminary point should be made. The Community institutions started the debates on non-economically active persons long before the adoption of the Single European Act. At that time, the 'internal market' did not yet exist. The SEA famously defined the internal market, but it also introduced the concept itself. Until then, the Rome Treaty only used the (undefined) concept of the 'common market'.

Today, the relationship between the common and internal markets has lost its relevance. In the preparatory works for the draft Constitutional Treaty, the Council Legal Service casually invited the drafters to change all references from common to internal market.[12] The current Treaties refer to the internal market alone. This chapter, however, explores the past. The question thus arises to what extent *common market* examples can shed a light on the subject matter dimension of the *internal market* competence. The answer logically depends on the relationship between the common and internal markets.

Several theories on this relationship existed.[13] Some scholars considered both concepts to be synonymous.[14] Some argued that the common market was wider, because it included the competition, transport, and agricultural policies.[15] And others still added that the internal market may indeed have been a narrowing in scope, but a deepening in ambition.[16]

One thing is certain: the introduction of the internal market concept was not an unconsidered decision. The drafters of the SEA explicitly wondered whether this concept was appropriate.[17] Regrettably, the preparatory documents do not reveal an explicit answer. That the Act did indeed introduce the internal market concept to the Treaty suggests that the drafters concluded that it was appropriate.

But even if common and internal market differed, the fundamental freedoms clearly featured in both. Chapter seven explains how the Rome Treaty's common market concept had different meanings. The common market referred to the four

[12] Convention Secretariat, Note on Part Two of the Constitution – Report by the working party of experts nominated by the Legal Services of the European Parliament, the Council and the Commission, CONV 618/03, 171.

[13] See S Šarčević, *Language and Culture in EU Law: Multidisciplinary Perspectives* (Routledge, 2015) 215 on the terminological confusion in general.

[14] C Barnard, *The Substantive Law of the EU* (OUP, 2016) 12; P Oliver, 'Introduction' in P Oliver (ed), *Oliver on Free Movement of Goods in the European Union* (Hart Publishing, 2010) 7.

[15] P Pescatore, 'Some Critical Remarks on the Single European Act' (1987) 24 *Common Market Law Review* 9, 11; K Mortelmans, 'The Common Market, the Internal Market, and the Single Market: What's in a Market?' (1998) 35 *Common Market Law Review* 101, 107.

[16] K Lenaerts, *European Union Law* (Sweet & Maxwell, 2011) 201; Weatherill, *The Internal Market as a Legal Concept* (n 6), 18.

[17] Groupe Union européenne, Projet de dispositions complétant le Traité CEE en vue de l'établissement du marché intérieur, UE(85)71, 2.

freedoms or to the entire Treaty system.[18] Before the SEA, the common market in the wide sense thus encompassed the common market in the narrow freedoms sense. After the SEA, the internal market replaced the latter concept. The case study of non-economically active persons is limited to that sphere. It may thus rely on the internal market as the natural successor to the common market. That is what will happen below.

2. *Social Security*

The Community institutions' first real debate on the competence to promote the free movement of non-economically active persons took place in the 1970s. A Council Regulation co-ordinated national social security rules to promote the free movement of workers.[19] Under the common market (services) legal basis, the Commission proposed to extend this Regulation to self-employed persons.[20] But the Council considered going further. Several Member States wanted to include non-economically active persons, such as students and 'housewives', as well.[21] From a social and political perspective, excluding this small number of persons seemed impossible.[22] From a legal perspective, the Member States did not see obstacles to an inclusion.[23] The Council Legal Service agreed.[24] At least at first, however, the Commission Legal Service did not.[25]

The question was not yet whether the free movement of non-economically active persons fell within the subject matter dimension of the common market competence. After all, the Council did not consider whether the Regulation's extension to such persons could be adopted under a common market legal basis. The Council only considered Article 235 TEEC as legal basis. This flexibility clause

[18] See, eg H Ehring, 'Allgemeine und Schlußbestimmungen (Art.235)' in H von der Groeben and H von Boeckh (eds), *Kommentar zum EWG Vertrag II* (Verlag August Lutzeyer, 1958) 448; L Ferrari Bravo and A Giardina, 'Art. 235' in R Quadri, R Monaco, and A Trabucchi (eds), *Trattato istitutivo della comunità economica europea: commentario* (Giuffrè, 1965) 1707; G Marenco, 'Les conditions d'application de l'article 235 du Traité CEE' (1970) 12 *Revue du marché commun* 147, 150.

[19] Regulation (EEC) No 1408/71 of the Council of 14 June 1971 on the application of social security schemes to employed persons and their families moving within the Community, OJ L149. Its legal bases were Articles 2 (tasks of the Community), 7 (non-discrimination), and 51 (free movement of workers in the common market) TEEC.

[20] Commission, Extension de la réglementation communautaire sur la sécurité sociale des travailleurs migrants à tous les assurés qui se déplacent à l'intérieur de la Communauté, COM(78)466.

[21] Working Party on Social Questions, Note on the Proposals on social security for self-employed persons 180/78, 4; Working Party on Social Questions, Note on the Proposals on social security for self-employed persons, 256/78, 4.

[22] Working Party on Social Questions, Note on the Proposals on social security for self-employed persons, 256/78, 4.

[23] Working Party on Social Questions, Note on the Proposals on social security for self-employed persons, 56/78, 3.

[24] Working Party on Social Questions, Note on the Proposals on social security for self-employed persons, 443/78, 2.

[25] ibid, 3; Working Party on Social Questions, Note on the Proposals on social security for self-employed persons, 256/78, 2.

allowed the Council to adopt measures 'to attain, in the course of the operation of the common market, one of the objectives of the Community'.[26] These measures had to be necessary to attain the objective, no more specific legal bases to adopt them could exist, and the Council had to decide by unanimity. Chapter seven explores Article 235 in detail. For now, it suffices to say that the clause initially conferred both competence and power. Whether the free movement of all persons fell within the scope of the common market competence was, therefore, superfluous.[27]

The Council Legal Service interpreted Article 235 and the Community's objectives widely. It emphasised that raising the standard of living in the Community was a Community objective under Article 2 TEEC.[28] More interestingly, it also referred to Article 3(c) TEEC. That Article listed, among the activities of the Community, 'the abolition, as between Member States, of obstacles to freedom of movement for persons, services and capital'.[29] According to the Council Legal Service, that notion of free movement of persons was not restricted to workers and self-employed persons.

Supported by its Legal Service, the Commission reasoned more cautiously. It did not accept the free movement of non-economically active persons as a Community objective.[30] The Treaty only protected such freedom for workers and self-employed persons.[31] Article 3(c) had to be read in the light of the specific Treaty articles on free movement; as they did not extend to non-economically active persons, neither could Article 3(c). The Commission Legal Service, therefore, rejected Article 235 as a legal basis.

The Council Legal Service won the debate. It convinced the Commission Legal Service that the promotion of free movement of all persons corresponded to an Articles 2 and 3(c) objective.[32] This did not, however, settle the competence

[26] Article 235 TEEC.

[27] The measure also had to pursue its objectives within the framework of the functioning of the common market. This condition was arguably fulfilled – as consumers, non-economically active persons received services in the common market. Chapter 7 explains that the common market condition was often ignored. Here, too, the Council and Commission Legal Services did not explicitly consider it.

[28] Working Party on Social Questions, Note on the Proposals on social security for self-employed persons, 1097/78, 6a; Working Party on Social Questions, Summary of proceedings on the Proposals on social security for self-employed persons, 4304/79, 3a.

[29] Working Party on Social Questions, Note on the Proposals on social security for self-employed persons, 1097/78, 6a.

[30] Working Party on Social Questions, Note on the Proposals on social security for self-employed persons, 256/78, 2.

[31] PJG Kapteyn, R Barents, and P VerLoren van Themaat, *Inleiding tot het recht van de Europese Gemeenschappen: na Maastricht* (Kluwer, 1995) 406; FG Jacobs, 'The Free Movement of Persons within the EEC' (1977) 30 *Current Legal Problems* 123, 124; P Craig, 'The Evolution of the Single Market' in C Barnard and J Scott (eds), *The Law of the Single European market: Unpacking the Premises* (Hart Publishing, 2002) 2; Rapport des chefs de délégation aux Ministres des Affaires Etrangères (1956) ('Spaak Report') 74.

[32] Working Party on Social Questions, Note on the Proposals on social security for self-employed persons, 9433/79, 6.

question altogether. The Member States were not in full agreement. Denmark argued that recourse to Article 235 required an economic objective.[33] The Legal Services replied that the proposal did indeed pursue an economic objective; non-economically active persons were consumers,[34] and thus 'potentially participat[ed] in economic life'.[35]

This reasoning was not new.[36] In *Luisi e Carbone*, the Court ruled that the movement of service recipients was 'the necessary corollary' of the freedom to provide services.[37] Much earlier, the *Spaak Report* had hinted at this idea when it referred to hotel services.[38] Nonetheless, the Council finally decided to limit the new measure to self-employed persons and their families alone.[39]

Thus, the question of non-economically active persons did not emerge as a common market competence question. Since Article 235 also granted competence, assessing whether such persons fell within the subject matter of the common market was not needed. The legal thinking, however, cautiously moved towards an affirmative answer. The Council and, later, Commission Legal Services saw Article 3(c) as an expression of free movement of persons in general. A logical (but unspoken) conclusion would then be that the subject matter of the common market included the free movement of persons in general too. Yet caution remained. The Legal Services' subsidiary argument on non-economically active persons illustrates how the common market's subject matter scope remained uncertain.

3. *Residence (1)*

A second example illustrates the same uncertainty. In 1979, the Commission proposed a general Residence Directive.[40] Nationals of the Member States, regardless of economic activity, would have the right to reside in another Member State. In the explanatory memorandum, the Commission justified Article 235 as legal basis

[33] P Lachmann, 'Some Danish Reflections on the Use of Article 235 of the Rome Treaty' (1981) 18 *Common Market Law Review* 447, 447.

[34] Working Party on Social Questions, Note on the Proposals on social security for self-employed persons, 9433/79, 6.

[35] Permanent Representatives Committee, Report on the Proposals on social security for self-employed persons, 10689/79, 4.

[36] W Van Gerven and P van den Bossche, 'Freedom of movement and equal treatment for students in Europe: an emerging principle?' in HG Schermers, C Flinterman, and AE Kellermann (eds), *Free movement of persons in Europe: legal problems and experiences* (Asser, 1993) 418–19.

[37] Joined Cases 286/82 and 26/83 *Luisi e Carbone v Ministero del Tesoro* [1984] ECR-00377 ECLI:EU:C:1984:35, para 10. See also Case 186/87 *Cowan v Trésor public* [1989] ECR-00195 ECLI:EU:C:1989:47. But see Opinion in Case 118/75 *Watson and Bellmann* [1976] ECR-01185 ECLI:EU:C:1976:79, 1204 for an early rejection of this approach.

[38] Spaak Report (n 31) 32; P Van Der Mei, *Free Movement of Persons within the European Community* (Hart Publishing, 2003) 50.

[39] Council Regulation (EEC) No 1390/81 of 12 May 1981 extending to self-employed persons and members of their families Regulation (EEC) No 1408/71 on the application of social security schemes to employed persons and their families moving within the Community, OJ L143.

[40] Commission, Proposal for a Council Directive on a right of residence for nationals of Member States in the territory of another Member State, COM(79)215.

on the ground that the 'freedom of movement for persons within the Community [was] one of the explicit objectives of the Community listed in Article 3 of the EEC Treaty'.[41]

While Title III implemented that objective for economically engaged persons, '[t]he Treaty contain[ed] … no specific powers with regard to persons not carrying on an economic activity';[42] hence the application of the flexibility clause. Again, the question of non-economically active persons was, therefore, not an internal market competence question. The main issue remained whether the free movement of such persons was a Community objective.[43]

Unsurprisingly, the Council Legal Service agreed with the Commission.[44] After all, it had defended precisely this reasoning in the social security file. Yet the Council Legal Service also made a concession. Its Opinion admitted that a contrary view could be reached. After all, the specific Treaty provisions guaranteeing free movement only did so for economically active persons.[45] So did the provisions conferring specific powers to act upon the institutions. 'The conclusion might therefore be drawn that free movement [was] an objective of the Community only insofar as economically active persons [were] concerned.'[46]

The Council Legal Service itself, of course, reached a different conclusion. It emphasised that Article 3(c) was not written narrowly.[47] The provision referred to persons in general and had to be interpreted literally. But the Legal Service did recognise the weakness in the argument that the Rome Treaty covered the free movement of *all* persons. The Treaty simply did not offer sufficient explicit support to avoid reasonable doubt. If the Community legislator really wanted to adopt the Residence Directive, it probably needed a stronger legal backing.

4. *The Single European Act*

This backing came with the Single European Act. During the Treaty negotiations, the Commission proposed an internal market definition that was clearly meant to transcend the economy.[48] Removing intra-Community barriers evidently was of great economic significance. But the Commission also emphasised the internal market's 'human significance'.[49] It formed an area where 'citizens of the Community

[41] ibid, 4.
[42] ibid.
[43] Groupe ad hoc "Droits spéciaux", Résultats des travaux sur les Droits spéciaux des citoyens, 5607/80, 2–3.
[44] Council Legal Service, Opinion on the Proposal for a Council Directive on a right of residence, 7084/80; H Taschner, 'Free movement of students, retired persons and other European citizens – a difficult legislative process' in HG Schermers, C Flinterman, and AE Kellermann (eds) (n 36) 430.
[45] Council Legal Service, Opinion on the Proposal for a Council Directive on a right of residence, 7084/80, 3.
[46] ibid.
[47] ibid, 5.
[48] Groupe restraint Union européenne, Vademecum sur le Marché Intérieur, UE(85)186, 1 and 3.
[49] ibid, 1 and 3.

had the possibility to circulate, reside or work as if they had remained in their own Member State'.[50] For the Commission, an important aspect of its proposed internal market definition was, thus, the clearer inclusion of free movement for all persons within the Community.[51]

Since the social security file, the Commission had been convinced that Article 3(c) extended to non-economically active persons. Logically, this meant that such persons fell within the subject matter of the common market. But the examples of the social security and residence proposals showed that uncertainty remained. The Commission Legal Service realised this.[52] Thus, the internal market definition served to remove the doubts. The free movement of non-economically active persons was to be a clear part of the internal market competence's subject matter dimension.

The Member States rigorously debated the proposed definition[53] and received explicit advice on its legal implications.[54] A Council Legal Service Opinion examined whether defining the internal market as 'an area without internal frontiers' or 'single market without internal frontiers' made any legal difference.[55] Although the Legal Service recognised that only the latter vocabulary hinted at an economic idea, it concluded that there was no substantive difference between the definitions.[56] After all, it had already expressed a consistent view that Article 3(c) of the Rome Treaty applied regardless of economic activity.[57] Defining the internal market as an area or as a market would not affect that interpretation. When they approved the Commission's definition, the Member States thus understood its wide meaning.[58]

Admittedly, the new Article 8a did not introduce an internal market with four freedoms, full stop. It only did so 'in accordance with the provisions of this Treaty'.[59] In that sense, Article 8a resembled Article 3(c). Yet these Articles differed in a fundamental way.[60] Article 3 TEEC acted as an introductory provision. It offered an overview of the Community's objectives and activities. If the operative part of the Treaty only addressed economically active persons, it was possible to read

[50] ibid.

[51] Commission, Note à l'attention de Monsieur le Président Delors, P1087/85, 3.

[52] Groupe Union européenne, Le grand marché intérieur, UE(85)55, 2–3.

[53] Commission, Compte rendu succinct de la 2ème réunion du Groupe de préparation de la Conférence des Gouvernements des Etats membres members, SG(85) D/11912, 5; Commission, Compte rendu succinct de la 2ème réunion du Groupe de préparation de la Conférence des Gouvernements des Etats membres membres, SG(85) D/12198, 5 and 8; Commission, Note sur la 5ème réunion du Groupe de préparation de la Conférence des Gouvernements des Etats members, SI(85)658, 2; Commission, Note sur la Réunion ministérielle de la Conférence inter-gouvernementale P/1404/85, 4–5.

[54] Service juridique du Conseil, Avis sur la Définition du marché intérieur, CONF-RGEM 118/85.

[55] ibid.

[56] ibid, 2.

[57] ibid, 3.

[58] But see J Cloos, G Reinesch, D Vignes, and J Weyland, *Le traité de Maastricht: genèse, analyse, commentaires* (Bruylant, 1993) 168 for a different opinion.

[59] Article 8a TEEC (SEA).

[60] E Grabitz, 'Die Einheitliche Europäische Akte: Rechtliche Bewertung' (1986) 9 *Integration* 95, 99; C-D Ehlermann, 'The Internal Market following the Single European Act' (1987) 24 *Common Market Law Review* 361, 366.

Article 3(c) in the same manner. Article 8a was different. It introduced the internal market's free movement of persons as a self-standing concept.[61] How that concept was to be translated in concrete measures depended on other Treaty provisions. But the concept of the internal market itself followed from Article 8a alone.

Thus, Article 8a suggested that the scope of the internal market competence extended to *all* persons. Its limitation clause only referred to power. Within the field of internal market competence, the Community institutions could only act 'in accordance with the provisions of [the] Treaty'.[62] Here, the distinction between competence and power comes to the front. With Article 8a, the Single European Act recognised or added non-economically active persons to the subject matter scope of the internal (and, therefore, common) market competence. It did not, however, introduce corresponding powers.

The SEA's new internal market power did not apply to the free movement of persons.[63] Article 100a authorised the Community legislator to harmonise national laws to ensure the establishment and good functioning of the internal market. Crucially, a qualified majority in the Council sufficed. This departure from unanimity voting significantly facilitated the decision-making process.[64] But it also meant that Member States could be bound by legislation which they objected to.

That was a sensitive issue. Article 100a did not specify which categories of national rules could be subject to harmonisation. No thematic limitation applied.[65] It sufficed that their disparities jeopardised, or risked jeopardising, the internal market. The drafters thus limited the scope of Article 100a.[66] The new harmonisation power did not apply to the entire subject matter scope of the internal market competence. Sensitive matters were excluded. The free movement of persons, including non-economically active persons, was one of them.[67]

Thus, for the purpose of this analysis, the SEA mattered in terms of competence. Non-economically active persons formed a part of the subject matter scope of the internal market competence. To ensure their free movement, however, the Community legislator had to invoke the pre-existing Treaty legal bases.[68] The competence evolution was not accompanied by an evolution of power. Article 8a delimitated the internal market's subject matter scope widely, without economic condition for persons. But it did not confer new powers to act within that extended field of competence.

[61] ibid.

[62] Article 8a TEEC (SEA).

[63] Article 100a(2) TEEC (SEA); J De Ruyt, *L'Acte Unique Européen* (Editions de l'Université de Bruxelles, 1989) 154–56.

[64] Présidence, Note sur le Marché intérieur, CONF-RGEM 94/85, 3.

[65] R Schütze, *European Union Law* (CUP, 2015) 534.

[66] Présidence, Note sur le Marché intérieur, CONF-RGEM 72/85, 3; Présidence, Note sur le Résultat des travaux de la Conférence des Représentants des Gouvernements des Etats members, CONF-RGEM 130/85, 7.

[67] Article 100a(2) TEEC (SEA).

[68] Présidence, Note sur le Résultat des travaux de la Conférence des Représentants des Gouvernements des Etats members, CONF-RGEM 130/85, 2; De Ruyt (n 63) 156.

5. From Residence (1) to Residence (2)

The 1979 proposal was never adopted. Several Member States insisted on watering down the proposed residence right by adding further restrictions and conditions.[69] They also continued to raise doubts over Article 235 as legal basis.[70] Eventually, the Commission withdrew its proposal.[71] In a change of tactics, it proposed three more targeted measures instead.[72] Each measure covered a different category of persons. The first applied to retired persons.[73] The second covered students.[74] The third granted a right of residence to non-economically active persons in general.[75]

A crucial distinction between the 1979 and 1989 general residence proposals lay in their legal bases. Instead of Article 235, the Commission now invoked Article 100 of the TEEC. It argued that both Article 3(c) and the new Article 8a 'clearly stat[ed] that all persons must enjoy freedom of movement within the Community'.[76] Since the SEA, the internal (and, therefore, common)[77] market had covered all persons. Article 100 thus applied.

This logic is somewhat puzzling. For the Commission, the SEA's entry into force warranted a legal basis shift from Article 235 to Article 100.[78] But the Commission and Council Legal Services had already argued that Article 3(c) included free movement of non-economically active persons long before the Act. This suggested that they considered such persons as part of the subject matter scope of the common market competence. And Article 100 was a common market power. Applying this logic consistently, the Commission could already have based its first residence proposal on Article 100. And that would have excluded the applicability of the residual flexibility clause altogether.

Why the Commission did not invoke Article 100 earlier remains unclear. In terms of power modalities, there was no difference between Articles 100 and 235. Both legal bases required unanimity in the Council. Both also demanded that the

[69] Taschner (n 44) 431.

[70] Groupe ad hoc "Droits spéciaux", Résultat des travaux sur la Proposition relative au droit de séjour, 8343/80, 1–2; Groupe ad hoc "Droits spéciaux", Compte rendu des travaux sur la Proposition relative au droit de séjour, 6911/83, 1; Présidence, Note sur la Proposition relative au droit de séjour, 7291/85, 6.

[71] Council, Press release on the 1316th Council meeting, 6341/89, 5.

[72] S O'Leary, 'The Free Movement of Persons and Services' in P Craig and G De Búrca (eds), *The Evolution of EU Law* (OUP, 1999) 381.

[73] Commission, Proposal for a Council Directive on the right of residence for employees and self-employed persons who have ceased their occupational activity, COM(89)275.

[74] Commission, Proposal for a Council Directive on the right of residence for students, COM(89)275.

[75] Commission, Proposal for a Council Directive on the right of residence, COM(89)275.

[76] ibid, 7; Working Party on Special Rights of Citizens, Summary of proceedings on the Proposals for Directives on the right of residence, 7842/89, 1–2.

[77] Here, the question of the distinction between common market and internal market reappears. Article 8a defined the internal market. Article 100, however, still referred to the common market. The Commission clearly reasoned that the latter concept included (at least?) the internal market freedoms. That view seems plausible.

[78] Working Party of Counsellors from the Permanent Representations on Special Rights of Citizens, Note on the Proposals for Directives on the right of residence, 8361/89, 2.

Council consult the Parliament. So, in practice, it did not matter much. Perhaps the reason was symbolic. After the SEA, the Commission felt strengthened in its free movement approach. The reasoning had long been that Article 3(c), and the common market, covered all persons; but Article 8a greatly increased its credibility. By adopting an internal market definition which referred to persons in general, the drafters of the Treaty seemed to confirm the Legal Services' view. The residence proposals' shift in legal basis reflected that important backing.

To a large extent, the Council Legal Service shared the Commission's reasoning. It confirmed that Article 8a reinforced the earlier interpretation of free movement for all persons under Article 3(c).[79] Nonetheless, it rejected Article 100 as a legal basis. Again, the distinction between competence and power helps to understand why. The Council Legal Service agreed that the proposed Directive fell within the internal market competence. But, it argued, the Article 100 power did not apply.

The proposal did indeed harmonise national laws to some extent. Its real impact on free movement, however, happened by granting a new right to the Community's citizens, rather than through the approximation of diverging national laws.[80] For the Council Legal Service, the proposed Directive, therefore, did not satisfy the harmonisation requirement of Article 100. It used a different power instrument. Much to the Commission's regret, Article 235 became the legal basis instead.[81]

This was not the end of the story. It continued with the negotiations of the Maastricht Treaty. Again, the free movement of *all* persons reached the agenda.[82] The outcome was the creation of an EU citizen, with (some) free movement rights regardless of economic activity.[83] There is no need to look into those further developments here. The point of this chapter has already been made: the case study of non-economically active persons illustrated that the internal (or common) market competence does indeed have a subject matter dimension; and that dimension has real legal importance.

B. Objectives

There is also a second competence dimension. A measure must not only relate to the subject matter of the competence it invokes; it must also pursue the objective(s)

[79] Council Legal Service, Opinion on the Proposals for Council directives on the right of residence, 8512/89, 2.

[80] ibid, 12.

[81] Vice-Président de la Commission M Bangeman, Lettre sur les Directives relatives au droit de séjour, 8156/90, 1; Taschner (n 44) 436.

[82] Discussions on the opportunity of free movement for all persons illustrate the SEA's ambiguity. See Council Ministers of Foreign Affairs, Note on the Preparation of the Intergovernmental Conference on Political Union, 10661/90, 9–10; General Secretariat, Note on Political Union – Outcome of the proceedings of the personal representatives of the Ministers for Foreign Affairs, 10356/90, Annex 3, 3.

[83] C Barnard, 'The Day the Clock Stopped: EU Citizenship and the Single Market' in P Koutrakos and J Snell (eds), *Research Handbook on the Law of the EU's Internal Market* (Edward Elgar Publishing, 2017) 105.

of that competence. For the internal market competence, that objective is clear.[84] Article 26 TFEU refers to 'the aim of establishing or ensuring the functioning of the internal market'.[85] A measure can only be an internal market competence measure if it seeks to promote the internal market. That went wrong in one of the most notorious competence sagas in EU law. For the first time, the Court struck down an internal market harmonisation measure because it did not contribute to the internal market.[86] As an illustration of competence's objectives dimension, this is the story of the Tobacco Advertising Directives.

1. The Tobacco Advertising Directive (I)

That the Court annulled the first Tobacco Advertising Directive is famous.[87] Less well known is what came before. Competence questions did not first arise in Court; they governed the Directive from its very conception. When the Commission presented its original tobacco advertising proposal, it invoked Article 100a as a legal basis.[88] By harmonising divergent national rules, the proposed Directive would remove obstacles to trade and thus promote the free movement of tobacco advertising products (not tobacco products) and ensure undistorted competition between tobacco advertisers (not tobacco producers).[89] But in the Council, not everyone agreed. From the start, several delegations refused to accept that the measure fell within the internal market competence.[90]

To understand the competence tensions, it is necessary to have a closer look at what the Commission proposed. Adopting the Tobacco Advertising Directive proved to be an onerous matter. The Member States not only started from very different views on the proposed measure's legality and desirability, but were also

[84] S Crosby, 'The single market and the rule of law' (1991) 16 *European Law Review* 451, 457.

[85] Article 26(1) TFEU.

[86] S Weatherill, *EU Consumer Law and Policy* (Edward Elgar, 2014) 14.

[87] Case C-376/98 *Germany/Parliament and Council* [2000] ECR I-08419 ECLI:EU:C:2000:544. See, eg R Barents, 'De tabaksrichtlijn in rook opgegaan' (2000) 12 *Nederlands tijdschrift voor Europees recht* 327; O Segnana, 'Le contentieux de la base juridique. A propos de l'annulation par la Cour de justice des CE de la directive relative à la publicité pour le tabac' (2001) 75 *Journal des Tribunaux: droit européen* 9; KJM Mortelmans and RH Van Ooik, 'Het Europese verbod op tabaksreclame: verbetering van de interne markt of bescherming van de volksgezondheid?' (2001) 50 *Ars Aequi* 114; TK Hervey, 'Up in smoke? Community (anti)-tobacco law and policy' (2001) 26 *European Law Review* 101; S Weatherill, 'European private law – Is there a future after the Tobacco Advertising decision' in PC Müller-Graff (ed), *Europäisches Integrationsrecht im Querschnitt* (Nomos, 2003) 93.

[88] Commission, Proposal for a Council Directive on the advertising of tobacco products in the press and by means of bills and posters, COM(89)163.

[89] ibid, 2.

[90] Working Party on Health Questions, Summary of proceedings on Proposal for a Tobacco Advertising Directive, 7833/89, 9a; Working Party on Health Questions, Summary of proceedings on Proposal for a Tobacco Advertising Directive, 9336/89, 2a.

not inclined to alter them.[91] To gain support, the Commission, therefore, amended its proposal several times.[92]

The original proposal laid down rules for warnings in advertising in the press and on bills and posters[93] and prohibited some forms of advertising.[94] A second proposal resembled the first, but only covered authorised advertising.[95] With the third proposal, the Commission shifted the approach to a general tobacco advertising ban.[96] The final Directive followed the same line; with some exceptions, it banned tobacco advertising and sponsorship altogether.[97]

The amendments failed to remove the competence-critical delegations' concerns. Essentially, they raised two objections. First, they argued that the proposed Directive's scope was too wide.[98] If the aim was to promote the internal market, the measure should only cover goods and services with a cross-border nature.[99] Newspapers and posters which did not ordinarily move within the internal market, therefore, had to remain outside the scope of the Directive. The shift to a general advertising ban only strengthened these concerns.[100]

Second, the delegations raised concerns on the possibility of more stringent national rules. In the original proposal, the Commission included a controversial provision. The first paragraph of the proposed Article 5 appeared to be a standard free movement clause.[101] Member States could not 'cite tobacco advertising as the reason for prohibiting or restricting the sale of newspapers … and posters

[91] Presidency, Note on the Amended proposal for a Tobacco Advertising Directive, 10657/94, 2.

[92] Commission, Amended proposal for a Council Directive on the authorized advertising of tobacco products in the press and by means of bills and posters, COM(90)147; Commission, Modified Proposal for a Council Directive on advertising for tobacco products, COM(91)111; Commission, Amended proposal for a Council Directive on the approximation of Member States' laws, regulations and administrative provisions on advertising for tobacco products, COM(92)196.

[93] Commission, Proposal for a Tobacco Advertising Directive on the advertising of tobacco products in the press and by means of bills and posters, COM(89)163, 6.

[94] ibid, 7.

[95] Commission, Amended proposal for a Council Directive on the authorized advertising of tobacco products in the press and by means of bills and posters, COM(90)147, 9. This allowed Member States to maintain or introduce a general tobacco advertising ban without the need for a clause allowing stricter national rules.

[96] Commission, Modified Proposal for a Council Directive on advertising for tobacco products, COM(91)111, 15; Commission, Amended proposal for a Council Directive on the approximation of Member States' laws, regulations and administrative provisions on advertising for tobacco products, COM(92)196, 8.

[97] Article 3 of Tobacco Advertising Directive I, 98/43/EC.

[98] General Secretariat, Introductory note on the Proposal for a Tobacco Advertising Directive, 6092/90, 2; Working Party on Health Questions, Outcome of proceedings – Amended proposal for a Tobacco Advertising Directive, 8077/91, 8; General Secretariat, Text tabled by the German delegation, 7788/93, Annex 9.

[99] ibid.

[100] Working Party on Health Questions, Outcome of proceedings on the Amended proposal for a Tobacco Advertising Directive, 5409/94, 5.

[101] Working Party on Health Questions, Summary of proceedings on the Proposal for a Tobacco Advertising Directive, 7833/89, 8a.

which comply with [the] Directive'.[102] But there was also a second paragraph: as long as they did not change the Directive's rules on advertising form and content, Member States could still introduce tobacco advertising measures inspired by public health.[103]

Article 5(2) served to reassure the Member States which already prohibited tobacco advertising altogether.[104] They could maintain their bans. From a public health perspective, the clause was thus desirable. But for the internal market, it raised difficult questions. The problem lay in Article 5(2)'s confusing wording.[105] In particular, it was not clear whether the Member States with more stringent rules could ban the marketing of Directive-compliant goods from other Member States based on non-compliance with their stricter national rules. This would hinder free movement. And that would be contrary to the internal market competence's objective of removing barriers to trade.[106]

Several delegations thus requested the deletion of the second paragraph.[107] They did so in vain; the final Directive still allowed Member States to apply stricter measures for public health reasons. Moreover, it did not include an equivalent of the original Article 5(1).[108] In the original proposal, the free circulation of Directive-compliant goods and services remained uncertain. The final Directive denied that free circulation outright. For the critical delegations, the proposed Directive, therefore, did not pursue an internal market competence objective. Instead, it aimed to reduce tobacco consumption to protect public health.[109]

The Council Legal Service agreed.[110] Initially, it had supported the Commission's proposal. In a very short Opinion, the Legal Service concluded that the first proposal fell within the internal market competence.[111] The Opinion simply followed the Commission's assessment that the absence of common tobacco advertising rules hindered the internal market, and failed to address the proposed Article 5.

When the Commission proposed a general ban, however, the Legal Service became more critical. It followed the critical delegations in their two major concerns. The Directive unlawfully covered goods and services which were 'not

[102] Commission, Proposal for a Council Directive on the advertising of tobacco products in the press and by means of bills and posters, COM(89)163, 7.

[103] ibid.

[104] Working Party on Health Questions, Summary of proceedings on the Proposal for a Tobacco Advertising Directive, 4562/90, 11a.

[105] ibid.

[106] Working Party on Health Questions, Summary of proceedings on the Proposal for a Tobacco Advertising Directive, 8063/89, 9a.

[107] Working Party on Health Questions, Summary of proceedings on the Proposal for a Tobacco Advertising Directive, 10989/89, 11a; Working Party on Health Questions, Summary of proceedings on the Proposal for a Tobacco Advertising Directive, 4562/90, 12a.

[108] Article 5 of Tobacco Advertising Directive I, 98/43/EC.

[109] General Secretariat, Situation report on the Amended proposal for a Tobacco Advertising Directive, 9457/92, 3.

[110] Council Legal Service, Opinion on the Amended proposal for Tobacco Advertising Directive (Legal basis), 10732/93, 7.

[111] ibid, 6.

routinely traded between the Member States' and did not secure the free movement of goods and services (such as newspapers) that did have an internal market dimension.[112] Its objective was to protect public health. And Article 100a could 'not be used as the legal basis for the adoption of measures whose princip[al] objective [was] health protection'.[113]

Yet the Community legislator adopted the Directive based on internal market powers within the internal market competence.[114] Sceptics could point out that she had no choice; the public health competence excluded harmonisation powers.[115] That is true. But the Directive's preparatory documents do show that competence mattered. The Commission Legal Service responded to the Council Legal Service's comments.[116] It argued that the proposed Directive did contribute to the internal market. In the absence of common rules, sectors in Member States which banned tobacco advertising would be competitively disadvantaged compared with sectors which could rely on such advertising for funding.

Admittedly, the Commission Legal Service did not engage with the Article 5 concerns. It also did not explain why, if the rationale was undistorted competition, the Directive had to cover sectors which did not financially depend on advertising. Nonetheless, the fact remains that the Member States in the Council did not simply disregard legal advice when they adopted the Directive. There was a legal debate on competence, with two opposing views. The qualified majority chose the view that supported adoption. Doing so meant that the measure was likely to go to Court.[117] Perhaps it also meant that the scope of the Community's competence was not very well understood. It did not, however, mean that competence did not matter.

After almost a decade of negotiations, the Community legislator adopted the Tobacco Advertising Directive. It banned tobacco advertising and allowed Member States to impose stricter rules. With Articles 100a, 57(2), and 66 as legal bases, it was presented as an internal market measure. Germany, one of the most critical delegations, voted against the Directive.[118] In a statement, it stressed that its legal basis doubts had not been removed.[119] Whether the Directive indeed pursued an internal market objective, and hence could fall under the internal

[112] ibid, 5, 9, and 10.

[113] ibid, 5.

[114] Article 100a and, to emphasise the link with services, Articles 57(2) and 66 of the TEC (Maastricht). See Permanent Representatives Committee, Introductory note on the Amended proposal for a Tobacco Advertising Directive, 12654/97, 2.

[115] Article 129 TEC (Maastricht).

[116] Working Party on Health Questions, Outcome of proceedings on the Amended proposal for a Tobacco Advertising Directive, 5409/94, 2–5.

[117] General Secretariat, Information note on the Proposal for a Tobacco Advertising Directive, 8401/98, 2.

[118] Council, Addendum to the Draft minutes of the 2109th Council meeting, 9280/98 Add1, 3. So did Austria.

[119] ibid, 4.

market competence, remained controversial. But a qualified majority sufficed.[120] A few months later, the Court received an application for annulment.[121]

2. Tobacco Advertising (I)

In Court, Germany repeated its earlier objections. Essentially, the Tobacco Adverting Directive did not pursue an internal market competence objective; it did not aim to establish or enhance the functioning of the internal market.[122] It covered situations without significant cross-border character. Typically, advertising media were not often traded between Member States,[123] and advertising service providers focused on their own national market.[124]

Moreover, even if the advertising market did lend itself to cross-border trade, the Directive failed to promote such trade. Rather, by banning virtually all tobacco advertising, it negated the free movement of advertising goods and services.[125] It also lacked a free movement clause to mitigate the impact of stricter national rules.[126] In summary, this was not an internal market measure. The Directive pursued public health objectives and unlawfully relied on internal market legal bases.[127]

Germany won the case. In line with the Advocate General's Opinion, the Court annulled the Directive on the ground that it could not be validly adopted under the invoked legal bases.[128] Importantly, the judgment confirmed that an internal market competence measure must aim to promote the internal market.[129] It must genuinely 'have as [its] object the establishment and functioning of the internal market'.[130] To satisfy this criterion, the measure had to either eliminate obstacles to free movement or remove distortions of competition.[131] The Directive did neither; at least not entirely.

The Court accepted that the ban promoted the free movement of newspapers, magazines, and periodicals.[132] After all, it prevented a newspaper from a Member

[120] S Weatherill, 'The Limits of Legislative Harmonization Ten Years after Tobacco Advertising: How the Court's Case Law has become a "Drafting Guide"' (2011) 12 *German Law Journal* 827, 830.
[121] Case C-376/98 *Tobacco Advertising I.*
[122] ibid, paras 23–24.
[123] ibid, paras 15–16.
[124] ibid, para 22.
[125] ibid, para 24.
[126] ibid, para 18.
[127] ibid, para 32.
[128] ibid, para 118; Opinion in Case C-376/98 *Germany v Parliament and Council* [2000] ECR I-08419 ECLI:EU:C:2000:324, para 181.
[129] Case C-376/98 *Tobacco Advertising I*, paras 83–85; Common Market Law Review, 'Editorial comments: Taking (the limits of) competences seriously' (2000) 37 *Common Market Law Review* 1301, 1304; M Ludwigs, 'Case C-380/03, Federal Republic of Germany v. European Parliament and Council of the European Union (Tobacco Advertising II)' (2007) 44 *Common Market Law Review* 1159, 1169.
[130] Article 100a(1) TEC (Maastricht).
[131] Case C-376/98 *Tobacco Advertising I*, para 95.
[132] ibid, para 98.

State allowing tobacco advertising from facing a marketing ban in another Member State on the ground that it contained a prohibited advertisement. Banning such advertising thus ensured the free movement of the advertising medium.[133] For other advertising media, such as posters, parasols, and ashtrays, however, the Directive did not aid free movement.[134]

Moreover, even trade in newspapers did not straightforwardly benefit from the Directive. Article 5 posed problems. By allowing Member States to impose stricter rules without a clause that ensured the free movement of products complying with the harmonised standards, the Directive did not promote the internal market.[135] The Commission, Council, and Parliament's attempts to explain Article 5 as securing such free movement did not convince the Court.[136]

The Directive also did not eliminate appreciable distortions of competition.[137] Again, its scope was too wide. The Court accepted that a tobacco advertising ban could sometimes be justified on competition grounds. Sports events could, for instance, be relocated to Member States allowing tobacco advertising, to the detriment of Member States with a ban.[138] Such specific examples, however, could not justify an outright ban.[139] The Directive, therefore, did not pursue an internal market competence objective through the competition side either. Articles 100a, 57(2), and 66 could not be its legal bases.[140]

The Court also made an important statement on power. As legal bases, the Community legislator invoked Article 100a on general harmonisation and Articles 57(2) and 66 on services. Although the Court mainly focused on Article 100a, it stressed that the internal market objectives requirement also applied to Articles 57(2) and 66.[141] That is important; it shows the dynamic between competence and power. To act within a certain field of competence, the Union often has several possible powers. Whichever of these powers it invokes, it must satisfy the requirements of the corresponding competence. *Tobacco Advertising I* illustrates this. Articles 100a, 57(2), and 66 all fell within the internal market competence. Thus, all measures adopted under these powers must aim to promote the internal market.

Power also played a second important role in the Directive's story. That the use of internal market powers necessitated the pursuit of an internal market competence objective has already been underlined above. Germany accused the Directive of pursuing a public health objective instead. Here, the fact that the Community legislator invoked a harmonisation power is crucial. Harmonisation entails the

[133] Ludwigs (n 129) 1169.
[134] Case C-376/98 *Tobacco Advertising I*, para 99.
[135] ibid, paras 103–04.
[136] ibid, para 102.
[137] ibid, para 114. See also para 107 for the appreciability requirement.
[138] ibid, para 110.
[139] ibid, para 111.
[140] ibid, para 115.
[141] ibid, para 87.

introduction of common rules to align diverging national rules. As Advocate General Fennelly explained in his Opinion, such national rules are adopted for a reason;[142] they pursue their own public interest objectives.

When the Community legislator then approximates these rules, it is logical and desirable that the same national public interest considerations underlie the approximating measure. The internal market may require common rules. It does not require the Community legislator to ignore substantive policy considerations when it adopts these common rules. On the contrary, it followed from the very nature of the power to harmonise that the Directive could also pursue a public interest objective. And this was especially clear for public health. Article 100a itself required the Community legislator to 'take as a base a high level of protection' when proposing harmonisation in the sphere of public health.[143]

It is, therefore, not surprising that the Court recognised that public health could be 'a decisive factor in the choices to be made'.[144] If the Community legislator claimed that its measure fell within the internal market competence, that measure had to aim to promote the internal market. But if the legislator invoked a harmonisation power to adopt that measure, it was obvious that the harmonised rules could simultaneously pursue an underlying policy objective.[145]

Thus, the Court did not annul the Tobacco Advertising Directive because it pursued a public health objective; it annulled the Directive because it pursued a public health objective without pursuing the objective of the internal market. To fall within a certain field of competence, a measure must pursue the objective of that competence. In *Tobacco Advertising I*, the Court found that the objectives dimension of the internal market competence had not been satisfied.

3. *The Tobacco Advertising Directive (II) and* Tobacco Advertising (II)

The Community legislator listened.[146] A few months after the Court's ruling, the Commission proposed a new Tobacco Advertising Directive.[147] The Directive again relied on Articles 100a (now 95), 57(2) (now 47(2)), and 66 (now 55) as legal bases.[148] But this time, its scope was more limited. There would be no general

[142] ibid, paras 64–65.
[143] Article 100a(3) TEC (Maastricht).
[144] Case C-376/98 *Tobacco Advertising I*, para 88.
[145] C Hillion, 'Tobacco Advertising: If you must, you may' (2001) 60 *The Cambridge Law Journal* 441, 488.
[146] Weatherill, 'The Limits of Legislative Harmonization Ten Years after Tobacco Advertising' (n 120) 849, F Amtenbrink and JF Appeldoorn, 'Is er leven na het Tabaksreclamearrest? De interpretatie van art. 95 EG en de hernieuwde poging van de Commissie inzake de tabaksreclame' (2001) 12 *Tijdschrift voor Europees en economisch recht* 413, 420.
[147] Commission, Proposal for a Directive of the European Parliament and of the Council on the approximation of the laws, regulations and administrative provisions of the Member States relating to the advertising and sponsorship of tobacco products, COM(2001)283.
[148] ibid, 13.

tobacco advertising ban. Instead, the proposed Directive banned most tobacco advertising in the press and on the radio.[149] It also banned tobacco sponsorship of cross-border events.[150] Crucially, Member States were not allowed to 'prohibit or restrict the free circulation of products or services which comply with [the] Directive'.[151] Unlike its annulled predecessor, the proposed Directive thus included a free movement clause.

As the Commission itself underlined, it had 'taken due account' of the Court's judgment.[152] The Council and the Parliament reflected the same determination to observe the principle of conferral. In the Council, the Member States asked the Legal Service's views on the new proposal's legal basis.[153] The Council Legal Service broadly approved of the Commission's effort. It did, however, insist on a few changes to fully align the new Directive with the judgment.[154] While the Court had accepted the usefulness of a tobacco advertising ban for 'periodicals, magazines, newspapers and other similar publications',[155] for instance, the Commission referred to 'press and other printed publications' instead.[156] '[T]o ensure that the Directive [was] fully compliant with its legal base', the Council Legal Service, therefore, proposed a modification.[157] The Parliament, too, stressed the need to stay within the scope of the internal market competence and powers.[158]

Not all the Legal Service's suggestions entered the *Official Journal*. The wider press reference, for instance, remained.[159] But that was but a detail. What mattered was that the second Tobacco Advertising Directive, unlike the first, aimed to promote the internal market. It only banned tobacco advertising where a ban would help free movement or undistorted competition. And it ensured the free movement of products and services which complied with its rules.[160] When Germany, again outvoted in the Council, submitted another annulment request, history thus did not repeat itself. The Court upheld the Directive.[161] The Tobacco Advertising

[149] ibid, 17.
[150] ibid.
[151] ibid, 18.
[152] ibid, 2.
[153] Council Legal Service, Opinion on the Proposal for a Tobacco Advertising Directive II, 12244/01, 1.
[154] ibid, 11.
[155] Case C-376/98 *Tobacco Advertising I*, para 98.
[156] Commission, Proposal for a Directive of the European Parliament and of the Council on the approximation of the laws, regulations and administrative provisions of the Member States relating to the advertising and sponsorship of tobacco products, COM(2001)283, 17.
[157] Council Legal Service, Opinion on the Proposal for a Tobacco Advertising Directive II, 12244/01, 11; Permanent Representatives Committee, Report on the Proposal for a Tobacco Advertising Directive II, 13503/01, 2.
[158] Council, Information note on the Proposal for a Tobacco Advertising Directive II, 14318/02, 1.
[159] Article 3 of Directive 2003/33/EC of the European Parliament and of the Council of 26 May 2003 on the approximation of the laws, regulations and administrative provisions of the Member States relating to the advertising and sponsorship of tobacco products, OJ L152/16.
[160] Case C-380/03 *Germany v Parliament and Council* [2006] ECR I-11573 ECLI:EU:C:2006:772, paras 73–75.
[161] ibid, para 160.

Directive (II) fell within the subject matter and – especially – the objectives scope of the internal market competence.

Together, the stories of non-economically active persons and the Tobacco Advertising Directives thus show that the internal market competence has a subject matter and an objectives dimension. It would be wrong, however, to think that this nuance only applies to the internal market. On the contrary, it governs EU 'competence' in general. All fields of competence have a subject matter and an objectives dimension. To illustrate this, the following section moves to the common commercial policy.

II. Common Commercial Policy

The common commercial policy competence concerns trade (however defined) between the EU and one or more third countries or organisations; and CCP measures may pursue a wider set of objectives than the promotion of international trade alone. The former is the subject matter dimension; the latter is the objectives dimension. Here, too, the concepts of 'competence' apply.

A. Subject Matter

Opinion 1/94 offers a clear example where the subject matter dimension of the common commercial policy competence needed clarification.[162] In this Opinion, the Court faced the question whether the CCP extended to trade in services. It gave a negative reply; the subject matter scope of the common commercial policy competence did not include services. It was for the Member States to change this; and they did.

1. Opinion 1/94

Opinion 1/94's context was international. Within the framework of the General Agreement on Tariffs and Trade (GATT), a round of multilateral negotiations had recently taken place. The Uruguay Round not only led to the creation of the World Trade Organization (WTO), but also introduced new domains to the international trade system.[163] One of these domains was services.[164] Annexed to the WTO Agreement appeared a General Agreement on Trade in Services (GATS).

[162] Opinion 1/94 *Accords annexés à l'accord OMC* [1994] ECR I-5267 ECLI:EU:C:1994:384.

[163] JH Jackson, 'The Evolution of the World Trading System – the Legal and Institutional Context' in D Bethlehem, I Van Damme, D McRae, and R Neufeld (eds), *The Oxford Handbook of International Trade Law* (OUP, 2009) 38.

[164] K Alexander and MT Andenas, The World Trade Organization and Trade in Services (Brill, 2008) 33.

At the Community level, the new agreement raised an important question. It was not clear whether GATS fell under the Community's exclusive CCP competence or not. During the Uruguay Round negotiations, the Commission had represented both the Community and its Member States as a sole negotiator.[165] But the Member States were not keen to extend this to the conclusion stage. They argued that the CCP did not extend to trade in services.[166] The Commission asked the Court for advice. In *Opinion 1/94*, the judges had to decide whether the Treaty conferred an exclusive CCP competence (and power) upon the Community to conclude the full GATS agreement.[167] Essentially, the question was whether the Community concept of international trade covered only goods, or also services.

The Treaty provisions on the CCP themselves did not give a conclusive answer. Article 110 TEC referred to 'international trade'.[168] This was an undefined legal concept.[169] It had the potential to evolve over time, incorporating different subject matters in parallel with the changing views on international trade in general. The Court recognised this. In several cases, it stressed that an effective commercial policy required a wide interpretation.[170] Limiting its scope to a traditional concept of international trade would render the CCP 'nugatory'.[171]

In that sense, it did not matter that the drafters of the Rome Treaty appeared to have only goods in mind when they designed the common commercial policy.[172] It is true that they mostly conceived the CCP to protect the common market, in which imported goods enjoyed free circulation.[173] At a time when international trade only focused on goods, they did not consider extending the CCP to services.[174] Nonetheless, Article 110 did not define the concept of

[165] JHJ Bourgeois, 'The EC in the WTO and Advisory Opinion 1/94: An Echternach procession' (1995) 32 *Common Market Law Review* 763, 763; D Lasok, *The Trade and Customs Law of the European Union* (Kluwer, 1998) 21.

[166] J Wouters, F Hoffmeister, G De Baere, and T Ramopoulos, *The Law of EU External Relations* (OUP, 2013) 378.

[167] Opinion 1/94, para 6.

[168] Article 110 TEC (Maastricht). See also the TEC's recital on the CCP.

[169] M Waelbroeck in M Melchior (ed), *Les relations extérieures de la communauté européenne unifiée: actes du troisième Colloque sur la fusion des Communautés européennes* (Institut d'études juridiques européennes de la Faculté de droit de l'Université de Liège, 1967) 266.

[170] K Lenaerts and E De Smijter, 'The European Community's Treaty-Making Competence' (1996) 16 *Yearbook of European Law* 1, 12.

[171] Opinion 1/78 *Accord international sur le caoutchouc naturel* [1979] ECR-02871 ECLI:EU:C:1979:224, para 44; Case 45/86 *Commission v Council* [1987] ECR-01493 ECLI:EU:C:1987:163, para 20.

[172] CWA Timmermans, 'Common Commercial Policy (Article 113 EEC) and International Trade in Services' in F Capotorti, C-D Ehlermann, J Frowein, F Jacobs, R Joliet, T Koopmans, and R Kovar (eds), *Du droit international au droit de l'intégration: Liber amicorum Pierre Pescatore* (Nomos, 1987) 684.

[173] Spaak Report (n 31) 62; Opinion 1/75 *Arrangement OCDE – Norme pour les dépenses locales* [1975] ECR-01355 ECLI:EU:C:1975:145; PJG Kapteyn, 'The Common Commercial Policy of the European Economic Community: Delimitation of the Community's Power and the European Court of Justice's Opinion of November 11, 1975' (1976) 11 *Texas International Law Journal* 485, 486; G Le Tallec, 'The Common Commercial Policy of the EEC' (1971) 20 *International and Comparative Law Quarterly* 732, 739.

[174] P Eeckhout, 'Constitutional Concepts for Free Trade in Services' in G De Búrca and J Scott (eds), *The EU and the WTO: Legal and Constitutional Issues* (Hart Publishing, 2002) 212.

international trade and Article 113 did not lay down an exhaustive list of trade matters.[175] Some scope to extend the CCP's subject matter to trade in services thus appeared to exist.[176]

The Court disagreed. In *Opinion 1/94*, it ruled that the Community did not enjoy exclusive competence (and power) to conclude GATS. The reason lay not in Articles 110 and 113 TEC themselves, but in the 'overall scheme of the Treaty'.[177] GATS identified four modes of service supply.[178] The first, cross-frontier supplies by a person established in one state to a consumer in another state, fell under the CCP.[179] Such services closely resembled trade in goods.[180] The other three modes, however, went beyond the scope of the CCP. They involved movement of persons, and that was a problem. Because the Treaty included specific chapters on free movement of natural and legal persons, those matters could not fall within the common commercial policy.[181]

This reasoning was not altogether new. Already, in the early days of the Community, debates on the role of services in the common commercial policy had taken place. Recognising that CCP provisions allowed a wide interpretation, many scholars argued that services could be included.[182] However, they also insisted on limits. Those matters which were already covered by distinct Treaty chapters could not fall under the CCP.[183] Thus, situations of establishment had to be excluded.[184] Using a similar logic, the Court excluded GATS' second, third, and fourth modes.

Of course, the mere fact that the Court's reasoning found its predecessor in earlier debates did not mean that it was valid. *Opinion 1/94* was open to some criticism. GATS aimed to secure free trade in services, not free movement of

[175] Kapteyn (n 173) 494.

[176] P Mengozzi, 'Trade in Services and Commercial Policy' in M Maresceau (ed), *The European Community's Commercial Policy after 1992: The Legal Dimension* (Martinus Nijhoff, 1993) 232.

[177] Opinion 1/94, para 42.

[178] ibid, para 43.

[179] ibid, para 44.

[180] RM Bierwagen, 'European Communities: Court of Justice Opinion 1/94 Concerning the Competence of the European Community to Conclude International Agreements Concerning Services and the Protection of Intellectual Property – Article 228(6) of the EC Treaty' (1995) 34 *International Legal Materials* 689, 692.

[181] Opinion 1/94, para 45.

[182] P Pescatore, 'Opinion 1/94 on Conclusion of the WTO Agreement: Is There an Escape from a Programmed Disaster?' (1999) 36 *Common Market Law Review* 387, 393; Le Tallec (n 173) 737; LJ Brinckhorst in M Melchior (ed), *Les relations extérieures de la communauté européenne unifiée: actes du troisième Colloque sur la fusion des Communautés européennes* (Institut d'études juridiques européennes de la Faculté de droit de l'Université de Liège, 1967) 231; U Everling in *Les relations extérieures de la communauté européenne unifiée* 208; Waelbroeck in *Les relations extérieures de la communauté européenne unifiée* 263.

[183] See Article 59(2) TEEC.

[184] P Pescatore, 'Les relations extérieures des communautés européennes: Contribution à la doctrine de la Personnalité des organisations internationales' (1961) 103 *Collected Courses of the Hague Academy of International Law* 3, 85; Brinckhorst (n 182) 231; Everling (n 182) 208; J Mégret, 'Le pouvoir de la Communauté économique européenne de conclure des accords internationaux' (1964) 75 *Revue du marché commun* 529, 532. See *a contrario* Waelbroeck in *Les relations extérieures de la communauté européenne unifiée* 264.

persons.[185] Arguably, however, there was an additional rationale behind its conclusion. As mentioned above, the CCP's concept of international trade was undefined, and hence potentially open to a wide interpretation. But that logic was somewhat affected by recent Treaty negotiations.[186] Not long before *Opinion 1/94*, the Member States signed the Maastricht Treaty. Including services under the CCP was an explicit option during the Treaty negotiations.[187] Crucially, the drafters rejected it.[188] In that context, the original scope for a wide interpretation of the concept of international trade was significantly reduced.[189]

2. *From Amsterdam to Lisbon*

A few years later, the Member States returned to the Treaty negotiations. Unsurprisingly, the Commission proposed to strengthen the Community's common commercial policy competence.[190] It pointed out that the CCP had been outdated since *Opinion 1/94*.[191] The international trade system had changed significantly and the CCP had not evolved with it.[192] It was for the drafters of the Treaty to remedy that. They were not all prepared to do so. Some Member States did indeed support an extension of the CCP's scope to services;[193] others, however, stressed the importance of *Opinion 1/94*.[194]

With the eventual Amsterdam Treaty, services did enter the scope of the CCP.[195] But they only did so dormantly. Article 133(5) allowed the Council to

[185] T Tridimas and P Eeckhout, 'The External Competence of the Community and the Case-Law of the Court of Justice: Principle versus Pragmatism' (1994) 14 *Yearbook of European Law* 143, 161–62; M Cremona, 'EC External Commercial Policy after Amsterdam: Authority and Interpretation with Interconnected Legal Orders' in JHH Weiler (ed), *The EU, the WTO, and the NAFTA: Towards a Common Law of International Trade?* (OUP, 2010) 11.

[186] P Eeckhout, 'Exclusive External Competences: Constructing the EU as an International Actor' in A Rosas, E Levits, and Y Bot (eds), *La Cour de Justice et la Construction de l'Europe: Analyses et Perspectives de Soixante Ans de Jurisprudence* (Asser Press, 2013) 618.

[187] Secretary-General of the Commission Mr Williamson, Translation of letter on the Intergovernmental Conference on Political Union, CONF-UP 1742/91, 6; Presidency, Draft Treaty on the Union, CONF-UP-UEM 2008/91, 38.

[188] M Maresceau, 'The Concept "Common Commercial Policy" and the Difficult Road to Maastricht' in M Maresceau (ed), *The European Community's Commercial Policy after 1992: The Legal Dimension* (Martinus Nijhoff, 1993) 17.

[189] A Dashwood, 'The limits of European Community Powers' (1996) 21 *European Law Review* 113, 119; V Engström, *Constructing the Powers of International Institutions* (Brill, 2012) 58; R Schütze, *From Dual to Cooperative Federalism: The Changing Structure of European Law* (OUP, 2009) 171; A-S Lamblin-Gourdin, 'Politique commerciale commune et protection juridique de l'innovation' (2010) 4 *Revue internationale de droit économique* 441, 453.

[190] Commission, Rapport sur le Fonctionnement du Traité sur l'Union européenne, SEC(95)731, 57; Presidency, External Economic Relations, CONF/3890/96, 2.

[191] Commission, Rapport sur le Fonctionnement du Traité sur l'Union européenne, SEC(95)731, 57.

[192] Presidency, Note on the Ministerial meeting on 28 October 1996 (External action), CONF/3956/96, 7; European Council, L'Union européenne aujourd'hui et demain, CONF/2500/96, 64.

[193] Groupe de réflexion, Rapport, SN520/1/95 Rev1, 8.

[194] ibid.

[195] D Leczykiewicz, 'Common Commercial Policy: The Expanding Competence of the European Union in the Area of International Trade' (2005) 6 *German Law Journal* 1673, 1675.

apply paragraphs 1 to 4 to international negotiations and agreements on services, to the extent that they were not yet covered.[196] Crucially, however, the Council had to act unanimously. In practice, unified Community action at the international trade in services stage thus remained very difficult,[197] especially in view of the Union's imminent enlargement.[198]

Thus, the CCP soon returned to the negotiation table.[199] The Nice Treaty added trade in services to its subject matter scope.[200] The exact outcome of these negotiations and the precise wording of these Treaty provisions has lost much of its relevance today; the Lisbon Treaty finally granted trade in service the same place in the CCP as trade in goods.[201] The EU now enjoys exclusive competence under the common commercial policy for all four GATS modes. Nonetheless, recalling the past remains interesting. It offers another helpful illustration of the relationship between competence and power.

The competence expansions of the Amsterdam and Nice Treaties went combined with a limitation in terms of power. Amsterdam's Article 133(5) only allowed the Council to apply paragraphs 1 to 4 to international negotiations and agreements on services. Nice's Article 133(5) included the same limitation.[202] This was important. The drafters of the Treaties agreed to add services to the (dormant) subject matter scope of the CCP. However, they only allowed the Community to act within that new field of competence with certain specified powers.[203] External measures were allowed; internal measures were not. The Lisbon Treaty finally removed this power limitation.[204]

[196] Article 133(5) TEC (Amsterdam); Cremona, 'EC External Commercial Policy after Amsterdam' (n 185) 18.

[197] C Herrmann, 'Common Commercial Policy after Nice: Sisyphus would have done a better job' (2002) 39 *Common Market Law Review* 7, 12.

[198] Commission, Note sur la Proposition de M Lamy sur la politique commerciale PRDS(99)3, 2; Commission, Adapter les institutions pour réussir l'enlargement – Avis de la Commission au titre de l'article 48 du Traité sur l'Union européenne, COM(2000)34, 28; Présidence, Rapport sur la Conférence intergouvernmentale sur la réforme institutionelle, CONFER/4750/00, 25.

[199] A Dimopoulos, 'The Common Commercial Policy after Lisbon: Establishing Parallelism between Internal and External Economic Relations' (2008) 4 *Croatian Yearbook of European Law and Policy* 102, 105.

[200] Article 133(5) TEC (Nice); Opinion 1/08 *Accords modifiant les listes d'engagements spécifiques au titre de l'AGCS* [2009] ECR-11129 ECLI:EU:C:2009:739; M Cremona, 'Balancing Union and Member State interests: Opinion 1/2008, choice of legal base and the common commercial policy under the Treaty of Lisbon' (2010) 35 *European Law Review* 678, 679. But see Article 133(6) TEC (Nice) on some sensitive services sectors falling under shared, rather than exclusive, Union competence.

[201] Dimopoulos, 'The Common Commercial Policy after Lisbon' (n 199) 106. The integral CCP is now an exclusive Union competence.

[202] M Cremona, 'The External Dimension of the Single Market: Building (on) the Foundations' in C Barnard and J Scott (eds), *The Law of the Single European Market: Unpacking the Premises* (Hart Publishing, 2002) 375.

[203] European Council, L'Union européenne aujourd'hui et demain, CONF/2500/96, 77.

[204] S Peers and Statewatch, 'EU Constitutional annotation no 2 – Part III, Title V: EU External Policies' (2003) 2.

Thus, the scope of the common commercial policy competence has long been a 'thorny question'.[205] *Opinion 1/94* provided an answer to an important subject matter question. Subsequent Treaty amendments gradually offered a different answer. The precise subject matter scope of the CCP competence is not essential to this chapter; what matters is that the question was raised. Competence has a subject matter dimension. *Opinion 1/94* and the subsequent Treaty amendments show this for the CCP.

B. Objectives

Questions also arose on the CCP's objectives dimension. Here, the CCP competence significantly differs from the internal market competence. The objective of the internal market competence is to ensure an area of free movement. For the common commercial policy, the objectives are wider. Within this field, the EU must promote, facilitate, or govern trade (or foreign direct investment).[206] This clearly goes further than the liberalisation of trade alone.[207]

There is no need to determine the exact scope of the CCP's objectives dimension here.[208] As mentioned before, this is not a chapter on the common commercial policy and the internal market; it is a chapter about competence. The purpose of this section is to show that the CCP competence, too, has an objectives dimension. Thus, what follows is a limited examination of the CCP's objectives. It focuses on one question in particular: whether a measure that aims to protect public health and/or the environment may fall within the scope of the common commercial policy. This question arose in a set of legal disputes.[209] They illustrate that the CCP competence does indeed have an objectives dimension.

1. Chernobyl

The first legal dispute dates back to the aftermath of the *Chernobyl* nuclear disaster. After the accident at the power station, the Community adopted a series of measures to avoid the import of agricultural products with dangerous levels of

[205] Opinion in Opinion 2/15 *Accord de libre-échange avec Singapour* [2016] ECLI:EU:C:2016:992, para 66.

[206] Opinion 2/00 *Protocole de Cartagena sur la prévention des risques biotechnologiques* [2001] ECR-09713 ECLI:EU:C:2001:664, 37; Case C-414/11 *Daiichi Sankyo and Sanofi-Aventis Deutschland* [2013] ECLI:EU:C:2013:520, para 51.

[207] A Dimopoulos, 'The Effects of the Lisbon Treaty on the Principles and Objectives of the Common Commercial Policy' (2010) 15 *European Foreign Affairs Review* 153, 162; C Kaddous, 'The Transformation of the EU Common Commercial Policy' in P Eeckhout and M Lopez-Escudero (eds), *The European Union's External Action in Times of Crisis* (Hart Publishing, 2016) 451.

[208] See eg Opinion 2/15 *Accord de libre-échange avec Singapour* [2017] ECLI:EU:C:2017:376, paras 139–67, and the contrasting Opinion of Advocate General Sharpston in Opinion 2/15, paras 478–83.

[209] Case C-62/88 *Greece v Council* [1990] ECR I-01527 ECLI:EU:C:1990:153; Opinion 2/00; Case C-94/03 *Commission v Council* [2006] ECR I-00001 ECLI:EU:C:2006:2.

radioactivity.[210] One of these measures was Council Regulation 3955/87.[211] It determined that the release into free circulation of agricultural products coming from third countries would be conditional upon compliance with certain maximum levels of radioactivity.[212] The motivation behind this measure was, of course, the protection of public health and the environment; but its legal basis was Article 113 TEEC.[213]

The Commission proposed to adopt the Regulation under the CCP competence.[214] This was not surprising; it had already suggested the same legal basis for the first Community measure which restricted agricultural imports after the disaster.[215] However, the Council had resisted the recourse to Article 113.[216] The preparatory documents do not show why it chose to base the first measure on the EEC Treaty in general. But they do briefly state why the Council did accept Article 113 for Regulation 3955/87. A qualified majority of Member States and the Commission emphasised that this legal basis was only justified because the measure fell within the commercial sphere completely.[217]

Not all Member States concurred with this assessment; Greece objected. It argued that the Regulation went beyond the scope of the CCP because it also covered elements of public health and consumer protection.[218] Thus, said Greece, Article 113 alone did not suffice as legal basis.[219] These concerns did not stop the Regulation. The Council adopted it under the CCP legal basis. In response, Greece went to Luxembourg.[220] It notably asked the Court to annul the Regulation on the ground of invalid legal basis.[221] Again, its argument was that the Regulation essentially aimed to protect public health.[222]

The Court upheld the Regulation. It emphasised that the contested measure laid down uniform import requirements.[223] It was thus 'intended to regulate trade

[210] Preamble of Council Regulation (EEC) No 3955/87 of 22 December 1987 on the conditions governing imports of agricultural products originating in third countries following the accident at the Chernobyl nuclear power-station, OJ L371.

[211] ibid.

[212] ibid, Article 2.

[213] ibid.

[214] Secrétariat Général du Conseil, Note sur l'Adoption d'un règlement du Conseil relatif aux conditions d'importations de produits agricoles originaires des pays tiers, 10572/87, 1.

[215] Commission, Proposition de Règlement du Conseil relative aux conditions d'importation de produits agricoles originaires des pays tiers, COM(86)318, 1.

[216] Council Regulation (EEC) No 3020/86 of 30 September 1986 extending Regulation (EEC) No 1707/86 on the conditions governing imports of agricultural products originating in third countries following the accident at the Chernobyl nuclear power-station, OJ L280.

[217] Secrétariat Général du Conseil, Note sur l'Adoption d'un règlement du Conseil relatif aux conditions d'importations de produits agricoles originaires des pays tiers, 10572/87, 3.

[218] ibid, Add1.

[219] ibid.

[220] Case C-62/88 *Greece v Council*.

[221] ibid, para 3.

[222] ibid, para 6; E-U Petersmann, *International and European Trade and Environmental Law After the Uruguay Round* (Springer, 1995) 147; P Eeckhout, *EU External Relations Law* (OUP, 2011) 41.

[223] Case C-62/88 *Greece v Council*, para 15.

between the Community and non-member countries'.[224] Article 113 applied. That the Regulation regulated international trade with the aim of protecting public health and the environment did not change that conclusion.[225] An objective of *regulating* trade with third countries sufficed. *Chernobyl* thus illustrated the very wide objectives scope of the CCP competence.

2. Opinion 2/00 *and* Commission v Council

Two cases further clarify the point. In *Opinion 2/00*, the Court ruled that the conclusion of the Cartagena Protocol on Biosafety fell under environmental policy and not the common commercial policy.[226] It reached a different conclusion in *Commission v Council*.[227] The Council should not have adopted the Rotterdam Convention on the Prior Informed Consent Procedure for certain hazardous chemicals and pesticides in international trade under an environment legal basis alone. The Decision fell within the scope of the CCP too. Interestingly, the Court also explained why the result in *Commission v Council* differed from that in *Opinion 2/00*: only the former concerned a measure which (also) aimed to govern international trade.

In *Opinion 2/00*, the Commission advocated a dual environment–CCP legal basis for the Cartagena Protocol's conclusion.[228] The Council, the Parliament, and the intervening Member States argued for Article 175 on the environment alone.[229] The Court agreed with the latter view. The judges stressed that the Cartagena Protocol, like the Convention on Biodiversity itself, pursued an environmental objective.[230] It aimed to 'ensur[e] an "adequate level" of protection in the field of the safe transfer, handling and use of LMOs' (living modified organisms).[231] The Protocol's content reflected that aim.[232]

Then, the judges addressed a Commission counter-argument. It is worth repeating the Court's paraphrasing of the counter-argument in full:

> The fact that provisions governing international trade in certain products pursue objectives which are not primarily commercial – such as protection of the environment or of human health, development cooperation, foreign and security policy objectives, or agricultural policy objectives – cannot, according to the Commission, have the effect of excluding the Community's exclusive competence and justifying recourse to, for example, Article 175 EC where the measures in question are intended specifically to govern the Community's external trade (see, to this effect … Chernobyl …). In reality,

[224] ibid, para 16.
[225] ibid, para 18.
[226] Opinion 2/00, para 42.
[227] Case C-94/03 *Commission v Council*, para 51.
[228] Opinion 2/00, para 20.
[229] ibid, para 21.
[230] ibid, paras 27 and 29.
[231] ibid, para 30.
[232] ibid, para 31.

> measures regulating international trade often pursue a wide range of different objectives, but this does not mean that they must be adopted on the basis of the various Treaty provisions relating to those objectives.[233]

Crucially, the Court did not contradict the Commission's assessment of the CCP's objectives scope. Instead, it underlined that the Protocol covered 'any form of movement of LMOs between States, whether or not the movements are for commercial purposes'.[234] In other words, the issue was not that the Protocol pursued an environmental objective; it was that it did not primarily regulate international trade. The common commercial policy's subject matter requirement was not fulfilled.

Commission v Council confirmed this interpretation. The Commission had proposed a Council approval Decision under Article 133 TEC for the Rotterdam Convention on the Prior Informed Consent Procedure for certain hazardous chemicals and pesticides in international trade.[235] The Council, however, changed this to Article 175.[236] Thus, the Commission requested the Decision's annulment for invalid legal basis.[237]

The Court started its analysis with a clear statement on the Convention's objective. 'It cannot be denied', it said, 'that the protection of human health and the environment was the most important concern in the mind of the signatories of the Convention'.[238] And its content reflected that.[239] However, the Convention 'also contain[ed] rules governing trade in hazardous chemicals and having direct and immediate effects on such trade'.[240] It aimed to protect public health and the environment 'through the adoption of measures of a commercial nature'.[241] In other words, the Rotterdam Convention aimed to regulate international trade. To the extent that it did so, Article 113 applied.[242]

That was the difference with the Cartagena Protocol. The Rotterdam Convention was a trade measure. It only applied to internationally traded chemicals.[243] By contrast, the Cartagena Protocol's application did not depend on commercial exchange. 'An explicit link between trade and the environment was', therefore, 'lacking in the Cartagena Protocol examined by the Court in Opinion 2/00'.[244] That, and not a different interpretation of the CCP's objectives dimension, explained why only one measure (partially) fell within the common commercial policy competence.

[233] ibid, para 35.
[234] ibid, para 38.
[235] Case C-94/03 *Commission v Council*, para 17.
[236] ibid, para 18.
[237] ibid, para 21.
[238] ibid, para 37.
[239] ibid, para 41.
[240] ibid, para 42.
[241] ibid, para 43.
[242] ibid, para 51.
[243] ibid, para 44.
[244] ibid.

Thus, *Chernobyl*, *Opinion 2/00*, and *Commission v Council* show that questions of competence's objectives dimension also arose in the CCP. *Opinion 1/94* did the same for the subject matter dimension. The conclusion is clear: the two dimensions of competence help explain what the EU may do in the context of the internal market, but they also matter elsewhere.

III. Conclusion

This chapter went from non-economically active persons to tobacco advertising, and from trade in services to radioactive agricultural products and biodiversity. Despite their differences, the legal disputes contribute to the same core argument. Competence is the field in which the Union may act. It has a subject matter dimension and an objectives dimension. To fall within a certain field of competence, a measure needs to fulfil both.

The examples of the non-economically active persons and trade in services both start with an ambiguous subject matter dimension. It was unclear whether the common market extended to non-economically active persons. And it was unclear whether the common commercial policy covered trade in services. Legislative development, Treaty changes, and Court rulings brought (more) clarity.

The tobacco advertising dispute tells a different story. Here, the issue was not that the internal market competence's objectives dimension was unclear and required specification. Without a doubt, an internal market measure had to aim to enhance the internal market. The EU legislator, however, failed to respect this in the first Tobacco Advertising Directive.

Finally, *Chernobyl*, *Opinion 2/00*, and *Commission v Council* illustrate a significant difference between the internal market and CCP competences. In the common commercial policy, a measure may do more than simply facilitate international trade; it may also regulate it. Yet those wide objectives do not mean that the common commercial policy competence knows no boundaries. Where the objectives dimension plays a limited limitative role, the subject matter dimension becomes crucial. A CCP measure must govern international trade. *Opinion 2/00* shows that this is not an empty statement.

Together, these legal disputes show that 'competence' is nuanced. Whether a measure complies with the principle of conferral does not depend on the application of a single test. Some cases will raise issues of subject matter; some will raise issues of objectives; and some, as the next chapter shows, will raise issues of power.

4

Power (and Competence)

Not all 'competence' questions are about competence. What follows is a chapter about power. Power is the second step in the 'competence' analysis. If the Union enjoys competence in a certain field, the question arises what it may do in that field, and how.[1] The answer to this question depends on the relevant power. Power is the actual authorisation to act. It does not belong to the Union as a whole, but to specific institutions. There are two power dimensions. One dimension governs the relevant power instruments; the other dimension governs the relevant types of legal act. There are also power modalities. They regulate the procedural side. They stipulate which institution(s) may act (or be involved in the acting) and by which voting majority.

These dimensions and modalities may be confusing. Like competence, power is best understood through practical application. This chapter, therefore, illustrates the theory of power through concrete legal disputes. For consistency with the previous chapter, these legal disputes are again derived from the internal market and the common commercial policy. More specifically, they concern a series of intellectual property measures adopted within the scope of the internal market competence and the CCP competence.

The first section of this chapter focuses on the internal market. It studies the legislative history of three (almost) Union-wide intellectual property measures: the EU trademark, the Community design, and the unitary patent.[2] Without much doubt, these measures fell within the scope of the internal market competence; but they triggered interesting questions on power.

The main question concerned power's instruments dimension. In the internal market, the best-known power instrument is that of harmonisation. The EU legislator introduces common rules to remove obstacles to free movement, and distortions of competition, that result from diverging national rules. However, the EU trademark, the Community design, and the unitary patent are not the product of harmonisation. They are (almost) Union-wide unitary intellectual property rights that exist alongside national rights. This also has consequences for the

[1] R Schütze, *Foreign Affairs and the EU Constitution – Selected Essays* (CUP, 2014) 250.

[2] Council Regulation (EC) No 40/94 of 20 December 1993 on the Community trade mark, OJ L11; Council Regulation (EC) No 6/2002 of 12 December 2001 on Community designs, OJ L3; Regulation (EU) No 1257/2012 of the European Parliament and of the Council of 17 December 2012 implementing enhanced cooperation in the area of the creation of unitary patent protection, OJ L361.

appropriate type of legal act. To introduce a unitary right, a regulation is more suitable than a directive that required national transposition.

Where relevant, this section also touches upon power's procedural modalities. These normally require less attention. Of course, which Union institution(s) may act matters. And the required voting majority is of great importance. But these are predominantly political questions. Once the drafters have tackled them, the Treaties normally clearly state who may act and by which majority. Still, it is worth paying attention to these modalities. The unitary patent illustrates that. Arguably, it was precisely the controversy around this patent's (failed) adoption that convinced the drafters to retain a unanimity rule and reserve powers to the Council.

The second section of this chapter shifts focus to the CCP. Showing that the relevance of power is not limited to the internal market, it revisits the more recent Geneva Act on the protection of geographical indications.[3] Both the opening of negotiations for the Act and the accession to the Act were annulled in Court.[4] The opening of negotiations for the Act was problematic in terms of competence and power. Although it aimed to facilitate international trade by protecting intellectual property rights, the Council had used an internal market power to adopt it. The accession to the Act was problematic in terms of power alone. Interestingly, the issue related to the power modality of which institution may act. By making far-reaching amendments to the Commission's proposal, the Council exercised a power that actually belonged to the Commission.

Thus, while the previous chapter explained the concept of competence, this chapter shifts focus. What follows is a story of the meaning of harmonisation as internal market instrument, the choice between directives and regulations, the requirements of qualified majority and unanimity, and the boundary between the Commission's right of initiative and the Council's right to amend. It is, in other words, a story about power.

I. Internal Market

A. Trademarks

The story begins with trademarks. A trademark is a sign that is 'capable of being represented graphically' and 'of distinguishing the goods or services of one

[3] Council Decision 8512/15 of 7 May 2015 authorising the opening of negotiations on a revised Lisbon Agreement on Appellations of Origin and Geographical Indications (unpublished); Council Decision (EU) 2019/1754 of 7 October 2019 on the accession of the European Union to the Geneva Act of the Lisbon Agreement on Appellations of Origin and Geographical Indications, OJ L271.

[4] Case C-389/15 *Commission v Council* [2017] ECLI:EU:C:2017:798; Case C-24/20 *Commission v Council* [2022] ECLI:EU:C:2022:911.

undertaking from those of other undertakings'.[5] For a long time, only national trademarks existed. Their application was limited to the territory of the registering Member State.[6] This negatively affected the free movement of marked goods in the common market.[7] In 1980, the Commission, therefore, proposed the introduction of a Community-wide trademark right.[8]

At least at the first sight, the proposal fell within the scope of the common market competence. It apparently satisfied both competence dimensions. The proposed measure concerned the free movement of marked goods in the common market and aimed to promote that free movement.[9] There is no need to explore this in more depth here.[10] This is a chapter about power; and questions of power did arise.

The following analysis touches upon these questions. It first introduces the 1980 proposal. It also introduces a connected proposal on the harmonisation of national trademark laws. Second, it examines the proposals' respective legal bases and the legal reasoning of the Commission and the Council (Legal Service). Third, it briefly examines to what extent the Single European Act affected the power dynamics.

1. *Two Proposals*

In 1980, the European Commission invited the Council to harmonise national trademark laws.[11] Differences between these laws hindered the free movement of marked goods and caused distortions of competition.[12] To promote the common market, the Commission, therefore, proposed harmonised rules on the trademark issues which most affected the free movement of marked goods.[13] These included, notably, the extent of trademark protection, the use of trademarks, and their cancellation.[14]

[5] See Article 4 of Regulation (EU) 2017/1001 of the European Parliament and of the Council of 14 June 2017 on the European Union trade mark, OJ L154 and Article 15 of the Agreement on Trade-Related Aspects of Intellectual Property Rights [1994].

[6] J Basedow, *The Law of Open Societies – Private Ordering and Public Regulation in the Conflict of Laws* (Brill, 2015) 214–18; See also Opinion in Joined cases C-267/95 and 269/95 *Merck v Primecrown* and *Beecham v Europharm* [1996] ECR-06285 ECLI:EU:C:1996:228, paras 89–90.

[7] N Reich, *Understanding EU Law – Objectives, Principles and Methods of Community Law* (Intersentia, 2003) 167.

[8] Commission, Proposal for a Council Regulation on the Community trade-mark, COM(80)635.

[9] ibid, 18, 53, and 54.

[10] See, eg G Bonet, 'Propriétés intellectuelles. La marque Communautaire: Règlement CEE n°40/94 du Conseil du 20 décembre 1993' (1995) 1 *Revue trimestrielle de droit européen* 31; B Van Reepinghen, 'Le règlement (CE) n° 40/94 sur la marque communautaire' (1995) 16 *Journal des Tribunaux: droit européen* 25.

[11] Commission, Proposal for a first Council Directive to approximate the laws of the Member States relating to trade-marks, COM(80)635.

[12] ibid, 13 and 53.

[13] ibid, 13; R Knaak, 'Trade mark protection and undistorted competition' in J Drexl, RM Hilty, L Boy, C Godt, and R Bernard (eds), *Technologie Et Concurrence – Mélanges en L'honneur de Hanns Ullrich* (Larcier, 2009) 125.

[14] Commission, Proposal for a first Council Directive to approximate the laws of the Member States relating to trade-marks, COM(80)635, 53.

But harmonisation alone would not suffice to guarantee the common market's smooth functioning. The perceived problem with the Member States' trademark rules was not just their diversity; it was, above all, their inherently limited territorial scope.[15] Nationally granted trademark protection only applied within the national territory.[16] It could not cover the Community in its entirety. To obtain trademark protection in every Member State, a registration in every Member State was required. Even if common rules were in place, this remained a costly endeavour. Moreover, the rules' territoriality failed to prevent that different persons obtained protection for identical or similar marks in different Member States.[17]

Thus, the Commission also submitted a second proposal. It invited the Council to introduce a Community trademark that would exist alongside the (harmonised) national trademarks.[18] Crucially, it would be a unitary Community right.[19] This meant that it would 'have identical effect throughout the Community'.[20] Only Community-wide registrations would be possible.[21] Transfers, surrenders, revocations, invalidations, and prohibitions of use would apply to the entire Community.[22]

2. *Two Powers*

The Commission did not propose to adopt the Trademark Directive and the Community Trademark Regulation under the same Treaty legal basis. Each measure reflected a different power within the common market competence. The reason for that change primarily lay in the different instruments used. Article 100 TEEC provided a legal basis for the harmonisation of national measures, but the Community trademark did not entail harmonisation. For this measure, the Commission, therefore, proposed the flexibility clause of Article 235 TEEC.[23]

Article 100 TEEC allowed the Council to 'issue directives for the approximation of such provisions laid down by law, regulation or administrative action in Member States as directly affect[ed] the establishment or functioning of the common market'.[24] Article 235 empowered the Council, '[i]f action by the Community should prove necessary to attain, in the course of the operation of the common market, one of the objectives of the Community … to take the

[15] ibid, 53; Opinion in Case C-10/89 *CNL-SUCAL/HAG* [1990] ECR I-03711 ECLI:EU:C:1990:359, para 55.

[16] AA Machnicka, 'Territorial Aspects of Community Trademarks – The Single Market's Splendid Sovereignty' (2014) 45 *International Review of Intellectual Property and Competition Law* 915, 916.

[17] ibid.

[18] Commission, Proposal for a Council Regulation on the Community trade-mark COM(80)635; M van Empel, 'The EEC Trade Mark Memorandum' (1978) 15 *Common Market Law Review* 57, 63–65.

[19] A Berthet and B Devevez, 'La marque communautaire: intérêt et mode d'emploi' (1997) 15 *Legicom* 23, 23; A Kur, T Dreier, and S Luginbuehl, *European Intellectual Property Law: Text, Cases and Materials* (Edward Elgar, 2013) 160.

[20] Commission, Proposal for a Council Regulation on the Community trade-mark, COM(80)635, 20.

[21] ibid.

[22] ibid.

[23] See Chapter 7.

[24] Article 100 TEEC.

appropriate measures'.[25] Importantly, it only applied in the absence of a specific Treaty power to act.[26]

With respect to their power modalities, Articles 100 and 235 were similar. Article 100 required unanimous voting in the Council.[27] So did the flexibility clause.[28] In both cases, the Council enacted the measure.[29] Article 235 always demanded the consultation of the European Parliament, but not the Economic and Social Committee.[30] Article 100 required the Council to consult both, but only if the implementation of the harmonising measure concerned entailed the amendment of national laws.[31] That was also the case for the trademark proposal.

Yet, for the purpose of this chapter, two crucial differences between Articles 100 and 235 existed. They concerned power's type of legal act dimension and its instrument dimension. First, Article 100 only authorised the adoption of directives.[32] Article 235, by contrast, empowered the Council to enact 'appropriate measures' without specifying a type of legal act.[33] Second, Article 100 only allowed the adoption of harmonising measures.[34] Harmonisation entails the introduction of common rules to replace future or present divergent national rules. A measure which did not introduce such common harmonisation rules could, therefore, not be adopted under Article 100.[35] Again, the flexibility clause was wider. It did not specify which power instruments the Council could use. '[A]ppropriate measures' covered more than harmonisation.

3. *Two Legal Analyses*

Both in the Commission and in the Council, in-depth discussions took place on the appropriate legal basis for the Community trademark. Both concluded that Article 235 applied. However, they reached this conclusion through different routes.

[25] Article 235 TEEC.

[26] ibid.

[27] First para of Article 100 TEEC.

[28] Article 235 TEEC.

[29] Articles 100 and 235 TEEC.

[30] Article 235 TEEC.

[31] Second para of Article 100 TEEC.

[32] R Monaco, 'Comparaison et rapprochement des législations dans le Marché commun européen' (1960) 16 *Revue internationale de droit comparé* 61, 67. See also the third para of Article 189 TEEC.

[33] T Konstadinides, *Division of Powers in European Union Law – The Delimitation of Internal Competence Between the EU and the Member States* (Wolters Kluwer, 2009) 25; A Tizzano, 'The Powers of the Community' in Commission (ed), *Thirty Years of Community Law* (Office for Official Publications of the EC, 1983) 56–57.

[34] Monaco (n 32) 65–66; A Limpens, 'Harmonisation des législations dans le cadre du Marché commun' (1967) *Revue internationale de droit comparé* 621, 624; AJ Easson, 'EEC Directives for the Harmonisation of Laws: Some Problems of Validity, Implementation and Legal Effects' (1981) 1 *Yearbook of European Law* 1, 1.

[35] TW Vogelaar, 'The Approximation of the Laws of Member States under the Treaty of Rome' (1975) 12 *Common Market Law Review* 211, 215.

The Commission conducted two 'competence' analyses before proposing the Community Trademark Regulation. In 1976, it presented its Memorandum on the creation of an EEC trademark.[36] This Memorandum introduced many of the legal considerations underlying the later Community trademark proposal. It explained that Article 100's limitation to harmonisation meant that it could not overcome the territoriality problem that threatened the common market.[37] Article 235, by contrast, could serve as a legal basis for the creation of a Community-wide intellectual property right.[38]

A few years later, the Commission published a more extensive legal basis analysis. Its Working Group on the Community Trademark had drafted a paper on the 'need for a European trade mark system' and the 'competence of the European Community to create one'.[39] The paper included an in-depth analysis of Article 235. More than 10 pages systematically verified whether all conditions for the application of the flexibility clause were fulfilled.

The first two conditions related to competence. First, the Working Group confirmed that '[t]he creation of a Community trade mark [was] designed to achieve … Community objectives which [were] explicitly laid down in the EEC Treaty'.[40] This concerned, notably, the abolition of obstacles to free movement and the guarantee of undistorted competition in the common market.[41] Second, it established that the attainment of Community objectives would occur 'in the course of the operation of the common market'.[42] A measure that aimed to promote the common market logically did so in the course of the common market.[43]

After also confirming the need for a Community trademark,[44] the paper finally addressed the absence of other powers to achieve the same objectives. It focused on Article 100 and the concept of harmonisation. Harmonisation, said the Working Group, 'neither … extend[ed] exclusive rights geographically to the territory of the other Member States nor … replace[d] them by exclusive rights which are effective throughout the Community'.[45] As a result, an Article 100 measure could not avoid that 'several persons acting independently could obtain protection in different Member States for the same or a similar trade mark and consequently prevent

[36] Commission, Memorandum on the creation of an EEC trade mark, SEC(76)2462.
[37] ibid, 12.
[38] Ibid, 14–15.
[39] Commission, Working Paper on the Competence of the Community to create a European trademark system and the need for such action, III/D/1294/79.
[40] ibid, 16.
[41] Articles 2 and 3(a),(c),(f) TEEC.
[42] Article 235 TEEC; Commission, Working Paper on the Competence of the Community to create a European trade mark system and the need for such action, III/D/1294/79, 16.
[43] ibid, 17. That the paper expressly addressed the common market condition was noteworthy. As Chapter 7 explains, the Community institutions tended to ignore it.
[44] ibid, 17–19.
[45] ibid, 20.

imports into their country of the marked goods in question'.[46] Harmonisation was, therefore, not an appropriate power instrument.

There was a second, subsidiary power reason not to use Article 100. A directive was not a desirable legal act to create the Community trademark. By requiring national implementation, it could 'give rise to identical law in all the States, but not to one law of the Community'.[47] To adopt a binding Community trademark that generally and directly applied in all Member States, a regulation was needed.[48] Only a regulation could ensure the unitary effect of the Community trademark. And Article 235's general reference to 'appropriate measures' covered such a measure.[49] Supported by the Working Group's recommendations, the Commission introduced its 1980 proposal for a Community trademark based on Article 235.

In the Council, however, things went less smoothly. From early on in the legislative proceedings, a few delegations objected to the use of Article 235.[50] Although the preparatory documents do not offer much information, it appears that their concerns especially related to the creation of a Community Trademarks Office responsible for administering the Community trademark.[51] According to the critical delegations, Article 235 could not act as legal basis for its creation. It is not clear if they also objected to the use of Article 235 to introduce a Community trademark as such.

In any event, the delegations' objections failed. The Council eventually did adopt the proposed Regulation under the proposed legal basis.[52] The Council Legal Service played a considerable role in the acceptance of Article 235. In a legal Opinion, it confirmed that the flexibility clause could be used to create and grant powers to the Community Trademark Office.[53] The Legal Service thus answered the critical delegations' most obvious concern. More importantly for this chapter, it also accepted that Article 235 was a valid legal basis for the adoption of the Community trademark.[54]

[46] ibid, 19.

[47] ibid, 20; Article 189 TEEC.

[48] Commission, Working Paper on the Competence of the Community to create a European trade mark system and the need for such action, III/D/1294/79, 20.

[49] ibid; Article 235 TEEC.

[50] Groupe de travail "Propriété Intellectuelle" (Marque), Sommaire des conclusions sur la Proposition de règlement sur la marque communautaire et proposition de directive rapprochant les législations des Etats membres sur les marques, 4268/82, 3; Présidence, Rapport sur la Proposition de règlement sur la marque communautaire et proposition de directive rapprochant les législations des Etats membres sur les marques, 9482/86, 3.

[51] Groupe de travail "Propriété intellectuelle" (Marque), Rapport sur l'état d'avancement des travaux: proposition de règlement du Conseil sur la marque Communautaire, 9277/84, 3.

[52] Council Regulation (EC) No 40/94 of 20 December 1993 on the Community trade mark, OJ L11.

[53] Council Legal Service, Opinion on the Proposal for a Council Regulation on the Community trade mark, 5837/85, 18.

[54] ibid. Unlike the Commission's Working Group, the Council Legal Service did not address the common market requirement.

Like the Commission and its Working Group, the Council Legal Service declared Article 100 to be inapplicable.[55] Yet there was a slight difference between the two approaches. The Commission primarily emphasised power's instrument dimension. They excluded Article 100 on the basis that the proposed Regulation did not harmonise national laws. The Council Legal Service did the reverse. It emphasised that Article 100 only empowered the Council to adopt directives.[56] The focus thus lay on the type of legal act dimension. Both institutions thus reached the same conclusion through different routes.

Arguably, the Commission's approach was preferable. The (absence of) harmonisation was decisive. Of course, the Council Legal Service correctly stated that only a regulation could introduce a true unitary right. But that, in itself, reflected the clear fact that the proposal did not entail harmonisation. Above all, the Community trademark highlighted the importance of power's instruments dimension. It contrasted harmonising measures with measures which introduced unitary Community rights. Both were common market powers, but Article 100 only covered the former.

B. Designs

Shortly before the adoption of the Community Trademark Regulation, the Commission submitted a proposal for a second Community-wide intellectual property right.[57] This time, it concerned designs. A design is 'the appearance of the whole or a part of a product resulting from the features of, in particular, the lines, contours, colours, shape, texture and/or materials of the product itself and/or its ornamentation'.[58] The proposed Community design mirrored the Community trademark's essential unitary character. It would 'have equal effect throughout the Community'.[59] Registrations, transfers, surrenders, and declarations of invalidity could only occur for the Community as a whole.[60] And it would co-exist with national designs.[61]

Yet a crucial difference distinguished the proposed design from the Community trademark. The Commission did not suggest Article 235 as legal basis.[62] Instead,

[55] ibid, 4.

[56] ibid.

[57] Commission, Proposal for a European Parliament and Council Regulation on the Community Design, COM(93)342.

[58] Article 3(a) of Council Regulation (EC) No 6/2002 of 12 December 2001 on Community designs, OJ L3.

[59] Commission, Proposal for a European Parliament and Council Regulation on the Community Design, COM(93)342, 54.

[60] ibid.

[61] ibid, 42. See also Commission, Proposal for a European Parliament and Council Directive on the legal protection of designs, COM(93)344.

[62] Commission, Proposal for a European Parliament and Council Regulation on the Community Design, COM(93)342, 50.

it opted for the new Article 100a. The following section analyses that legal basis choice in relation to power. The Commission's proposal legal basis did not, however, survive. The arrival of *Opinion 1/94* emphasised the inapplicability of Article 100a. That is the second part of the analysis.

1. *From 235 to 100a*

Like the Community trademark, the Community design was conceived as a (now) internal market measure. The same drawbacks of territoriality convinced the Commission of the need for a Community-wide design system.[63] Again, the aim was to ensure the free movement of protected goods and to guarantee undistorted competition.[64] At the level of competence, therefore, nothing had changed.

Nothing appeared to have changed at the level of power either. The proposed Community Design Regulation used the creation of a Community-wide intellectual property right as a power instrument to promote the internal market. It did not harmonise Member State laws. This combination of a regulation and no harmonisation had excluded Article 100 as a legal basis for the Community trademark; it logically did the same for the Community design. Recourse to the flexibility clause remained a necessity.

But the Commission found an alternative legal basis. The Single European Act's new Article 100a authorised internal market harmonisation by mere Council qualified majority voting.[65] Moreover, it referred to 'measures' in general.[66] By contrast with Article 100, the new internal market legal basis thus offered the Community legislator a choice between different types of legal act. It is true that the drafters of the Treaty had declared that the Commission should prioritise directives for proposals which entailed the amendment of national laws.[67] But this did not mean that regulations could not be adopted at all.[68] Article 100a applied for directives, but also for regulations.

Despite the new opening for regulations, the Commission's reliance on Article 100a remained questionable.[69] After all, it had not just rejected Article 100 for the Community trademark on type of legal act grounds; the main reason was the power instrument used. Article 100 required harmonisation, and a Community-wide intellectual property right did not entail harmonisation. Since

[63] ibid, 1.

[64] ibid.

[65] Article 100a TEEC (SEA). See J De Ruyt, *L'Acte unique européen – Commentaire* (Editions de l'Université de Bruxelles, 1989) 166.

[66] ibid.

[67] Member States, Declaration on Article 100A of the EEC Treaty, EC Bulletin Supplement 2/86, 24; K Lenaerts, *European Union Law* (Sweet & Maxwell, 2011) 298; De Ruyt (n 65) 168.

[68] P Oliver, *Free movement of goods in the E.E.C.: under Articles 30 to 36 of the Rome Treaty* (European Law Centre, 1988) 21; J Basedow, 'A Common Contract Law for the Common Market' (1996) 33 *Common Market Law Review* 1169, 1188.

[69] I Roudard, 'The proposed community design regulation and directive' (1999) 10 *Computer Law & Security Review* 26, 28.

Article 100a depended no less on that power instrument, the legal basis appeared just as inapplicable. Yet the Commission concluded otherwise.

In essence, the Commission proposed a different interpretation of 'harmonisation'. It did not deny that Article 100a only empowered the Council to adopt harmonising measures. But it argued that the Community design could be classified as harmonisation.[70] According to the Commission, Article 100a harmonisation was 'not restricted to amending national law';[71] it 'cover[ed] also supplementing national provisions or the replacement of national provisions'. Since '[t]he creation of a Community design supplement[ed] national provisions on the protection of design', concluded the Commission, it could 'be considered as an "approximation" of the law of the Member States in this area within the meaning of Article 100a EEC'.[72]

Perhaps the Commission genuinely believed its wide reading of the concept of harmonisation. Perhaps its legal basis choice stemmed from pragmatism rather than conviction. It is, in any case, hard to ignore the power modality advantages of Article 100a compared with Article 235. The latter legal basis required unanimity in the Council; the former only a qualified majority. A procedural power dimension may thus have steered the Commission's choice of legal basis. Soon, however, that choice would be undermined. With two rulings, the Court consolidated the use of Article 235 as a legal basis for Community-wide intellectual property rights.

2. Opinion 1/94 *and* Spain v Council

A few years after its initial proposal, the Commission reconsidered its legal basis position. It submitted an amended Community design proposal with the flexibility clause as legal basis.[73] The reason for the shift to (now) Article 308 TEC was clear.[74] *Opinion 1/94* had confirmed the Community trademark approach.[75] The internal market harmonisation legal bases did not apply to the creation of Community-wide intellectual property rights.

In chapter three, *Opinion 1/94* already illustrated the subject matter dimension of the common commercial policy competence. Here, the focus shifts to power. In their analysis of the Agreement on Trade-Related Aspects of Intellectual Property Rights (TRIPS), the judges clearly distinguished between the harmonisation of intellectual property rules and the creation of a Community-wide intellectual

[70] Commission, Proposal for a European Parliament and Council Regulation on the Community Design, COM(93)342, 3.

[71] ibid.

[72] ibid.

[73] Commission, Amended proposal for a Council Regulation (EC) on Community Design, COM(1999)310; Presidency, Report on the Amended proposal for a Council Regulation on Community designs 12420/00, 2.

[74] Commission, Amended proposal for a Council Regulation (EC) on Community Design, COM(1999)310.

[75] Opinion 1/94 *Accords annexés à l'accord OMC* [1994] ECR I-5267 ECLI:EU:C:1994:384.

property right. Articles 100 and 100a applied to the former; Article 235 applied to the latter:

> [A]t the level of internal legislation, the Community is competent, in the field of intellectual property, to harmonize national laws pursuant to Articles 100 and 100a and may use Article 235 as the basis for creating new rights superimposed on national rights, as it did in Council Regulation (EC) No 40/94 of 20 December 1993 on the Community trade mark.[76]

A second ruling confirmed this distinction. In *Spain v Council*, Spain requested the annulment of a Council Regulation that introduced a supplementary protection certificate for medicinal products.[77] The certificate served to compensate pharmaceutical companies for the difference in time between the start of a new medicinal product's patent protection and its market authorisation.[78] Because of the lengthy duration of research and testing, that difference was often significant.[79] The supplementary protection certificate, therefore, extended the protection for up to five years;[80] and it did so on the basis of Article 100a.

Among other arguments, Spain claimed that the Council should have used Article 235 as a legal basis.[81] The Court did not accept this; it repeated that the flexibility clause might constitute the legal basis 'for creating new rights superimposed on national rights'.[82] That did not, however, matter for the contested Regulation. The judges emphasised that it was 'undisputed that in this case the contested regulation [did] not create a new right'.[83] Not everyone agreed that the supplementary protection certificate did not constitute a new right.[84] But the underlying idea remained clear: Community-wide intellectual protection right was not harmonisation; it required Article 235 as internal market legal basis.

The Commission understood this. Encouraged by the European Parliament, it changed the proposed Community Design's legal basis from Article 100a to Article 308 TEC.[85] The new legal basis reflected the power instrument chosen. It entailed no change in the type of legal act, but a significant change at the procedural level. Qualified majority in the Council became unanimity. Co-operation

[76] ibid, para 59.

[77] Case C-350/92 *Spain v Council* [1995] ECR I-01985 ECLI:EU:C:1995:237, para 1; Council Regulation (EEC) No 1768/92 of 18 June 1992 concerning the creation of a supplementary protection certificate for medicinal products, OJ L182.

[78] J Mischo, 'The Contribution of the Court of Justice to the Protection of the "Federal Balance" in the European Community' in D O'Keeffe (ed), *Judicial Review in European Union Law – Essays in Honour of Lord Slynn* (Kluwer Law International, 2000) 61.

[79] Recitals of Council Regulation (EEC) No 1768/92 of 18 June 1992 concerning the creation of a supplementary protection certificate for medicinal products, OJ L182.

[80] ibid, Article 13.

[81] Case C-350/92 *Spain v Council*, para 25.

[82] ibid, para 23.

[83] ibid, para 27.

[84] R Schütze, *European Constitutional Law* (CUP, 2012) 157.

[85] Commission, Amended proposal for a Council Regulation (EC) on Community Design, COM(1999)310, 2.

with the European Parliament became consultation. And there was no longer a requirement to consult the Economic and Social Committee.

C. Patents

A third proposal for a Community-wide intellectual property right proved less successful. In 2000, the Commission proposed the creation of a Community patent.[86] Again, the proposal's context was the internal market competence. The new patent would eliminate distortions of competition and ensure the free movement of patented goods in the internal market.[87] Again, it concerned an intellectual property right with a unitary character.[88] And, again, the Community patent would co-exist with national patents.[89] Evidently, the Commission thus chose Article 308 TEC as its legal basis.[90] It continued what had already 'been done in relation to the Community trade mark and Community designs'.[91]

The reality turned out differently. The Community patent 'met with insuperable resistance in the Council'.[92] Unlike the Community trademark and the Community design, it never came into existence. After 'a long history of fruitless proposals and failed initiatives', the Commission ultimately withdrew its proposal in 2012.[93] The full details of these proceedings are not relevant here;[94] this is a chapter about power, not about the Community patent. Only those issues which add to the power analysis deserve a mention.

There were two such issues. First, a language controversy prevented the proposal's unanimous adoption under Article 308 TEC and likely convinced the drafters to retain the unanimity rule for language aspects in the new power to create Union-wide intellectual property rights. Second, the Court explicitly confirmed that this new power was an internal market power.

[86] Commission, Proposal for a Council Regulation on the Community patent, COM(2000)412.
[87] ibid, 6.
[88] ibid, 9 and 38.
[89] ibid, 6.
[90] J Pila, 'An Historical Perspective I: The Unitary Patent Package' in J Pila and C Wadlow (eds), *The Unitary EU Patent System* (Hart Publishing, 2015) 14; Belgian Delegation to the Working Party on Intellectual Property (Patents), Note on the Institutional aspects of the EC's accession to the European Patent Convention, 13742/01, 3.
[91] Belgian Delegation to the Working Party on Intellectual Property (Patents), Note on the Institutional aspects of the EC's accession to the European Patent Convention, 13742/01, 3.
[92] Opinion in Case C-431/05 *Merck Genéricos Produtos Farmacêuticos* [2007] ECR I-07001 ECLI:EU:C:2007:48, para 49.
[93] C Seville, 'Developments (and Non-Developments) in the Harmonisation of EU Intellectual Property Law' (2009) 11 *Cambridge Yearbook of European Legal Studies* 87, 113; R Schütze, *European Union Law* (OUP, 2021) 576; Commission, Withdrawal of obsolete Commission proposals (2012) OJ C156.
[94] See, eg S Peers, 'The Constitutional Implications of the EU Patent' (2011) 7 *European Constitutional Law Review* 229; O Bossung, 'A union patent instead of the community patent: Developing the European patent into an EU patent' (2003) 34 *International Review of Intellectual Property and Competition Law* 1.

1. *From Unanimity to Qualified Majority (and Unanimity)*

The proposed Community patent raised a difficult question:[95] which language requirements would have to be fulfilled in an application for patent protection and in related proceedings? From an internal market perspective, less was more; translations are costly and time-consuming.[96] This became very clear when the Member States first tried to create a unitary patent. Their Luxembourg Convention did not receive sufficient ratifications.[97] Concerns regarding the Convention's insistence on translations in all Community languages were seen as a major reason for its failure.[98]

In its 2000 proposal, the Commission, therefore, advanced a more limited scheme.[99] To be protected throughout the Community, it would suffice that a patent had been granted in one of the working languages of the European Patent Office responsible for administering the Community patent and had been translated into the Office's two other working languages.[100] The Commission thus limited the patent's languages to English, French, and German.[101] Further translation requirements would, however, protect alleged patent infringers in legal proceedings.[102]

The Council objected. The proposed language arrangements constituted one of the proposal's most controversial aspects.[103] If the Council could reach an agreement at all, it certainly did not appear likely to follow the Commission's proposal. A 2003 common political approach stipulated that patent claims would have to be translated into all Community languages.[104] This again raised fears of an overly costly patent system. In response, the Commission reiterated its belief that a more optimal compromise between legal certainty and low transaction costs was possible.[105]

[95] This was not the only controversy, but the only one that matters for this chapter. Presidency, Reflection paper on the Community patent, 8375/1/02, 1 lists the four main issues. See also T Jaeger, 'The EU Patent: *Cui Bono et Quo Vadit?*' (2010) 47 *Common Market Law Review* 63.

[96] Commission, Proposal for a Council Regulation on the Community patent, COM(2000)412, 10.

[97] Convention establishing a Community patent [1976] OJ L17.

[98] Peers (n 94) 232.

[99] Commission, Proposal for a Council Regulation on the Community patent, COM(2000)412, 12; Bossung (n 94) 2.

[100] Commission, Proposal for a Council Regulation on the Community patent, COM(2000)412, 12.

[101] Kur, Dreier, and Luginbuehl (n 19) 151.

[102] Commission, Proposal for a Council Regulation on the Community patent, COM(2000)412, 12.

[103] Presidency, Note on the Language arrangements for the Community patent, 11056/01; Presidency, Note on the patent: Presidency compromise proposal concerning translations, 15111/03; Presidency, Working document 'Towards a Community patent: Translation arrangements and distribution of fees', 8928/08; C Geiger, 'The construction of intellectual property in the European Union: search for coherence' in C Geiger (ed), *Constructing European Intellectual Property – Achievements and New Perspectives* (Edward Elgar, 2013) 14.

[104] General Secretariat, Note on the Community patent: common political approach, 7159/03, 2. See also Peers (n 94) 234; A Ilardi, *The New European Patent* (Hart Publishing, 2015) 22.

[105] Commission, Communication to the European Parliament and the Council – Enhancing the patent system in Europe, COM(2007)165, 4–5; Ilardi (n 104) 25–26.

Then, the Treaties changed. The Commission originally proposed the Community patent as an Article 308 measure. But the Lisbon Treaty introduced a specific legal basis for the creation of Union-wide intellectual property rights. In the internal market chapter, a new Article 118 allowed the Council and the Parliament to act through the ordinary legislative procedure.[106] Crucially, a qualified majority in the Council sufficed. Yet there was an important exception: for the adoption of language arrangements, the Council would merely consult the Parliament and could only act unanimously.[107]

The roots of this new legal basis date back to the draft Constitutional Treaty. The idea was to limit recourse to Article 308 by adding specific legal bases, especially for non-harmonisation measures within the internal market competence.[108] These included the creation of unitary intellectual property rights. The draft Constitutional Treaty thus introduced Article 118's predecessor.[109] It also introduced the specific unanimity rule for language arrangements. Some drafters had feared that this would undermine swift decision-making.[110] Still, it did not come as a surprise. After all, the preparations of the Constitutional Treaty coincided with the rising controversies on the Community patent and its language arrangements.

For the Commission's proposal, the shift from the flexibility clause to Articles 118(1) and 118(2) had an important consequence. Before, a single legal act could create a Community patent and lay down its language arrangements; Article 308 applied the same power modalities to both. Post-Lisbon, that changed.[111] Article 118(1) empowered the Council and the Parliament to adopt the measure; Article 118(2) only so empowered the Council. A qualified majority sufficed for Article 118(1); Article 118(2) required unanimity. This made the legal bases mutually incompatible.[112]

The Commission realised this. Soon after the entry into force of the Lisbon Treaty, it submitted a new proposal. It concerned the language arrangements of the (now) European Union patent.[113] In the proposal, the Commission highlighted the consequence of the power modality differences between Articles 118(1) and 118(2). 'Due to the change of legal basis for the creation of the EU patent following the entry into force of the Lisbon Treaty', it said, 'the translation arrangements for the

[106] Article 118(1) TFEU.

[107] Article 118(2) TFEU.

[108] Convention Secretariat, Final report of Working Group V, CONV 375/1/02 Rev1, 8; Convention Secretariat, Note on Part Two of the Constitution – Report by the working party of experts nominated by the Legal Services of the European Parliament, the Council and the Commission, CONV 618/03, 29.

[109] Convention Praesidium, Cover note on the Draft sections of Part Three with comments, CONV 727/03.

[110] L Hjelm-Wallén and S-O Petersson, Suggestion for amendment of Article: III-65, CONV 2002–2003; G Lennmarker, Suggestion for amendment of Article: III-65, CONV 2002–2003; GM de Vries and TJAM de Bruijn, Suggestion for amendment of Article: III-65, CONV 2002–2003.

[111] J-C Piris, *The Lisbon Treaty – A Legal and Political Analysis* (CUP, 2010) 323.

[112] M Kellerbauer, 'Articles 114–118' in M Kellerbauer, M Klamert, and J Tomkin (eds), *The EU Treaties and the Charter of Fundamental Rights: A Commentary* (OUP, 2019) 1267.

[113] Commission, Proposal for a Council Regulation (EU) on the translation arrangements for the European Union patent, COM(2010)350.

EU patent that were initially present in the Commission proposal of 2000 must now become the subject of a separate proposal'.[114]

The proposal would never be adopted. The failure of the patent project quickly became undeniable. This prompted a number of Member States to propose a different approach.[115] They requested the Commission to initiate proceedings for an enhanced co-operation measure.[116] A unitary patent could thus be created for those Member States willing to participate. The Commission accepted. It first proposed the Council to authorise the enhanced co-operation.[117] Then, it issued the substantive proposals; and, crucially, there were two. One proposal introduced a unitary patent;[118] the other concerned its language arrangements.[119]

Yet a return to the Community Trademark Regulation illustrates that these distinct power modalities are not always observed. In 2015, the EU legislator adopted an amendment to the Regulation.[120] It concerned, among others, the trademark's language arrangements.[121] Nonetheless, the Council and the Parliament adopted the full amending act under Article 118(1). And the Council did not vote by unanimity. The preparatory documents equally ignore Article 118(2). Of course, adopting a single legal act was considerably more practical, but Article 118's distinct power modalities simply did not allow it.

2. *An Internal Market Power (Instrument)*

A second point should be made; it concerns power's instrument dimension. From the beginning, this chapter qualified the creation of Community- or Union-wide intellectual property rights as exercises of an internal market power. The aim always was the promotion of free movement and undistorted competition in the common or internal market. *Opinion 1/94* confirmed this for the flexibility clause. The Court gave an equivalent confirmation for Article 118 TFEU.

[114] ibid, 3.

[115] Peers (n 94) 236.

[116] Ilardi (n 104) 29.

[117] Council Decision 2011/167/EU of 10 March 2011 authorising enhanced cooperation in the area of the creation of unitary patent protection, OJ L76.

[118] Commission, Proposal for a Regulation of the European Parliament and of the Council implementing enhanced cooperation in the area of the creation of unitary patent protection, COM(2011)215.

[119] Commission, Proposal for a Council Regulation implementing enhanced cooperation in the area of the creation of unitary patent protection with regard to the applicable translation arrangements, COM(2011)215.

[120] Regulation (EU) 2015/2424 of the European Parliament and of the Council of 16 December 2015 amending Council Regulation (EC) No 207/2009 on the Community trade mark and Commission Regulation (EC) No 2868/95 implementing Council Regulation (EC) No 40/94 on the Community trade mark, and repealing Commission Regulation (EC) No 2869/95 on the fees payable to the Office for Harmonization in the Internal Market (Trade Marks and Designs), OJ L342.

[121] ibid, Article 1(102). See also Case C-147/13 *Spain v Council* [2015] ECLI:EU:C:2015:299, paras 65–75 on the meaning of 'language arrangements'.

In the Council, two delegations objected to the adoption of the unitary patent under the enhanced co-operation mechanism.[122] Italy and Spain continued to campaign for an EU-wide compromise. When their efforts proved in vain, they announced legal action against the Council's authorisation decision.[123] One line of their argumentation is especially interesting from a power and competence perspective: both Member States argued that the Council could not have authorised the enhanced co-operation, because Article 118 fell within the Union's exclusive competition competence.[124]

The Court did not accept this argument. It recalled the text of Article 26(1) TFEU:[125] 'The Union shall adopt measures with the aim of establishing or ensuring the functioning of the internal market, in accordance with the relevant provisions of the Treaties.'[126] This reference to the 'relevant provisions of the Treaties' was important. It made clear that:

> [C]ompetences falling within the sphere of the internal market are not confined to those conferred by Articles 114 TFEU and 115 TFEU relating to the adoption of harmonisation measures but cover also any competence attaching to the objectives set out in Article 26 TFEU, such as the competences conferred on the Union by Article 118 TFEU.[127]

It is regrettable that the Court referred to the competences of the internal market; from the perspective of the concepts of 'competence', it instead meant powers. But the underlying idea was sound. Article 118, too, '[fell] within the ambit of the functioning of the internal market'.[128] Just like Articles 114 and 115, it was an internal market power in a field of internal market competence.

II. Common Commercial Policy

Not all intellectual property measures fall within the scope of the internal market competence; to the extent that they specifically relate to international trade, they fall within the scope of the common commercial policy instead. That includes the

[122] Presidency, Note on the Unitary patent proposals: political orientation/exchange of views, 10401/11, 4; Presidency, Note on the Unitary patent proposals: political orientation/exchange of views, 10629/11, 4.

[123] Presidency, Note on the Unitary patent proposals: common approach, 11328/11, 4; Action brought on 3 June 2011 – *Kingdom of Spain v Council of the European Union* (Case C-274/11); Action brought on 10 June 2011 – *Italian Republic v Council of the European Union* (Case C-295/11).

[124] Joined Cases C-274/11 and C-295/11 *Spain and Italy v Council* [2013] ECLI:EU:C:2013:240, para 10.

[125] ibid, para 20.

[126] Article 26(1) TFEU.

[127] Joined Cases C-274/11 and C-295/11 *Spain and Italy v Council*, para 21.

[128] ibid, para 18.

more recent Geneva Act on geographical indications.[129] Both the opening of negotiations and the accession to the Act proved problematic in terms of 'competence'.

The opening of negotiations for the Act was largely a problem of competence. However, it raised an interesting point of power too. It confirmed that the protection of intellectual property rights can also be a power instrument within the CCP. The accession to the Act was solely a problem of power. By making a far-reaching amendment to the Commission's proposal, the Council exercised a power that actually belonged to the Commission. The following sections explain both the problem of competence and the problem of power.

Before doing so, however, it is useful to briefly introduce the Act itself. It revises the Lisbon Agreement; this Agreement was (and is) an intellectual property agreement concluded under the auspices of the World Intellectual Property Organization.[130] It established an international registration system for appellations of origin.[131] Members to the Agreement undertook to protect these appellations on their territory. Since only states could accede to it, the EU was not a member.

Almost 60 years later, work began to revise the original Lisbon Agreement. The revision served to complement and clarify the Agreement.[132] It extended the scope of protection from appellations of origin to geographic indications in general.[133] Crucially for the EU, it also allowed the accession of international organisations.[134] This revision became known as the Geneva Act. In 2015, the parties to the Lisbon Agreement convened a diplomatic conference to consider and adopt the Act. The EU also received an invitation to the conference.

A. Geographical Indications: Opening of Negotiations

The Commission recommended the Council to authorise the opening of negotiations for the Geneva Act.[135] As legal bases, it proposed Articles 207 (CCP) and 218

[129] Geneva Act of the Lisbon Agreement on Appellations of Origin and Geographical Indications [2015].

[130] A Rosas, 'Mixity and the Common Commercial Policy after Opinion 2/15' in M Hahn and G Van der Loo, *Law and Practice of the Common Commercial Policy – The First 10 Years After the Treaty of Lisbon* (Brill, 2020) 35; G Miribung, 'Changes happen slowly – some comments on geographical indications between the Geneva Act and Regulation 2019/1753' (2020) 1 *European Food and Feed Law Review* 25, 28.

[131] J Pila and P Torremans, *European Intellectual Property Law* (OUP, 2019) 445–46.

[132] Case C-389/15 *Commission v Council*, para 18.

[133] In summary, Swiss-made watches and Cassis de Dijon are geographical indications. A geographical indication is 'a sign used on goods that have a specific geographical origin and possess qualities or a reputation due to that place of origin' (WIPO, 'Understanding Industrial Property' (2015) 19). Appellations of origin constitute a category of geographic indications. Here, '(t)he quality or characteristics of (the protected good) must result exclusively or essentially from its geographical origin' ('What is the difference between a geographical indication and an appellation of origin' (WIPO), www.wipo.int/geo_indications/en/faq_geographicalindications.html). Parma ham, for instance, must be produced in Parma, from Parma pigs.

[134] Case C-389/15 *Commission v Council*, para 18.

[135] Commission, Recommendation for a Council Decision authorizing the opening of negotiations on a Revised Lisbon Agreement on Appellations of Origin and Geographical Indications, COM(2015)142.

(international agreements) TFEU. The Council disagreed;[136] in its view, the Act did not fall within the scope of the CCP competence, because it did not aim to facilitate international trade. Instead, it laid down a 'uniform procedural framework for the protection of appellations of origin and geographical indications'.[137] The Council thus based its Decision on Articles 114 (internal market harmonisation) and 218 instead.[138] In response, the Commission contested the Decision in Court.

The Court found that the Geneva Act did indeed fall within the scope of the CCP. It was 'essentially intended to promote, facilitate or govern trade' and had 'direct and immediate effects on trade'.[139] In line with the Paris Convention and the Lisbon Agreement, the Act aimed to 'encourage the participation, on an equal footing, of the relevant economic operators in trade between [its] members' by ensuring homogeneous standards of protection.[140] These standards of protection and the single registration mechanism also directly affected international trade, especially 'in the light of the key role that the protection of intellectual property rights plays in trade in goods and services in general, and in combatting unlawful trade in particular'.[141]

Thus, the Court annulled the Decision because the Council had erred on the applicable competence. Interestingly, however, the Court also made a point of power. It did not treat intellectual property rights as aspects of competence. Its ruling made no attempt to establish whether the concept of international trade covered intellectual property rights as such. Put differently, it did not examine whether the subject matter scope of the CCP competence extended to intellectual property rights. Instead, the Court treated the protection of geographical indications (and intellectual property rights more generally) as a power instrument.

The Geneva Act fell within the scope of the CCP, because mutually protecting geographical indications was a means to facilitate international trade in goods and services.[142] Here, a parallel emerges with the (common and) internal market examples examined earlier in this chapter. Harmonising existing intellectual property rights and introducing new Union-wide intellectual property rights was a means to promote the internal market. Similarly, ensuring a shared protection of intellectual property rights between international trading partners was a means to promote international trade.

[136] Council, 2539th meeting of the Permanent Representatives Committee held in Brussels on 29 April 2015, 8382/15, 12.
[137] Case C-389/15 *Commission v Council*, para 43.
[138] Council Decision 8512/15 of 7 May 2015 authorising the opening of negotiations on a revised Lisbon Agreement on Appellations of Origin and Geographical Indications as regards matters falling within the competence of the European Union.
[139] Case C-389/15 *Commission v Council*, paras 49–50.
[140] ibid, paras 57–60.
[141] ibid, paras 67–72.
[142] See, for similar reasoning, Case C-414/11 *Daiichi Sankyo and Sanofi-Aventis Deutschland* [2013] ECLI:EU:C:2013:520; and Case C-137/12 *Commission v Council* [2013] ECLI:EU:C:2013:675.

B. Geographical Indications: Accession

A few years later, the Council adopted a Decision on the EU's accession to the Geneva Act.[143] This time, it used the correct legal bases. As proposed by the Commission, it adopted its Decision under Articles 207 and 218(6)a TFEU. The Decision did, however, derogate from the proposal on a fundamental point: the Commission only proposed the EU's accession to the Act; the Council amended the proposal to also allow Member States to accede.

It did so for two practical reasons.[144] First, as mentioned, several Member States were already party to the Lisbon Agreement. The Council wanted to ensure the continuity of the protection of appellations of origin that were already registered in these Member States. Second, as an international organisation, the Union would not enjoy any voting rights in the Geneva Act's assembly. The Act did not grant international organisations a voting right in their own right; it only allowed them to exercise the votes of their Member States. Thus, if no Member State was a party to the Act, the EU could not vote.

The Commission strongly objected.[145] Exceptionally, it was prepared to accept that those Member States who had already joined the Lisbon Agreement could also accede to the Geneva Act. However, allowing all Member States to accede was unacceptable. When the Council refused to change its approach, the Commission warned it would consider legal action.[146] And, indeed, it soon challenged the Decision in Court.

Again, the Court sided with the Commission.[147] It annulled the Decision on the grounds of a lack of power. With its amendment, the Council had exercised a power that belonged to the Commission.[148] To understand this, it is necessary

[143] Council Decision (EU) 2019/1754 of 7 October 2019 on the accession of the European Union to the Geneva Act of the Lisbon Agreement on Appellations of Origin and Geographical Indications, OJ L271.

[144] Presidency, Proposal for a Council Decision on the accession of the European Union to the Geneva Act of the Lisbon Agreement on Appellations of Origin and Geographical Indications – Examination of the compromise text, 5714/19, 4; Presidency, Proposal for a Council Decision on the accession of the European Union to the Geneva Act of the Lisbon Agreement on Appellations of Origin and Geographical Indications – Preparation of the request for the consent of the European Parliament, 6877/19, 5; M Chamon, 'Commission challenges authorisation granted to Member States to exercise EU exclusive competences' (EU Law Live, 2020), www.eulawlive.com/analysis-commission-challenges-authorisation-granted-to-member-states-to-exercise-eu-exclusive-competences-by-merijn-chamon.

[145] General Secretariat of the Council, Draft Council Decision on the accession of the European Union to the Geneva Act of the Lisbon Agreement on Appellations of Origin and Geographical Indications – Statements, 12384/19 Add2, 1–2.

[146] ibid.

[147] Case C-24/20 *Commission v Council* [2022] ECLI:EU:C:2022:911.

[148] The Commission also claimed a violation of Article 2(1) TFEU. Within an exclusive EU competence, Member States may only adopt binding acts 'if so empowered by the Union or for the implementation of Union acts'. The Commission argued that the Council had exceeded the limits of its power to empower the Member States. Advocate General Szpunar agreed: the empowerment was disproportionate. The objective to ensure continuity of protections and a Union voting right was valid, but the Council could have achieved it by only authorising the Member States party to the Lisbon

to recall Article 293 TFEU. This provision sets out how the Council may amend Commission proposals and how the Commission may alter its own proposals. In most cases, including the contested Decision, the Council may only amend a Commission proposal by unanimity (unless the Commission agrees with the amendments).[149] The Commission may alter its proposal at any time, as long as the Council has not acted.[150]

The issue was not that the Council had failed to act unanimously; in fact, it had approved the Decision by unanimity. However, that did not suffice. The Court emphasised that Article 293 must be read together with the principles of conferred powers and institutional balance under Article 13 TEU and the Commission's general power of initiative under Article 17(2) TEU.[151] In that context, the Council did not enjoy an unlimited power to amend a Commission proposal under Article 293. The Council could not alter the proposal's 'raison d'être' – its subject matter and objective.[152]

Yet that was precisely what the Council had done. The Court emphasised that the Geneva Act fell within the scope of the Union's exclusive CCP competence.[153] In principle, the EU alone should act within such an exclusive competence. The Commission could, nonetheless, propose to empower the Member States to act. This special political choice reflected the Commission's view of the Union's general interest and fell within its power of initiative.[154] For the Geneva Act, the Commission opted only to propose the EU's accession and explicitly objected to a general option for the Member States to accede. By nonetheless foreseeing such an option, the Council distorted the proposal's subject matter and objective.[155]

In essence, the problem related to power's modality of which institution may act. The Council exercised a power held by the Commission. Under Article 293, the Council enjoys a discretionary power to amend a Commission proposal. However, it lacks a power to alter that proposal's subject matter or objective; that

Agreement to accede to the Act. The Court upheld the first plea, so did not need to rule on this point. For more details, see Opinion in Case C-24/20 *Commission v Council* [2022] ECLI:EU:C:2022:404, paras 91–120; and T Verellen, 'The distortion theory in EU treaty-making: Commission v. Council (Geneva Act)' (2022) 60 *Common Market Law Review* 1705, 1708–09.

[149] Article 293(1) TFEU.

[150] Article 293(2) TFEU.

[151] Case C-24/20 *Commission v Council*, paras 83–85.

[152] ibid, paras 93–94.

[153] ibid, paras 97–102; P Krajewski, 'The European Commission as a Driver of EU Trade Policy: Executive Leadership by Technocratic Means' in C Eckes, P Leino-Sandberg, and AW Ghavanini (eds), *Dynamics of Powers in the European Union* (Hart Publishing, 2024) 105.

[154] Case C-24/20 *Commission v Council*, paras 103–04.

[155] ibid, paras 105–08. This reasoning can be traced back to the Court's judgments in Case C-408/95, *Eurotunnel and Others v SeaFrance* [1996] ECR I-06315 ECLI:EU:C:1997:532, paras 37–39; and Case C-409/13 *Council v Commission* [2015] ECLI:EU:C:2015:217. See M Chamon, 'Reinforcing the Community Method – the Commission as a veto player in EU external relations' (EU Law Live, 2022), www.eulawlive.com/op-ed-reinforcing-the-community-method-the-commission-as-a-veto-player-in-eu-external-relations-by-merijn-chamon. See also K Lenaerts, P Van Nuffel, and T Corthaut, *EU Constitutional Law* (OUP, 2021) 542.

power belongs to the Commission, as part of its power of initiative.[156] Any practical voting difficulties or continuity issues related to an EU-only accession could not change that conclusion. After all, it followed directly from Article 13(2) and its principle of conferred powers.

The Court thus annulled the Decision to the extent that it authorised all Member States to accede to the Geneva Act. However, it maintained the annulled provisions' effects until the adoption of an amendment to the Decision. This was to allow the Council, within a reasonable time period and based on a new Commission proposal, to authorise only those Member States who were already party to the Lisbon Agreement to accede to the Act. The Commission had explicitly agreed to such a compromise during the Luxembourg proceedings. Soon, as proposed by the Commission, the Council adopted the more limited authorisation.[157]

Fundamental questions remain. These include whether the Court got the balance right, and the impact of its ruling in other contexts, notably in shared fields of competence.[158] This chapter does not seek to provide an answer. Its point has already been made: the Geneva Act confirms the relevance of power as a 'competence' concept.

III. Conclusion

Power is the authorisation to act in a certain field of competence. It has an instruments dimension and a type of legal act dimension. It also has procedural modalities. The European Union trademark, the Community design, and the unitary patent illustrate these dimensions and modalities in the field of the internal market. Geographical indications show that power's dimensions and modalities also matter in the field of the common commercial policy.

The first two legal disputes focused on the power dimensions. For the trademark and the design, the main issue concerned the power instrument used. Unitary intellectual property rights aim to promote the internal market, but not by harmonising national laws. The internal market harmonisation power, therefore, did not apply. The choice of power instrument also influenced the relevant type of legal act; to create a unitary right, a regulation is more appropriate than a directive.

The third legal dispute also looked at the power modalities. When the Commission proposed the Community patent, the power instrument distinction between the creation of a unitary intellectual property right and the harmonisation of national intellectual property rules was established. So was the choice for a

[156] See Verellen (n 148) 1714.

[157] Council Decision (EU) 2023/1051 of 22 May 2023 amending Decision (EU) 2019/1754 on the accession of the European Union to the Geneva Act of the Lisbon Agreement on Appellations of Origin and Geographical Indications, OJ L141.

[158] See Chamon, 'Reinforcing the Community Method' (n 155); and Verellen (n 148).

regulation. But the entry into force of the Lisbon Treaty did highlight the importance of power's modalities.

The fourth legal dispute showed that power also matters outside the internal market competence. The opening of negotiations of the Geneva Act confirmed that the protection of intellectual property rights may also be a CCP power instrument. The accession to the Act illustrated that the power modality of which institution may act may often be straightforward, but can nonetheless raise real legal conflicts.

Thus, power is the second concept of 'competence'. Competence is the field in which the European Union may act; but to act in that field, it needs power. Power is the EU institutions' actual authorisation to act. This chapter showed that authorisation in practice.

PART 3

Evaluative

So far, the approach has been descriptive. Part 1 returned to the ECSC. It showed that the European project always was a legal project, based on the principle of conferral, and introduced the distinction between competence and power. Part 2 followed the same approach. It turned to the more recent history and present of Community and Union law. It first gave an overview of the common language of 'competence'. Then, using real legal disputes from the internal market and common commercial policy, it illustrated the main concepts of competence and power.

This Part 3 uses a different approach. It argues why the concepts of 'competence' matter. It does so through two new legal disputes. To show that the concepts are relevant today, both legal disputes are recent. As in Part 2, they concern the internal market and the CCP. And both make the same argument. They both present a dispute in which the 'competence' debate is unsatisfactory, and in which thinking in terms of competence and power provides a more convincing alternative. The approach thus becomes evaluative. In the previous part, the concepts of 'competence' were introduced. This part shows their benefits.

5

The Benefits of 'Competence' (1): Posted Workers

This chapter illustrates the benefits of the concepts of 'competence'. It concerns a particularly controversial legal dispute. In the context of EU 'competence', strained legal reasoning is always problematic. The principle of conferral is a cornerstone of Union law and must be seen to be respected.[1] This requires a solid explanation why the Union does or does not have competence and power to adopt a certain measure. When such legal reasoning appears to be absent, tensions arise. This is especially the case in a context where the interests of two groups of Member States seem to be diametrically opposed. And that was precisely the context of the recent posted workers cases.[2]

When an undertaking established in one Member State sends workers to another Member State to provide a service, the question arises of which labour rules apply. Since 1996, the Posted Workers Directive has answered that question.[3] It initially determined that a limited set of host Member States rules applied as minimum standards for posted workers.[4] In 2018, the EU legislator amended the Directive.[5] They increased the list of matters in which host state rules applied. This was not uncontroversial.

On the one hand, Member States with less stringent rules wanted to ensure that their undertakings could provide services without incurring additional labour costs. They feared that minimum host state standards would remove an important competitive advantage for companies looking to provide their services in other Member States, and thus create a considerable obstacle to the free movement of their service providers.[6] On the other hand, Member States with a higher level of

[1] Article 5(1)–(2) TEU (Lisbon); K Lenaerts, P Van Nuffel, and T Corthaut, *EU Constitutional Law* (OUP, 2021) 84.

[2] S O'Leary and SI Sanchez, 'Free Movement of Persons and Services' in P Craig and G De Búrca (eds), *The Evolution of EU Law* (OUP, 2021) 531.

[3] Directive 96/71/EC of the European Parliament and of the Council of 16 December 1996 concerning the posting of workers in the framework of the provision of services, OJ L18.

[4] ibid, Article 3.

[5] Directive (EU) 2018/957 of the European Parliament and of the Council of 28 June 2018 amending Directive 96/71/EC concerning the posting of workers in the framework of the provision of services, OJ L173.

[6] General Secretariat, Note on the Proposal for an amended Posted Workers Directive (yellow card), 9970/16, 4; General Secretariat, Note on the Proposal for an amended Posted Workers Directive

worker protection wanted to protect their undertakings against competition from undertakings subjected to less protective rules.[7] They emphasised the need to fight social dumping and unfair competition.

Eventually, the EU legislator amended the Posted Workers Directive.[8] She increased the application of host state rules. Several Member States responded by expressing their regret that the EU legislator had not found a proper balance between the free movement of services and the protection of workers.[9] Poland and Hungary went further: they denounced the amendment as a 'protectionist tool' that would be 'highly detrimental to the competitiveness of the Union as a whole', and voted against it.[10] When the Council adopted the amending act anyway, both Member States initiated annulment proceedings.[11] Importantly, they claimed that the Directive was invalidly adopted within the internal market competence.

The Court did not agree; it upheld the Directive.[12] But its reasoning was not convincing. And the reason why is crucial. EU competences have a subject matter and an objectives dimension. The posted workers cases fail to properly recognise the latter. First, the judges conflated competence objectives with horizontal Treaty objectives. They identified worker protection as a valid internal market competence aim alongside the aim to promote the provision of services in that market. Second, the Court did not examine whether the contested Directive actually pursued an internal market competence objective. Together, these issues cast doubt over its conclusion that the Directive fell within the internal market competence and was lawfully based on the internal market powers invoked.

The chapter proceeds as follows. The first section gives an overview of the original and amended Posted Workers Directives, and of the two judgments. The second section argues that the Court's legal 'competence' reasoning is unconvincing, because it misidentifies the internal market competence's objectives and fails to verify whether the contested Directive actually pursues them. The third section completes the legal basis analysis. It shows the existence of an additional, unexplored line of legal basis reasoning which was forgotten in the judgments.

(yellow card), 9309/16, 3; 'Going Posted' (*The Economist*, 7 July 2016), www.economist.com/europe/2016/07/07/going-posted.

[7] S Evju, 'Revisiting the Posted Workers Directive: Conflict of Laws and Laws in Contrast' (2010) 12 *Cambridge Yearbook of European Legal Studies* 151, 169; P Rodière, 'Le droit européen du détachement de travailleurs: fraude ou inapplicabilité?' (2016) 7/8 *Droit Social* 598, 599.

[8] Directive (EU) 2018/957 amending the Posted Workers Directive.

[9] General Secretariat, I/A Note on the Proposal for an amended Posted Workers Directive (adoption and statements), 9383/18 Add1; Council, Note on the Proposal for an amended Posted Workers Directive (voting result), 10422/18, 2.

[10] General Secretariat, I/A Note on the Proposal for an amended Posted Workers Directive (adoption and statements), 9383/18 Add1, 5.

[11] Action brought on 2 October 2018 – *Hungary v European Parliament and Council of the European Union* (Case C-620/18); Action brought on 3 October 2018 – *Republic of Poland v European Parliament and Council of the European Union* (Case C-626/18).

[12] Case C-620/18 *Hungary v Parliament and Council* [2020] ECLI:EU:C:2020:1001; Case C-626/18 *Poland v Parliament and Council* [2020] ECLI:EU:C:2020:1000.

Together, these sections show the benefits of the concepts of 'competence', and the need for a more rigorous and precise legal 'competence' reasoning.

I. Posted Workers: The Directives and the Judgments

Before examining where the Court's reasoning went wrong from a 'competence' perspective, the scene must be set. Thus, the following analysis is descriptive. It first explains the original Posted Workers Directive and its amendment. Second, it gives an overview of the judges' legal basis reasoning in *Poland* and *Hungary*.

A. The (Amended) Posted Workers Directive

In the European Union, posting of workers 'has always been a sensitive issue'.[13] It involves the interests of posting undertakings (who favour the application of home state rules under the principle of mutual recognition), local undertakings (who fear competitors bound by potentially lower labour rules), and posted workers (who wish to be protected by strong labour rights). Aligning these apparently opposed interests is not an easy task.[14]

In 1996, the Community legislator made a first attempt at reconciliation; it adopted the original Posted Workers Directive.[15] The Directive required Member States to ensure that undertakings guaranteed their posted workers some employment rules of the Member State where the posted work was carried out (the host Member State). Article 3(1) listed these rules.[16] In the construction sector, undertakings also had to guarantee the terms and conditions of employment laid down in universally applicable collective agreements.[17]

No minimum time threshold existed. The Directive applied from the first day of posting, even if the posting work was only scheduled for a short period. Two provisions did, however, nuance this strict rule. First, a supplier of goods could post specialist workers to assemble and/or install the goods within eight days, without having to pay them the host Member State's minimum rates of pay, and without having to comply with local rules on minimum paid leave.[18] This exception did not apply for construction suppliers.[19] Second, Member States could opt not to require

[13] Opinion in Case C-620/18 *Hungary v Parliament and Council* [2020] ECLI:EU:C:2020:392, para 17.
[14] Evju (n 7) 169; Rodière (n 7) 599.
[15] Posted Workers Directive 96/71/EC.
[16] ibid, Article 3(1).
[17] ibid and Annex.
[18] ibid, Article 3(2).
[19] ibid and Annex.

posting undertakings to comply with their minimum rates of pay if the posting did not exceed one month.[20] Overall, these exceptions remained narrow.

The Posted Workers Directive was, however, limited in one crucial aspect: its Article 3(1) list was exhaustive.[21] A host Member State could not require a posting employer to comply with its employment rules on matters excluded from the list.[22] As a result, significant discrepancies continued to exist between the working conditions of posted and local workers, especially regarding pay. In many Member States with higher labour standards, especially those receiving large numbers of posted workers from lower-standard Member States, that became an issue. These Member States increasingly complained of social dumping and unfair competition.[23]

To address their concerns, the EU legislator adopted the contested Directive.[24] Just like the original Directive, it was based on internal market (services) legal bases.[25] Three amendments are especially relevant to the Polish and Hungarian cases. First, the application of collective agreements with universal applicability is no longer limited to the construction sector.[26] For all matters on Article 3's list, and for all sectors, laws and such agreements both apply. Second, Article 3(1)c no longer refers to minimum rates of pay.[27] Instead, host Member States shall ensure that posting undertakings comply with local remuneration rules. Third, the 2018 Directive introduced a new category of long-term posting. If a posting effectively lasts longer than 12 months, nearly all employment rules of the host Member State apply.[28] However, this period is extended to 18 months if the posting undertaking submits a motivated notification to the host Member State concerned.[29]

Finally, to complete the legislative context, it is important to remember the adoption of a connected posted workers' instrument. In 2014, the EU legislator

[20] ibid, Article 3(3)–(4).

[21] Case C-341/05 *Laval un Partneri* [2007] ECR I-11767 ECLI:EU:C:2007:809, paras 74 and 81; V Hatzopoulos, 'Actively talking to each other: the Court and the political institutions' in M Dawson, B de Witte, and E Muir (eds), *Judicial Activism at the European Court of Justice* (Edward Elgar, 2013) 21.

[22] Unless the employer and the employee chose the law of the host Member State as the law applicable to the employment contract. See (at the time of the adoption of the Directive) Article 3 of the Convention on the Law Applicable to Contractual Obligations [1980] OJ L266.

[23] P Syrpis, 'Should the EU be attempting to harmonise national systems of labour law?' in M Andenas and CB Andersen (eds), *The Theory and Practice of Harmonisation* (Edward Elgar, 2012) 467; M Khan, 'Posted Worker Problems' (*Financial Times*, 24 October 2017), www.ft.com/content/6ed52842-b89b-11e7-9bfb-4a9c83ffa852.

[24] Directive (EU) 2018/957 amending the Posted Workers Directive; Z Adams, C Barnard, S Deakin, and SF Butlin, *Deakin and Morris' Labour Law* (Hart Publishing, 2021) 79–80.

[25] Articles 53(1) and 62 TFEU.

[26] Article 3(1) of Directive (EU) 2018/957 amending the Posted Workers Directive; J-P Lhernould, 'Directive (EU) 2018/957 of 28 June 2018 amending Directive 96/71/EC concerning the posting of workers in the framework of the provision of services: What will change in 2020?' (2019) 20 *ERA Forum* 249, 255.

[27] Article 3(1)c of Directive (EU) 2018/957 amending the Posted Workers Directive.

[28] ibid, Article 3(1a).

[29] ibid.

adopted a Directive on the enforcement of the Posted Workers Directive.[30] On the one hand, the Enforcement Directive aimed to prevent abuse of the posting rules.[31] For that purpose, it notably included provisions on the identification of a genuine posting.[32] On the other hand, the 2014 Directive also served posting service providers. It facilitated the application of Article 3 of the Posted Workers Directive by obliging Member States to create a single national website with free information on the applicable terms and conditions of employment and relevant collective agreements.[33]

B. *Poland* and *Hungary*

Poland and Hungary challenged the 2018 Directive in Luxembourg. They raised several claims.[34] This analysis focuses on one of them. Both Member States argued that the EU legislator invalidly based the Directive on Articles 53(1) and 62 TFEU. They based their reasoning on an assessment of the internal market competence's objectives dimension. For Poland and Hungary, the contested Directive did not aim to contribute to the free movement of services in the internal market;[35] rather than promoting this freedom, it restricted it.[36] As the Directive essentially aimed to protect workers, and thus pursued a social policy objective, it fell outside the scope of the internal market competence.[37]

The Court did not accept this.[38] It began its analysis by repeating its well-known jurisprudence on the choice of legal basis. The EU decision-maker may only choose a legal basis on the basis of 'objective factors that are amenable to judicial review', including 'the aim and the content of the measure'.[39] The Court also accepted the relevance of 'the legal framework within which new rules are situated'.[40] Finally, it reminded that the EU legislator 'cannot be denied the possibility of adapting [an] act to any change in circumstances or advances in knowledge'.[41]

[30] Directive 2014/67/EU of the European Parliament and of the Council of 15 May 2014 on the enforcement of Directive 96/71/EC concerning the posting of workers in the framework of the provision of services and amending Regulation (EU) No 1024/2012 on administrative cooperation through the Internal Market Information System ('the IMI Regulation'), OJ L159.

[31] S Feenstra, 'Resolving the Viking/Laval Conundrum' in F Vandenbroucke, C Barnard, and G De Baere (eds), *A European Social Union After the Crisis* (CUP, 2017) 324.

[32] Article 4 of the Posting Enforcement Directive 2014/67/EU.

[33] ibid, Article 5(2).

[34] Case C-620/18 *Hungary*, para 22; C-626/18 *Poland*, para 22.

[35] Case C-620/18 *Hungary*, para 28; C-626/18 *Poland*, para 39.

[36] C-626/18 *Poland*, para 42.

[37] Case C-620/18 *Hungary*, para 28; C-626/18 *Poland*, para 40.

[38] P Melin, 'Overview of recent cases before the Court of Justice of the European Union (September 2020–December 2020)' (2021) 23 *European Journal of Social Security* 81, 82.

[39] Case C-620/18 *Hungary*, para 38; C-626/18 *Poland*, para 43.

[40] Case C-620/18 *Hungary*, para 39; C-626/18 *Poland*, para 44.

[41] Case C-620/18 *Hungary*, para 41; C-626/18 *Poland*, para 46.

Then, the judges focused on the internal market (services) legal bases. Article 53(1) and 62 TFEU empowered the EU legislator to promote the free movement of services by co-ordinating heterogeneous national rules.[42] But that did not mean that the legislator did not have to respect the general interest and the social objectives of Article 9 TFEU.[43] 'It followed', ruled the judges, that:

> [T]he coordination measures adopted by the EU legislature, on the basis of Article 53(1) TFEU, read together with Article 62 TFEU, must not only have the objective of making it easier to exercise the freedom to provide services, but also of ensuring, when necessary, the protection of other fundamental interests that may be affected by that freedom.[44]

The Court thus had to assess whether the contested Directive still applied the right balance between, 'on the one hand, the need to promote the freedom to provide services and to ensure a level playing field, and, on the other, the need to protect the rights of posted workers'.[45] The Court proceeded to make this assessment on the basis of the Directive's objective, content, and context.

First, the objective; by adopting the Directive, the EU legislator aimed to ensure the free movement of services on a fair basis.[46] Free movement of services on a fair basis meant two things. It meant preventing that competition between service providers within one Member State would be based on substantially different employment terms and conditions merely because one service provider was located in a different Member State from the other.[47] It also meant increasing the protection of posted workers.[48] To achieve both, the EU legislator aimed to align the working conditions for local and posted workers as much as possible.[49]

Second, the content; here, the Court confirmed that the amendments introduced by the contested Directive did indeed contribute to the objective to ensure the free movement of services on a fair basis, as described above.[50] This was so, notably, for the new rules on remuneration and long-term posting.[51]

Third, the context; the contested Directive had to be seen in the context of the original Posted Workers Directive. The latter Directive already aimed to prevent that competition within one Member State would be based on substantially different employment terms and conditions.[52] The 2018 Directive adapted this original system to new circumstances.[53] Since 1996, the Union's expansion had significantly increased the disparities between Member State terms and conditions of

[42] Case C-620/18 *Hungary*, paras 44–45; C-626/18 *Poland*, paras 49–50.
[43] Case C-620/18 *Hungary*, para 46; C-626/18 *Poland*, para 51.
[44] Case C-620/18 *Hungary*, para 48; C-626/18 *Poland*, para 53.
[45] Case C-620/18 *Hungary*, para 49; C-626/18 *Poland*, para 54.
[46] Case C-620/18 *Hungary*, para 51; C-626/18 *Poland*, para 56.
[47] ibid.
[48] ibid.
[49] Case C-620/18 *Hungary*, para 52; C-626/18 *Poland*, para 57.
[50] Case C-620/18 *Hungary*, para 57; C-626/18 *Poland*, para 62.
[51] Case C-620/18 *Hungary*, paras 55–56; C-626/18 *Poland*, paras 60–61.
[52] Case C-620/18 *Hungary*, para 60; C-626/18 *Poland*, para 65.
[53] Case C-620/18 *Hungary*, para 61; C-626/18 *Poland*, para 66.

employment, especially with regard to rates of pay.[54] In that context, the Court concluded that:

> [T]he EU legislature could take the view that it was necessary to adjust the balance at the heart of Directive 96/71 by strengthening the rights of posted workers in the host Member State in order that competition between undertakings posting workers to that Member State and undertakings established in that State should develop on a more level playing field.[55]

II. Unconvincing Judgments

The previous section described the Court's ruling. It is now time to consider whether its reasoning was convincing. The answer is negative. In essence, the Court failed to pay due account to the internal market competence's objectives dimension. It erred in two ways. First, the judges conflated the internal market competence's objectives with the Treaties' horizontal objectives. Second, they did not examine whether the contested Directive actually promoted the internal market.

A. Competence Objectives and Horizontal Objectives

The concepts of 'competence' help to explain where the Court went wrong. To act, the EU needs power in a certain field of competence. Each EU competence has a subject matter and an objectives dimension. For the internal market competence, these dimensions are defined in Article 26 TFEU. An EU internal market measure must relate to (one of) the fundamental freedoms of the internal market, and must aim to promote (one of) these freedoms in the internal market.[56]

Once the Union's competence in a certain field has been established, the question of power arises. In the field of the internal market, the EU has a wide range of powers. There is, of course, the general power under Article 352 TFEU and the harmonisation power under Article 114 TFEU. But the EU legislator can also rely on more specific internal market legal bases. To adopt and amend the Posted Workers Directive, she invoked the power to co-ordinate Member State rules on the provision of services.[57] This is a specific power. It applies to an aspect of the subject matter of the internal market competence (services).[58] And it serves to pursue, specifically, the aim of promoting the free movement of services in the internal market.

[54] Case C-620/18 *Hungary*, paras 62-63; C-626/18 *Poland*, paras 67–68.
[55] Case C-620/18 *Hungary*, para 64; C-626/18 *Poland*, para 69.
[56] Article 26(1)–(2) TFEU.
[57] Articles 53(1)–62 TFEU; Articles 57(2)–66 TEC (Maastricht).
[58] Articles 53(1) TFEU and 57(2) TEC (Maastricht), on their own, apply to establishment.

In *Poland* and *Hungary*, much of this was unproblematic. The Posted Workers Directive and its amendment co-ordinated the employment rules which Member States apply to EU service providers who post workers to their territory.[59] Clearly, such co-ordination related to the free movement of services within the internal market.[60] In other words, the original and contested Directives fell within the subject matter dimension of the internal market competence. If the objectives dimension was satisfied too, Articles 53(1) and 62 indeed authorised the EU legislator to adopt the Directives. Thus, the Polish and Hungarian cases were not about power or subject matter; they were about objectives. The real question was whether the amendment to the Posted Workers Directive did indeed aim to promote the free movement of services.

The Court failed to provide a satisfactory answer. The first problem with its approach was that it conflated one of the specific objectives of the internal market competence (facilitating the free movement of services) with one of the Treaty's horizontal objectives (guaranteeing adequate social protection). The judges built on the idea of free movement of services *on a fair basis*, which wrongly seemed to put the objective to protect posted workers on the same footing as the internal market competence objective. The posting undertakings' freedom to provide services was thus balanced with the protection of workers.

This approach contradicted the Union's system of 'competence'. A field of EU competence has an objectives dimension and a subject matter dimension. To fall within a certain competence, a measure must principally pursue the objective of that competence. For the internal market competence, that objective is clear: 'establishing or ensuring the functioning of the internal market'.[61] The specific establishment legal basis of Article 53(1) TFEU reflects that objective. It allows the EU legislator to co-ordinate national laws, but only '[i]n order to make it easier for persons to take up and pursue activities as self-employed persons'.[62] The same applies to services.[63] Because it was based on Articles 53(1) and 62 TFEU, the contested Directive had to aim to facilitate the free movement of services.

Of course, that did not mean that other policy objectives could not play any role in the contested Directive. Indeed, the Treaty includes horizontal clauses which require the Union to take certain interests and values into account in all its policies and activities. Article 9 TFEU is such a clause. When the EU legislator co-ordinates national measures to facilitate the provision of services, it 'shall take into account requirements linked to the promotion of a high level of employment, the guarantee of adequate social protection, the fight against social exclusion, and

[59] Recital 13 of the Posted Workers Directive 96/71/EC; R Schütze, *European Union Law* (OUP, 2021) 682 and 684.

[60] Case C-113/89, *Rush Portuguesa v Office national d'immigration* [1990] ECR I-01417 ECLI:EU:C:1990:142, para 12.

[61] Article 26(1) TFEU.

[62] Article 53(1) TFEU.

[63] Article 62 TFEU.

a high level of education, training and protection of human health'.[64] That includes (posted) worker protection.

Yet, an important limitation must be respected. The Treaty's horizontal clauses may not expand the scope of a Union competence;[65] their objectives only play a subsidiary role. Chapter three illustrated this. To ensure the free movement of (among others) newspapers and magazines, the Community legislator harmonised the rules on tobacco advertising. To function smoothly, the internal market required common rules. The content of these common rules, however, was not important from a competence perspective.

That is where the horizontal objectives came in. Because the Community was under a general obligation to maintain high levels of public health protection in all its policies, the legislator opted for an advertising ban. This did not imply a balancing of internal market and public health objectives at the level of competence. The horizontal objectives only became relevant when the Community legislator, facing several internal-market-facilitating policy choices, had to decide which one was preferable.

Here, the reasoning of the Court in *Poland* and *Hungary* differed from the reasoning described above. When the Court stated that the contested Directive 'must not only have the objective of making it easier to exercise the freedom to provide services, but also of ensuring, when necessary, the protection of other fundamental interests that may be affected by that freedom', the protection of posted workers became more than a secondary objective.[66] It ceased to simply point to the desirable mode of facilitating the free movement of services. On the contrary, the objective of the internal market competence itself had to be balanced with the objective of worker protection.[67]

Admittedly, the Court itself seemed to nuance this to some extent. Elsewhere, the judgment mentioned that the contested Directive enhanced the protection of posted workers. But it 'always [did so] in a way that [was] consistent with the objective of ensuring that the freedom to provide services in the host Member State can be exercised fairly".[68] Upon closer inspection, however, this statement is rather circular. After all, the judgment also underlined that protecting posted workers is, in itself, a means to facilitate the free movement of services on a fair basis.[69] Thus, the conclusion remains the same. The Court reviewed the contested Directive's legal basis without paying due regard to the internal market competence's objectives dimension. It failed to apply the nuance of the concepts of 'competence'.

[64] Article 9 TFEU.

[65] C Barnard and G De Baere, 'Towards a European Social Union: achievements and possibilities under the current EU constitutional framework' (2014) *Euroforum Seminars on a European Social Union* 1, 36.

[66] Case C-620/18 *Hungary*, para 48; C-626/18 *Poland*, para 53.

[67] Case C-620/18 *Hungary*, paras 50–51.

[68] Case C-620/18 *Hungary*, para 53.

[69] Case C-620/18 *Hungary*, para 51.

B. The Internal Market Objective

There is a second reason why the Court's reasoning in *Poland* and *Hungary* fails to convince. It again relates to the internal market competence's objectives dimension. The previous section argued that the judges erred a first time by misidentifying that competence's objectives. As mentioned above, worker protection should not be considered at the level of competence. But even ignoring that, the Court's reasoning remains problematic. Even assuming that the judges identified the correct competence objective (they did not), they neglected to verify whether the contested Directive actually pursued that objective.

1. No Actual Pursuit of Free Movement on a Fair Basis

Since the Court failed to recognise that only the promotion of free movement and undistorted competition constituted valid competence objectives, it cannot be expected to have judicated on the actual pursuit of those objectives either. Thus, it is useful to first examine whether the Court verified the contested Directive's actual pursuit of the incorrectly identified set of objectives; that is, a balance between free movement and posted worker protection.

The Court conducted its balancing exercise in three core paragraphs. First, it found that the contested Directive aimed to strike a balance between ensuring that undertakings can post workers to other Member States to provide services there, on the one hand, and protecting posted workers' rights, on the other hand.[70] Second, it put forward the idea of 'freedom to provide services on a fair basis' as a compromise between these balanced interests.[71] 'Fair' meant that competition within one Member State could not be based on substantially different mandatory terms and conditions of employment. Third, the Court concluded that the contested Directive aimed to promote such fair free movement of services. The Directive ensured 'that the terms and conditions of employment of posted workers [were] as close as possible to those of workers employed by businesses established in the host Member State'.[72]

As a first point, it is difficult not to observe that the judges devoted only a very small part of their judgments to the identification of the appropriate balance between free movement and worker protection. They nowhere explain how they arrived at the subsequent steps in their reasoning. It is not clear why the result of the exercise of weighing an undertaking's freedom to provide services with its own (posted) workers against the protection of these workers should be that local and posted workers' terms and conditions of employment cannot differ much.

[70] Case C-620/18 *Hungary*, para 50.
[71] Case C-620/18 *Hungary*, para 51.
[72] Case C-620/18 *Hungary*, para 52.

Moreover, the reality is that the contested Directive did not do what the Court said it did. The amended Posted Workers Directive did not really ensure that posted workers' terms and conditions of employment were as close as possible to those of local workers in the same Member State.[73] To an extent, a considerable alignment indeed took place; but it was specifically limited to certain situations. The contested Directive only closed the gap when the standards in the host Member State were higher than those in the home Member State. In the reverse scenario, nothing changed. Article 3 guaranteed that posted workers would enjoy, for the matters listed, at least the same protection as local workers.[74] It did not say that terms and conditions of employment for posted and local workers were to be the same or even just more closely aligned, as such.

Thus, even assuming that ensuring the free movement of services on a fair basis was an objective of the internal market competence (it was not), *Poland* and *Hungary* remain problematic. The Court did not only misidentify this objectives dimension; it also failed to convincingly verify whether the contested Directive actually pursued the (incorrectly identified) alternative objectives.

2. *Actual Pursuit of (Some) Free Movement*

The next question is, of course, whether the judgments nonetheless support a conclusion that the contested Directive did aim to promote the free movement of service in the internal market. Again, problems arise. While the Court explained why the amended Posted Workers Directive promoted the provision of services by some undertakings, it ignored the apparently significant barriers imposed on others. A balancing exercise should have been conducted to establish whether the contested Directive *overall* promoted the free movement of services. This did not happen.

As mentioned above, the Court emphasised that the (amended) Posted Workers Directive (sometimes) aligned the labour standards of home and host Member States.[75] This indeed facilitated the provision of (some) services in the internal market. For a posting undertaking established in a Member State with higher labour standards, it became easier to compete, in another Member State with higher labour standards, with a posting undertaking in a Member State with lower labour standards. And the contested Directive especially promoted the service provision by the local undertakings of these higher-standard Member States. Within their Member State, and for the matters listed in Article 3, they did not face competition from posting undertakings based on lower terms and conditions of employment.

[73] ibid.
[74] Article 3(1) of Directive (EU) 2018/957 amending the Posted Workers Directive.
[75] Case C-620/18 *Hungary*, paras 51 and 60; C-626/18 *Poland*, paras 56 and 65.

Thus, the Directive protected the provision of services by undertakings established in Member States with higher labour standards against standard-based competition from undertakings established in Member States with lower labour standards. As such, this approach was valid. In the internal market, distortions of competition must be addressed. The Court has long ruled that 'the elimination of barriers' and 'fair competition' are both 'necessary for bringing about a single market'.[76] In *Tobacco Advertising I*, it identified 'distortions of competition' alongside 'obstacles to the exercise of fundamental freedoms' as grounds for the application of the internal market harmonisation legal basis.[77] The same applied to the services legal bases.[78] The EU legislator might use her internal market powers to protect service providers against distortions of competition coming from disparate labour standards. Such an objective fell within the scope of the EU's internal market competence.

Yet there was a problem. The Court failed to verify whether the contested Directive *actually* promoted services in the internal market. To do so, it had to take into consideration another internal market interest involved: that of the posting undertakings established in Member States with lower labour standards. In the context of posting, two valid interests are diametrically opposed.[79] On the one hand, posting undertakings want to send their workers to other Member States to provide a service. Requiring these undertakings to comply with employment rules in the host Member State hinders their free movement. On the other hand, undertakings established in the host Member State may struggle to compete with posting undertakings who are not bound by the local rules. Posting undertakings established in other Member States with higher labour standards, too, face competition from posted workers sent from Member States with lower standards.

The problem with the Court's reasoning was that it only addressed the interests of undertakings established in Member States with higher levels of worker protection. Limiting local competition based on labour costs benefitted local undertakings and posting undertakings established in such Member States. For posting undertakings established in lower-standard Member States, however, providing services became more difficult.[80] Before, their relatively more stringent

[76] Case 32/65 *Italy v Council of the EEC and Commission of the EEC* [1966] ECR-00563 ECLI:EU:C:1966:42, para 405.

[77] Case C-376/98 *Germany/Parliament and Council* [2000] ECR I-08419 ECLI:EU:C:2000:544, para 84.

[78] ibid, para 87.

[79] TK Hervey, '"Adjudicating in the Shadow of the Informal Settlement?": The Court of Justice of the European Union, "New Governance" and Social Welfare' (2010) 63 *Current Legal Problems* 92, 124–25; D Carter, 'Equal Pay for Equal Work in the Same Place: Assessing the Revision to the Posted Workers Directive' (2018) 14 *Croatian Yearbook of European Law and Policy* 31, 47; A Lubow and SK Schmidt, 'A hidden champion? The European Court of Justice as an agenda-setter in the case of posted workers' (2020) *Public Administration* 321, 326; Evju (n 7) 169.

[80] M De Vos, 'Free Movement of Workers, Free Movement of Services and the Posted Workers Directive: a Bermuda Triangle for National Labour Standards?' (2006) 7 *ERA Forum* 356, 361; P Davies, 'The Posted Workers Directive and the EC Treaty' (2002) 31 *Industrial Law Journal* 298, 306.

employment obligations placed local undertakings at a disadvantage. With the Posted Workers Directive, that disadvantage shifted to the side of the posting undertakings.[81]

Of course, such rebalancing of advantages and disadvantages was not unique. EU internal market legislation often places a new burden on some undertakings. It is, moreover, precisely the point of such legislation. If regulatory differences lead to distortions of competition, because undertakings in one Member State are bound by rules which do not apply in others, these differences must be removed. And that means either lowering the bar or, in the spirit of the EU's horizontal objectives, raising standards throughout the Union.

Thus, even before the specific environment competence, the Community legislator adopted measures on air pollution and water quality.[82] Before these measures, some undertakings did not have to comply with such environmental standards, but others did. The legislator's intervention made the situation of the former undertakings less advantageous. Overall, however, common market competition became fairer. Undertakings no longer competed, or struggled to compete, on the basis of divergent regulatory standards. A level playing field was established.

Arguably, that is where the contested Directive differed. It did not genuinely level the playing field. Posting undertakings shall comply with labour standards of host Member States.[83] Especially for pay, that may be problematic. Economic disparities mean that the same sum is not worth the same in all Member States. The burden of compliance with a certain minimum wage does not equally rest on undertakings established in 'weaker' and 'stronger' economies. A glance at minimum wages in the Union explains why. Even considering price differences between the Member States, the highest national minimum wage was approximately two-and-a-half times higher than the lowest, in 2025.[84]

This was less problematic in the past. The original Directive only required posting undertakings to comply with host laws on minimum rates of pay. But the 2018 amendment required a posting undertaking to remunerate its posted workers in at least the same manner as a local service provider.[85] This included other elements of remuneration, such as overtime rates and holiday allowances.[86] Moreover, this did not only apply to remuneration rules laid down by Member State laws and

[81] R Giesen, 'Posting: Social Protection of Workers vs. Fundamental Freedoms?' (2003) 40 *Common Market Law Review* 143, 145.

[82] See, eg Council Directive 84/360/EEC of 28 June 1984 on the combating of air pollution from industrial plants, OJ L188; Council Directive 76/464/EEC of 4 May 1976 on pollution caused by certain dangerous substances discharged into the aquatic environment of the Community, OJ L129.

[83] Giesen (n 81) 145.

[84] 'Minimum Wage Statistics' (Eurostat), ec.europa.eu/eurostat/statistics-explained/index.php?title=Minimum_wage_statistics#Minimum_wages_expressed_in_purchasing_power_standards.

[85] Article 3(1)(c) of Directive (EU) 2018/957 amending the Posted Workers Directive.

[86] Commission, Practical Guide to Posting (2019) 9–10. Posting undertakings also could not include the allowances they paid to their posted workers for travel, board, and lodging expenses in the remuneration calculus; see Recital 18 and Article 3(7) of Directive (EU) 2018/957 amending the Posted Workers Directive; Lhernould (n 26) 52.

regulations, but also to those determined in universally applicable collective agreements. Overall, the contested Directive led to a much greater alignment of local and posted workers' pay than the 1996 version. The balancing test should have reflected that.

A further point also merited attention. Unlike local service providers, posting employers had to comply with two sets of legal rules.[87] The Directive, however, did not approach a particular Member States' labour standards as an integrated whole. It did not recognise that national legislators might balance higher protection in one area with lesser rights in another. On each individual matter, the posting undertaking had to guarantee their posted workers the level of protection of the host Member State. That could mean, for example, complying with one Member State's rules on leave and another's on pay. The posting undertaking could thus face higher standards than similar undertakings both at home and in the host Member State.[88]

To fall within the internal market competence, the contested Directive had to pursue an internal market objective; it had to 'actually contribute … to the improvement of the internal market'.[89] Considering both the internal market advantages and disadvantages, the overall effect had to be a facilitation of the provision of services. Perhaps the contested Directive had that overall result; perhaps it did not. The issue is that the Court did not appear to consider this. Its balancing test focused on the protection of undertakings from higher-standard Member States against lower-standard competition. The interests of posting undertakings from Member States with lower employment standards, by contrast, did not noticeably feature in the weighing exercise.

Admittedly, the Court did address the issue of potential detrimental effects on some posting undertakings elsewhere in the judgments: not under the legal basis claims, but under Poland and Hungary's argument that the contested Directive infringed Article 56 TFEU. Here, too, the Court found against the applicants. It did not accept that the contested Directive, and specifically its new rules on remuneration, infringed the free movement of services.[90]

More specifically, the judges ruled that the additional financial and administrative burdens for service providers of Member States with lower employment standards were the consequence of the very objective of the contested Directive.[91]

[87] De Vos (n 80) 363; B de Witte, 'The Freedom to Provide Services: The Controversial Freedom?' in S Garben and I Govaere (eds), *The Internal Market 2.0* (Hart Publishing, 2020) 142; B de Witte, 'Non-market values in internal market legislation' in NN Shiubhne (ed), *Regulating the Internal Market* (Edward Elgar Publishing, 2006) 82.

[88] Davies (n 80) 306; C Kilpatrick, 'Internal market architecture and the accommodation of labour rights: As good as it gets?' in P Syrpis (ed), *The Judiciary, the Legislature and the EU Internal Market* (CUP, 2012) 213.

[89] Case C-376/98 *Germany/Parliament and Council* [2000] ECR I-08419 ECLI:EU:C:2000:544, para 23.

[90] Case C-620/18 *Hungary*, para 125; C-626/18 *Poland*, para 101.

[91] C-626/18 *Poland*, para 103.

Moreover, the Directive did not exclude all cost based competition.[92] Cost-based competition remained possible through other factors, such as worker productivity and efficiency. Nothing in the contested Directive suggested that the EU legislator viewed such a competitive advantage as unfair.[93] Thus, the Directive did not distort competition in the internal market; Article 56 TFEU was not infringed.

This reasoning cannot convince. First, the fact that other factors of cost-based competition remained possible did not exclude a loss of competitive advantage. Second, and more importantly, the Court was wrong to say that the additional burdens on posting undertakings logically followed from the Directive's objectives. As an internal market measure, its objectives demanded the very opposite. Promoting the free movement of undertakings established in lower-standard Member States should have been part of the Directive's balancing test itself. Apparently, it was not. That is the second reason why *Poland* and *Hungary* conflict with competence's objectives dimension.

III. A Forgotten Argument

Thus, the Court's reasoning failed to convince. It incorrectly identified the internal market competence's objectives and did not show how the amended Posted Workers Directive actually pursued these objectives. An imprecise 'competence' analysis was not able to recognise the nuances of the legal problem concerned. Thinking in the concepts of 'competence' could have prevented this. If competence's objectives dimension is clearly identified, mistakes as to its substance may be avoided.

It is important to note that these errors did not automatically mean that the contested Directive was unlawful. The Court could still have found that, on balance, the measure promoted the internal market. In that context, it may be helpful to remember that the posting rules were not just about avoiding unfair labour-standard competition. A second internal market rationale existed: the Community legislator adopted the original Posted Workers Directive to provide legal certainty on the applicable labour standards. This rationale did not explicitly feature in the two judgments. The following section recalls it.

Admittedly, this section does not raise new issues on competence's objectives dimension. It also does not focus in depth on the other concepts of 'competence'. Nonetheless, the analysis remains relevant. This chapter explains these concepts' benefits through an example of inadequate legal 'competence' reasoning. That example is the Court's legal basis analysis of the amended Posted Workers Directive. It is, therefore, necessary to give a full picture of that legal basis analysis. And that includes pointing out which major element the Court overlooked.

[92] Case C-620/18 *Hungary*, para 128; C-626/18 *Poland*, para 106.
[93] C-626/18 *Poland*, para 122.

A. Co-ordination and Conflict of Laws

In the original Posted Workers Directive, the Community legislator used a co-ordination power to (allegedly) aim to promote the free movement of services in the internal market. With the 2018 amendment, it exercised the same co-ordination power.[94] Rather than harmonising Member States' employment rules, the original and amending Directives co-ordinated these rules. Essentially, they introduced a conflict-of-laws rule.[95] They identified which labour rules applied for the matters listed in Article 3. If the host Member States offered greater protection than the home Member State, the former's rules applied; if not, the posted workers concerned continued to enjoy the protection of their home state.

The Council Legal Service highlighted this during the legislative proceedings of the contested Directive.[96] In a legal Opinion, it considered that 'there [was] no legal obstacle to making use of the technique of a conflict-of-law rule among provisions that pursue objectives pertaining to the freedom to provide services'.[97] Thus, the Legal Service confirmed that the EU legislator may rely on conflict-of-laws measures as a tool to promote the internal market. In other words, it is a valid power instrument within the internal market competence.

That the 1996 Directive identified which Member State's rules applied to a posting scenario raises the question of whose rules applied before. And that question is crucial; it reveals that the Posted Workers Directive has a second internal market rationale. To fully understand it, it is necessary to go back in time. Two main legal events characterised the context in which the Community legislator adopted the 1996 Directive: the Court of Justice's judgments in *Seco* and *Rush Portuguesa*, and the conclusion of the Rome Convention.[98]

1. Seco *and* Rush Portuguesa

Although its foundations date back earlier,[99] the Posted Workers Directive's story seems to have really begun in Luxembourg.[100] In *Seco*, two French companies

[94] On the possibility of harmonisation in this context, see: Social Questions Working Party, Outcome of proceedings on the Proposal for an amended Posted Workers Directive, 7399/16, 6; F Rödl, 'The Labour Constitution' in A von Bogdandy and J Bast (eds), *Principles of European Constitutional Law* (Hart Publishing, 2010) 636–37.

[95] Opinion in Case C-341/05 *Laval un Partneri* [2007] ECR I-11767 ECLI:EU:C:2007:291, para 58; Opinion in Case C-319/06 *Commission v Luxembourg* [2007] ECR I-04323 ECLI:EU:C:2007:516, para 36; M Schmidt, *Das Arbeitsrecht der Europäischen Gemeinschaft* (Nomos, 2001) 254 and 259.

[96] Council Legal Service, Opinion on the Proposal for an amended Posted Workers Directive (possibility to introduce a conflict-of-law rule), 9544/16.

[97] ibid, 11.

[98] Case C-113/89 *Rush Portuguesa*; Joined Cases 62 and 63/81 *Seco v EVI* and *Desquenne & Giral* [1982] ECR-00223 ECLI:EU:C:1982:34; Convention on the Law Applicable to Contractual Obligations [1980] OJ L266.

[99] Evju (n 7) 154; DS Martinsen, *An Ever More Powerful Court? The Political Constraints of Legal Integration in the European Union* (OUP, 2014) 188.

[100] O De Schutter, 'Transborder provision of services and "social dumping": rights-based mutual trust in the establishment of the Internal Market' in I Lianos and O Odudu (eds), *Regulating Trade in*

had posted workers to Luxembourg to provide a railway repair service.[101] The Luxembourgish authorities required the companies to pay Luxembourgish social security contributions, even though their posted workers already enjoyed social security benefits in France and would not enjoy benefits in Luxembourg.[102] Among other arguments, Luxembourg argued that this was necessary to 'offset … the economic advantages' which the French companies enjoyed.[103] After all, they were not bound by the Luxembourgish rules on a minimum wage.

The Court did not agree. Imposing host Member State social security contributions in addition to such contributions at home restricted the undertakings' freedom to provide services.[104] And the restriction did not benefit the workers concerned, so it was not justified.[105] The Court did, however, accommodate Luxembourg's minimum wage concerns. It emphasised:

> It is well-established that Community law [did] not preclude Member States from applying their legislation, or collective labour agreements entered into by both sides of industry relating to minimum wages, to any person who is employed, even temporarily, within their territory, no matter in which country the employer is established, just as Community law [did] not prohibit Member States from enforcing those rules by appropriate means.[106]

Thus, the Court did not insist on mutual recognition of home labour rules.[107] Instead, it accepted that a host Member State could require posting undertakings to guarantee their posted workers the local minimum wage.[108] The problem with Luxembourg's approach was that it was too sweeping and did not consider whether the undertakings concerned had satisfied the minimum wage rules or not.

A second judgment crucially expanded this case law. In *Rush Portuguesa*, the Court ruled that France could not require a Portuguese company to obtain work permits for its workers sent to carry out a service there.[109] Already during Portugal's transition period towards Community membership, the free movement of services applied and prevented such a requirement. But the Court went on. It added:

> Community law does not preclude Member States from extending their legislation, or collective labour agreements entered into by both sides of industry, to any person who is employed, even temporarily, within their territory, no matter in which country the employer is established.[110]

Services in the EU and the WTO: Trust, Distrust and Economic Integration (CUP, 2012) 351; De Vos (n 80) 361.

[101] Joined Cases 62 and 63/81 *Seco v EVI* and *Desquenne & Giral*, para 2.

[102] V Hatzopoulos, *Regulating Services in the European Union* (OUP, 2012) 199.

[103] Joined Cases 62 and 63/81 *Seco v EVI* and *Desquenne & Giral*, 13.

[104] ibid, para 9.

[105] ibid, para 10.

[106] ibid, para 14.

[107] F de Witte, 'The architecture of the EU's social market economy' in P Koutrakos and J Snell (eds), *Research Handbook on the Law of the EU's Internal Market* (Edward Elgar, 2017) 127.

[108] Opinion in Case C-620/18 *Hungary*, para 27.

[109] Case C-113/89 *Rush Portuguesa*, para 12.

[110] ibid, para 18.

It was an obiter dictum in response to French concerns.[111] Nonetheless, it had an impact. Whereas the statement in *Seco* was limited to rules on minimum wages, the *Rush Portuguesa* dictum concerned the host Member State's (labour) rules in general. Empowered by the Court's statement, host Member States increasingly extended their national labour standards to posted workers.[112] This alarmed the Commission.[113] One year after the judgment in *Rush Portuguesa*, it introduced its proposal for a Posted Workers Directive.[114] At this point, the importance of a second legal event becomes clear.

2. Rome

In 1980, the EEC Member States concluded a Convention on the law applicable to contractual obligations.[115] The Rome Convention was a conflict-of-laws instrument.[116] It determined the law applicable to contractual obligations. Article 6 of the Convention specifically addressed employment contracts. Contract parties enjoyed the freedom to choose the applicable law.[117] In the absence of such a choice, the law of the country where the employee habitually performed his work applied.[118] Crucially, that law applied 'even if [the employee was] temporarily employed in another country'.[119] Thus, under the Rome Convention, posted workers normally continued to enjoy the labour law protection of their home Member State alone.

Nonetheless, the Directive did not ban host Member States from enforcing their own labour laws altogether. Article 7 allowed 'another country with which the situation has a close connection' to impose its 'mandatory rules' on the employment contract, even if the parties had chosen a different applicable law.[120] A host Member State could, therefore, compel posting undertakings to comply with its mandatory labour laws; and the Rome Convention did not specify which rules qualified as mandatory.[121]

The Posted Workers Directive did. It co-ordinated the laws of the Member States, 'to lay down a nucleus of mandatory rules for minimum protection to be observed in the host country by employers who post workers to perform temporary

[111] ibid.
[112] Davies (n 80) 300; Lubow and Schmidt (n 79) 327.
[113] Davies (n 80) 300; Lubow and Schmidt (n 79) 327.
[114] De Schutter (n 100) 351; De Vos (n 80) 361.
[115] Convention on the Law Applicable to Contractual Obligations [1980] OJ L266.
[116] Commission, Proposal for a Council Directive concerning the posting of workers in the framework of the provision of services, COM(91)230, 12.
[117] Articles 4 and 6(2) of the Posted Workers Directive.
[118] ibid, Article 6(2)a.
[119] ibid.
[120] ibid, Articles 6(1) and 7.
[121] J-J Kuijpers, *EU Law and Private International Law – The Interrelationship in Contractual Obligations* (Brill, 2011) 87.

work in the territory of a Member State where the services are provided'.[122] In other words, the 1996 Directive laid down that the provisions on the matters included on the Article 3 list were mandatory rules.[123] But it also went further. The Rome Convention merely allowed host countries to apply such rules to posting undertakings; the Posted Workers Directive required them to do so.[124]

B. Free Movement Through Legal Certainty

Here, the second internal market rationale underlying the posted workers measures becomes clear. In the past, posting undertakings found it difficult to predict which rules applied to their posted worker's employment situation.[125] There was no single rule which determined which laws of the host Member State constituted mandatory rules under Article 7 of the Rome Convention. Backed by *Seco* and *Rush Portuguesa*, each Member State could adopt its own approach. The resulting inability to easily ascertain the applicable terms and conditions in advance posed a threat to the internal market.[126] It made the provision of services in other Member States more difficult.

By introducing a conflict-of-laws rule, the Community legislator provided legal certainty.[127] At least from that perspective, the Posted Workers Directive and its 2018 amendment benefited all service providers in the internal market. This explains why the Article 3 list could only be exhaustive.[128] In its controversial *Laval* ruling, the Court confirmed this.[129]

Many scholars expressed their surprise with the ruling.[130] They emphasised that Article 3(7) of the Directive stated that the preceding paragraphs of Article 3 'shall not prevent application of terms and conditions of employment which are more favourable to workers'.[131] But Article 3(7) did not mean that Member States could also impose their labour laws on matters other than those listed. It only

[122] Recital 13 of the Posted Workers Directive.

[123] Kuijpers (n 121) 237.

[124] C Barnard, 'Fifty Years of Avoiding Social Dumping?' in M Dougan and S Currie (eds), *50 Years of the European Treaties: Looking Back and Thinking Forward* (Hart Publishing, 2009) 324.

[125] Commission, Proposal for a Council Directive concerning the posting of workers in the framework of the provision of services, COM(91)230, 2,13, and 16.

[126] ibid.

[127] N Countouris and S Engblom, 'Civilising the European Posted Workers Directive' in M Freedland and J Prassl (eds), *Viking, Laval and Beyond* (Hart Publishing, 2014) 281; De Schutter (n 100) 351; Opinion in Case C-346/06 *Rüffert* [2007] ECR I-01989 ECLI:EU:C:2007:541, para 74.

[128] Countouris and Engblom (n 127) 81.

[129] Case C-341/05 *Laval un Partneri*, paras 73 and 80; R Zahn, 'Revision of the Posted Workers Directive: A Europeanisation Perspective' (2017) 19 *Cambridge Yearbook of European Legal Studies* 187, 195.

[130] S Deakin, 'Regulatory competition after Laval' (2008) 10 *Cambridge Yearbook of European Legal Studies* 581, 596; C Barnard, 'Viking and Laval: An Introduction' (2008) 10 *Cambridge Yearbook of European Legal Studies* 463, 475; Kilpatrick (n 88) 848.

[131] Article 3(7) of the Posted Workers Directive.

meant that, for the Article 3 matters, host Member State rules applied to the extent that they were more favourable to posted workers than their home rules. Only that interpretation upheld the legal certainty which the Directive aimed to ensure. Without 'transparency in the system', the Posted Workers Directive would have lost an important internal market competence justification.[132]

Admittedly, the Community legislator itself had not wholeheartedly followed this reasoning. Article 3's exhaustive or illustrative nature was one of the most contentious points of the Council debates.[133] A majority of Member States refused to accept an exhaustive list.[134] Others voiced their opposition against an illustrative list.[135] Not surprisingly, this included Greece and Portugal, the two Member States with the lowest minimum wages in the Community at that time.[136] Equally unsurprisingly, the Commission generally sided with the Member States favouring an exhaustive list.[137] Although they were prepared to examine the possibility of a non-exhaustive list,[138] they warned that a purely illustrative list would be contrary to the internal market.[139]

In the end, the Council reached a compromise. An additional paragraph to Article 3 would allow host Member States to also impose their terms and conditions of employment for matters not included on the list.[140] However, they could only do so on public policy grounds. The Commission was prepared to accept the compromise.[141] The new provision introduced but a narrow exception, which later

[132] L Azoulai, 'The Court of Justice and the social market economy: The emergence of an ideal and the conditions for its realization' (2008) 45 *Common Market Law Review* 1335, 1352; C Barnard, 'The Protection of Fundamental Social Rights in Europe after Lisbon: a Question of Conflicts of Interests' in S de Vries, U Bernitz, and S Weatherill (eds), *The Protection of Fundamental Rights in the EU After Lisbon* (Hart Publishing, 2013) 39.

[133] Presidency, Note on the Proposal for a Posted Workers Directive, 9789/92, 2; Presidency, Note on the Proposal for a Posted Workers Directive (policy debate), 10323/92, 2; General Secretariat, Introductory note on the amended Proposal for a Posted Workers Directive, 5709/95, 3; General Secretariat, Introductory note on the amended Proposal for a Posted Workers Directive, 8116/95, 2.

[134] Working Party on Social Questions, Summary of proceedings on the Proposal for a Posted Workers Directive, 7344/92, 1; Working Party on Social Questions, Outcome of proceedings on the Proposal for a Posted Workers Directive, 9712/93, 13; General Secretariat, Introductory note on the amended Proposal for a Posted Workers Directive, 5709/95, 3.

[135] ibid.

[136] Commission, Proposal for a Council Directive concerning the posting of workers in the framework of the provision of services, COM(91)230, 4–5; Working Party on Social Questions, Summary of proceedings on the Proposal for a Posted Workers Directive, 8146/92, 13; Working Party on Social Questions, Outcome of proceedings on the Proposal for a Posted Workers Directive, 9712/93, 13.

[137] Working Party on Social Questions, Summary of proceedings on a Proposal for a Directive on subcontracting, 4165/92, 16; Secrétariat Général, Note introductive sur la Proposition modifiée de directive "Détachement de travailleurs", 10898/94, 5.

[138] Working Party on Social Questions, Summary of proceedings on the Proposal for a Posted Workers Directive, 8255/92, 13.

[139] Secrétariat Général, Note introductive sur la Proposition modifiée de directive "Détachement de travailleurs", 10898/94, 5.

[140] Council, Common position on the Proposal for a Posted Workers Directive, 6689/2/96 Rev2 Add1, 5.

[141] ibid.

received a narrow interpretation in Court.[142] Thus, despite some disagreements in the Council, the Community legislator adopted the Posted Workers Directive without an explicitly illustrative list. On the contrary, Article 3(10) suggested that the list was exhaustive; and *Laval* confirmed this.

This legal certainty rationale also explains why the EU legislator did not supplement the contested Directive's internal market legal basis with a social policy legal basis. In the Council, the Swedish delegation had suggested such an addition, because it believed that the proposal pursued both free movement of services and worker protection objectives.[143] The European Parliament later made a similar request.[144] But both the Commission and the Parliament's own Legal Service rejected such an addition.[145] Article 153(2)(b) only allowed the EU legislator to lay down minimum requirements.[146] Host Member States would then be free to generally impose their stricter employment rules.[147] That would undermine the whole legal certainty logic of the Directive.

Thus, the Posted Workers Directive and its amendment should not be seen through the lens of (un)distorted competition alone. They also aimed to promote the internal market by providing legal certainty. That the Court never raised this in *Poland* and *Hungary* is regrettable. By failing to do so, it ignored an important internal market rationale underlying the posted workers regime. Considering the controversy around the contested Directive and its legal basis, acknowledging its role in ensuring legal certainty would have been desirable.

IV. Conclusion

The judgments in *Poland* and *Hungary* are examples of flawed 'competence' reasoning. The principle of conferral is a foundational cornerstone of EU law. A nuanced and precise 'competence' analysis is essential to ensure that the Union stays within the competences and powers conferred upon it by the Member States in the Treaties. This is especially the case in the context of sensitive measures that divide the Member States. The amending Posted Workers Directive is such a measure. Yet *Poland* and *Hungary* are not examples of such nuanced and precise legal reasoning.

From the perspective of the concepts of 'competence', the Court incorrectly interpreted the internal market competence's objectives dimension. As the Treaties

[142] Case C-319/06 *Commission v Luxembourg* [2008] ECR I-4323 ECLI:EU:C:2008:350; Martinsen (n 99) 197.

[143] General Secretariat, Note on the Proposal for an amended Posted Workers Directive, 8740/16, 2.

[144] European Parliament Committee on Employment and Social Affairs, Report on the Proposal for an amended Posted Workers Directive, A8-0319/2017, 5 and 40–41; Presidency, Note on the Proposal for an amended Posted Workers Directive, 6783/18 Add1, 2.

[145] Lubow and Schmidt (n 79) 330; Lhernould (n 26) 250.

[146] Article 153(2)(b) TFEU.

[147] Lubow and Schmidt (n 79) 330.

currently stand, a measure adopted under Articles 53(2) and 62 TFEU must aim to promote the provision of services in internal market. That is the objective of the EU's internal market (services) competence. Protecting posted workers is an important Treaty objective. It cannot, however, extend the scope of the Union's existing competences. If it had properly recognised this objectives dimension, the Court's judgments would have been more convincing.

Moreover, a measure cannot merely claim to pursue a certain objective; it must *actually* do so. When assessing the amending Posted Workers Directive, the Court should have verified whether the contested Directive, all elements considered, made the provision of services easier. It was right to consider the advantages for service providers established in host Member States with higher labour standards. But it should also have paid due regard to the disadvantages for their competitors from Member States with lower labour standards.

Finally, the posted workers cases show the value of a wider 'competence' approach. At first sight, the Posted Workers Directive addressed the internal market through the lens of undistorted competition. Focusing on the question of power, however, shows an additional side. Co-ordinating national rules in a conflict-of-laws measure was necessary to enhance legal certainty for all posting service providers. The Court did not address this rationale, because it focused on the Directive's (alleged) role in ensuring undistorted competition alone.

This chapter does not apply its own balancing exercise. Whether, all things considered, the contested Directive did or did not fall within the internal market competence is not the issue here. The Court has spoken. But the chance exists that, in the future, a similar case will test the limits of the internal market competence's objectives dimension. Should this case arise, it would be preferable if the Court applied a more convincing 'competence' reasoning. The concepts of 'competence' would be a good start.

6

The Benefits of 'Competence' (2): Sanctions and Trade

This chapter offers a second illustration of the merits of the concepts of 'competence'. On 24 February 2022, Russia brought war back to Europe. After the unlawful annexation of Crimea in 2014 and the deployment of troops to the self-proclaimed independent republics of Donetsk and Luhansk in February 2022, Russian armed forces launched a full-scale invasion of Ukraine on that day. The aggression was unprovoked and is still ongoing today. Millions of Ukrainians fled the country. Many others were killed, often as civilians, and by Russian war crimes.

The European Union condemned Russia's aggression and responded with sanctions. It did so in two steps. First, the Council invoked Article 29 TEU.[1] Within the common foreign and security policy (CFSP) competence, Article 29 empowers the Council to 'define the approach of the Union to a particular matter of a geographical or thematic nature'.[2] On this basis, the Council introduced sanctions against Russia for its actions against Ukraine.[3] Second, the Council gave EU-wide effect to these sanctions by regulations based on Article 215 TFEU.[4] Article 215(1) notably empowers the Council to restrict economic or financial relations with a third country, when needed to implement a CFSP decision.[5]

These two steps reflect a well-established EU sanctions practice.[6] As Russia continues its aggression, the sanctions package grows.[7] Today it includes, for instance, export bans for dual-use goods, import bans for seaborne crude oil

[1] See, eg Council Decision (CFSP) 2022/327 of 25 February 2022 amending Decision 2014/512/CFSP concerning restrictive measures in view of Russia's actions destabilising the situation in Ukraine, OJ L48.

[2] Article 29 TEU (Lisbon).

[3] And against Belarus and several Russian and Belarusian persons.

[4] See, eg Council Regulation (EU) 2022/328 of 25 February 2022 amending Regulation (EU) No 833/2014 concerning restrictive measures in view of Russia's actions destabilising the situation in Ukraine, OJ L49.

[5] Article 215(2) TFEU empowers the Council to adopt restrictive measures against natural or legal persons and groups or non-State entities. This chapter focuses on sanctions against countries.

[6] K Lenaerts, P Van Nuffel, and T Corthaut, *EU Constitutional Law* (OUP, 2021) 362.

[7] For a more detailed discussion, see A Matthaiou and I Van Damme, 'The Administration and Enforcement of EU Sanctions Revisited' in I Govaere, S Garben, and E Spaventa, *The Impact of War (in Ukraine) on the EU* (Hart Publishing, 2025) 185–215.

products, and bans on the sale of aircraft and aircraft parts and equipment. All these measures are based on Articles 29 and 215.

In that context, a recent proposal may be surprising. On 17 June 2025, the Commission proposed phasing out Russian natural gas imports.[8] The proposed Regulation would gradually ban the import of natural gas from Russia into the EU, with a full stop in 2028. Such a measure would fit into the growing sanctions package. It seems obvious that the Council may ban the import of Russian gas, based on Articles 29 and 215. In fact, since the proposed import ban, the Council has banned the import of Russian liquified natural gas based on these provisions, as a CFSP sanction.[9] Yet, for the proposed import ban, the Commission suggests the common commercial policy competence's Article 207(2) TFEU as legal basis instead.[10]

In its proposal, the Commission does not explain its legal basis choice in much detail. It simply states that measures banning Russian gas imports are 'trade measures under the Union's common commercial policy'.[11] It does not include a detailed assessment of Article 207's requirements. It also does not explain why Article 207(2) would apply, despite the existence of Articles 29 TEU and 215 TFEU, and despite seemingly contradictory statements from the Commission in the past.[12]

That is regrettable. Today, the delimitation and relationship between sanctions and trade remain unclear. A proper 'competence' analysis is, therefore, needed. This is especially important for the proposed import ban. Here, the choice of legal basis has practical power implications. For Article 207(2), a qualified majority in the Council suffices. Article 29, by contrast, requires unanimity.[13] And, notably due to Hungarian and Slovakian opposition, reaching the latter appears implausible.[14]

[8] Commission, Proposal for a Regulation of the European Parliament and of the Council on phasing out Russian natural gas imports, improving monitoring of potential energy dependencies and amending Regulation (EU) 2017/1938, COM(2025)828 final/2.

[9] Council Decision (CFSP) 2025/2032 of 23 October 2025 amending Decision 2014/512/CFSP concerning restrictive measures in view of Russia's actions destabilising the situation in Ukraine, OJ L2025/2032; Council Regulation (EU) 2025/2033 of 23 October 2025 amending Regulation (EU) No 833/2014 concerning restrictive measures in view of Russia's actions destabilising the situation in Ukraine, OJ L2025/2033.

[10] This chapter only examines those aspects of the proposal that concern the import of (piped) natural gas. The Commission also proposes to ban the provision of liquefied natural gas services to Russian entities (although, as mentioned above, the Council has in the meantime adopted such a ban based on Articles 29 and 215 instead), and to take measures to end the import of Russian oil – both based on Article 207 TFEU. In addition, it includes aspects that do not specifically relate to international trade. Member States would also need to prepare diversification plans addressing the phase-out of Russian gas imports. These diversification plans relate to energy policy and would, therefore, be based on Article 194 TFEU.

[11] Import ban proposal, COM(2025)828 final/2, 7.

[12] For a sceptical take, see V Szép and L Schaupp, 'Energy Sanctions Reloaded: Navigating the Trade-Sanctions Divide in the EU's Proposed Gas Ban' (Verfassungsblog, 2025), verfassungsblog.de/energy-sanctions-russia-eu.

[13] Article 31(1) TEU (Lisbon).

[14] 'Hungary and Slovakia withhold support as EU proposes ban on Russian gas and oil by 2027' (*EU Insider*, 16 June 2025), www.euinsider.eu/news/hungary-and-slovakia-withhold-support-as-

A convincing 'competence' analysis is, therefore, essential to avoid the impression that the CCP legal basis merely serves to circumvent CFSP vetoes.[15] That analysis is missing, at least from the Commission.

This chapter aims to fill the gap. It examines the proposed import ban based on the concepts of 'competence'. It consists of four sections. The first section points out the flaws in the Commission's 'competence' reasoning. The second section shows that the proposed import ban indeed falls within the scope of the CCP competence and (arguably) the powers under Article 207(2). The third section explains that the proposal also falls within the scope of the CFSP competence and the powers under Articles 29 and 215. The fourth section explores the relationship between Article 207 and Articles 29 and 215. This section finds that the CFSP sanctions legal bases (arguably) do not undermine the EU legislator's powers under Article 207(2), and vice versa. Two equally valid alternatives exist. With some caveats, the chapter thus concludes that the Commission chose a correct legal basis.

At the time of writing, the proposed import ban's prospects remain unclear. The same applies to the Council and the Parliament's own legal basis analyses, which therefore do not feature in the assessment. That does not undermine this chapter's relevance. Using the concepts of 'competence', a clearer understanding of the delimitation and relationship between sanctions and trade is important for the response to Russia's aggression. It also matters for potential future trade restrictions on other third countries that violate international law or threaten its security. Such measures must be based on solid 'competence' foundations. This chapter illustrates how the concepts of 'competence' can contribute to the analysis.

I. The Commission's (Incomplete and Imperfect) Analysis

This first section points out three issues with the Commission's legal basis justification. First, the proposal explains why the import ban falls within the CCP competence, but fails to show that the Council and the Parliament also have the power to adopt it under Article 207(2). Second, the proposal remains silent on the relationship between Article 207, on the one hand, and Articles 29 and 215, on the other hand. And when the Commission later sought to explain why the proposed import ban could not have been based on the latter provisions, it

eu-proposes-ban-on-russian-gas-and-oil-by-2027; 'EU plans ban on new Russian gas contracts using trade law' (*Financial Times*, 16 June 2025), www.ft.com/content/8b005c13-2088-47cd-aa47-9163e36efa4a.

[15] The Slovak and Hungarian Parliaments accused the Commission of such circumvention in their Reasoned opinions on the application of the Principles of Subsidiarity and Proportionality. See Council Secretariat, Slovak Parliament – Reasoned opinion on the application of the Principles of Subsidiarity and Proportionality, 12264/25, 2; Hungarian Parliament – Reasoned opinion on the application of the Principles of Subsidiarity and Proportionality, 13560/25, 7–8.

misidentified their objectives scope and applied a non-existent power instrument limitation. Third, the Commission's current choice of Article 207 seems to contradict a recent prior legal basis analysis.

A. The Proposal

As mentioned, the Commission proposes to ban Russian gas imports based on Article 207 TFEU. More precisely, its proposal points to Article 207(2) TFEU. This provision empowers the Council and the Parliament to adopt internal CCP regulations (as opposed to the conclusion of trade agreements): 'T]he European Parliament and the Council, acting by means of regulations in accordance with the ordinary legislative procedure, shall adopt the measures defining the framework for implementing the common commercial policy.'[16]

The proposal does not justify this CCP legal basis choice in detail. It simply notes that measures banning Russian gas imports are 'trade measures under the Union's common commercial policy'.[17] That explanation is only partially satisfactory. As section II explains in more detail, the proposed Regulation indeed falls within the scope of the CCP competence. It specifically relates to international trade. Moreover, an import ban is a valid power instrument within the CCP competence, and Article 207(2) expressly empowers the Council and the Parliament to adopt regulations.

However, Article 207(2) also includes an important power limitation; it applies to 'measures defining the framework for the implementation of the CCP'.[18] This means that the Council and the Parliament only enjoy a power under Article 207(2) to adopt framework measures. Yet the proposed import ban is a detailed rule that applies to a specific good and a specific third country. This raises the question whether it really qualifies as a framework measure. The Commission, however, remains silent on this requirement in its proposal.

B. The Response

The proposal also remains silent on the relationship with sanctions adopted under Articles 29 and 215. However, the Commission did briefly address this relationship in response to a Parliamentary question. Perhaps not surprisingly, the question was raised by a Member of Parliament from Slovakian prime minister Fico's party.[19]

[16] Article 207(2) TFEU.

[17] Import ban proposal, COM(2025)828 final/2, 7.

[18] Article 207(2) TFEU.

[19] E Kaliňák, Question for written answer E-002510/2025 to the Commission, 23 June 2025. The question merely refers to media reports on a planned Commission proposal based on a CCP legal basis, and not to the proposal itself (which had already been published at the time).

It accused the Commission of using Article 207 to bypass Article 29's veto requirement. The Commission denied the allegations. Although brief, its response gives an insight into the Commission's views on the relationship between Article 207 and the CFSP sanctions legal bases.

The Commission argued that the proposed import ban and sanctions adopted under Articles 29 and 215 pursued different objectives:

> The proposed Regulation is fully in line with EU law, and it has a different legal basis and a different purpose than EU restrictive measures under Common Security and Foreign Policy, that aim at incentivising changed behaviour. This proposal's purpose is to put an end to market distortions in the EU caused by Russia, which has proved to be an unreliable energy trading partner, to the detriment of EU's economic and energy security.[20]

Again, this reasoning is not convincing. First, it is not entirely accurate to claim that the proposal aims to end market distortions in the EU. The proposal does indeed refer to market distortions as a result of dependencies on Russian gas.[21] Its core aim, however, is to protect the Union against the weaponisation by Russia of its energy resources. The proposal notably stresses that 'the Russian Federation systematically used existing dependencies on Russian gas supplies to harm the Union's economy'.[22] In that context, '[m]aintaining energy supplies from Russia would expose the Union to continued economic and security risks'.[23]

Thus, the proposal essentially aims to protect the EU's security and independence in line with Article 21 TEU. Article 21 lays down the EU's external action objectives. These objectives are not explicitly linked to a specific competence field.[24] Article 205 confirms their relevance for the CCP competence. However, they clearly matter for the CFSP competence too.[25] Just like a CCP measure, a CFSP measure may aim to protect the EU's security and independence.

Moreover, the Treaties do not support the Commission's claim that EU sanctions under the CFSP must aim to incentivise changed behaviour. It is true that the Council's non-binding sanctions guidelines state that sanctions 'are imposed by the EU to bring about a change in policy or activity by the target country'.[26] And, as the Court confirmed, many sanctions do indeed seek to bring about such

[20] Answer given by Mr Jørgensen on behalf of the European Commission, E-002510/2025, 14 August 2025.

[21] See especially Recital 6 of the Import Ban Proposal, COM(2025)828 final/2.

[22] ibid, Recital 2.

[23] ibid, Recital 7.

[24] M Cremona, 'External Relations of the European Union: The Constitutional Framework for International Action' in P Craig and G De Búrca (eds), *The Evolution of EU Law* (OUP, 2021) 476; RA Wessel, 'General principles in EU common foreign and security policy' in KS Ziegler, PJ Neuvonen, and V Moreno-Lax (eds), *Research Handbook on General Principles in EU Law: Constructing Legal Orders in Europe* (Edward Elgar, 2022) 611.

[25] Article 23 TEU (Lisbon).

[26] General Secretariat, Sanctions Guidelines – update, 5664/18, 5.

a change.[27] However, neither Article 29 nor Article 215 imposes incentivisation as a requirement for their application.

Article 29 states that:

> The Council shall adopt decisions which shall define the approach of the Union to a particular matter of a geographical or thematic nature. Member States shall ensure that their national policies conform to the Union positions.[28]

Article 215 states that:

> Where a decision, adopted in accordance with Chapter 2 of Title V of the Treaty on European Union, provides for the interruption or reduction, in part or completely, of economic and financial relations with one or more third countries, the Council, acting by a qualified majority on a joint proposal from the High Representative of the Union for Foreign Affairs and Security Policy and the Commission, shall adopt the necessary measures. It shall inform the European Parliament thereof.[29]

On these bases, the Council may decide to restrict trade relations with a third country to induce it to change its behaviour. But it may also impose such a restriction for foreign policy and security reasons without directly seeking a change of behaviour. That includes an import ban to protect the EU's economic and energy security against the weaponisation by Russia of its energy resources. Contrary to the Commission's response, the presence or absence of a behaviour – changing aim is, therefore, not decisive for the choice of legal basis.

Neither is the fact that the proposed import ban is designed to apply permanently. In the context of the Council's decision-making process, the Commission repeated its behaviour – changing argument and further added that Articles 29 and 215 only empower the Council to adopt temporary measures: 'While sanctions are coercive foreign policy measures and, by nature, temporary, the [import ban] proposal pursues trade … goals and is meant to apply on a permanent basis.'[30] In essence, the Commission thus argued that the Council's powers under Articles 29 and 215 only extend to instruments that are limited in time.

This argument is not convincing either. Most CFSP sanctions do indeed apply for a limited period.[31] And the Council's non-binding guidelines do emphasise

[27] Case C-681/23 P *Gutsierev v Council* [2025] ECLI:EU:C:2025:327, para 41; Case T-65/18 RENV *Venezuela v Council* [2023] ECLI:EU:T:2023:529, para 42.

[28] Article 29 TEU (Lisbon).

[29] Article 215(1) TFEU. Article 215(2) is not relevant to this chapter, as it concerns sanctions against natural or legal persons and groups or non-State entities. Article 215(3) requires the Council to include legal safeguards in its sanctions decisions.

[30] Permanent Representatives Committee (Part 1), Proposal for a Regulation of the European Parliament and of the Council on phasing out Russian natural gas imports, improving monitoring of potential energy dependencies and amending Regulation (EU) 2017/1938 – General approach, 13869/25, 3.

[31] See, eg in the context of Russia's aggression against Ukraine, Council Decision (CFSP) 2022/327 of 25 February 2022 amending Decision 2014/512/CFSP concerning restrictive measures in view of Russia's actions destabilising the situation in Ukraine, OJ L48. Not all CFSP sanctions measures include an expiration data – see, eg the sanctions against North Korea, Council Decision (CFSP) 2016/849/CFSP of 27 May 2016 concerning restrictive measures against the Democratic People's Republic of Korea and repealing Decision 2013/183/CFSP, OJ L141.

the need to regularly review sanctions.[32] But this does not mean that Articles 29 and 215 only empower the Council to adopt temporary measures. The text of these provisions does not include such a requirement. Neither does the case law of the Court. To the extent that the Court underlined that certain sanctions are temporary, it did so based on the specific measures concerned, and not based on Articles 29 and 215 themselves.[33] Of course, a temporary limitation may be needed for proportionality reasons. From a power perspective, however, it is not required.

Thus, the Commission's response failed to clearly acknowledge that the proposal essentially aimed to protect the Union's security and independence. It also identified a non-existent difference in the CCP and CFSP competences' objectives scopes. In reality, both CCP measures and CFSP sanctions may aim to protect the EU's security and independence. Moreover, the Council's powers under Articles 29 and 215 are not limited to temporary measures.

C. The ECI

There is also a third issue: the Commission's choice of Article 207(2) is difficult to align with its legal basis analysis in a recent legal dispute. This concerned the registration of a proposed European Citizens' Initiative (ECI). The proposed ECI asked the Commission to propose a ban on 'importing products originating in illegal settlements in occupied territories and exporting to such territories'.[34]

Under the ECI Regulation, the Commission may only register an ECI if the Commission does not manifestly lack the power to propose the measure concerned. The question thus arose whether the Commission reasonably enjoyed the power to propose the measure concerned. The ECI organisers argued it did; they pointed to the CCP competence.[35] Within that field of competence, the Commission enjoys the power to propose trade measures.

The Commission disagreed. It found that '[a] legal act covering the subject matter of the proposed citizens' initiative could only be adopted on the basis of Article 215 TFEU'. However, Article 215 required a pre-existing CFSP Decision. The Commission noted that such a Decision did not exist and that it lacked the power to propose it. That power belonged to the High Representative of the Union for Foreign Affairs and Security Policy, and the Member States. The Commission thus refused to register the proposed ECI.

In response, the ECI organisers went to Luxembourg. The General Court annulled the Commission's refusal on the ground of inadequate motivation.[36]

[32] General Secretariat, Sanctions Guidelines – update, 5664/18, 6 and 14.

[33] See, eg Case T-262/15 *Kiselev v Council* [2017] ECLI:EU:T:2017:392, para 124; See Joined Cases C-402/05 P and C-415/05 P, *Kadi and Al Barakaat* [2008] ECR I-6351 ECLI:EU:C:2008:461, para 358.

[34] Recital 2 of Commission Decision (EU) 2019/1567 of 4 September 2019 on the proposed citizens' initiative entitled 'Ensuring Common Commercial Policy conformity with EU Treaties and compliance with international law', OJ L241.

[35] ibid.

[36] Case T-789/19, *Moerenhout v Commission* [2021] ECLI:EU:T:2021:260.

Despite the proposed ECI's reference to the CCP competence, the Commission had failed to explain why the proposed measure could not be based on Article 207.[37] To be clear, the Court did not rule that Article 207 applied; it only required the Commission to properly explain why that provision in its view did not apply.

Following the ruling, the Commission adopted a new Decision. This time, it did register the ECI. The Commission agreed that the proposed measure would 'have a specific link with international trade and as a consequence would fall within the scope of Article 207 TFEU even if it pursues foreign policy objectives'.[38] However, it also stressed that the ECI organisers had clarified their original initiative. The initiative now 'ask[ed] for a trade measure that is general in nature and that does not target a specific country or territory'.[39]

That specification raises questions. It suggests that the Commission considered that Article 207 could not provide a legal basis for an import ban with a foreign policy and security objective that targets a specific country. Implicitly, its Decision favours Articles 29 and 215 for such a measure. Yet, four years later, the Commission proposed to ban the import of Russian gas based on Article 207.

A contradiction thus presents itself. The Commission's justification for the Russian import ban as a CCP measure is difficult to align with its position on the ECI. That does not mean that Article 207 is not a valid legal basis for the former. But it does show that a better 'competence' reasoning is needed. The following sections aim to provide this. They analyse the import ban proposal through the concepts of 'competence'.

II. Trade

Since the Commission has proposed the import ban on the basis of Article 207(2), it is logical to start the 'competence' assessment here. Despite the Commission's imperfect justification, the proposed import ban indeed falls within the scope of the CCP competence. Under a broad interpretation, Article 207(2) also empowers the Council and the Parliament to adopt it.

A. Competence

First, the question arises whether the Commission's proposal falls within the CCP competence as defined in Title II of Part V of the TFEU. The answer is affirmative: the

[37] ibid, para 45.

[38] Recital 12 of Commission Implementing Decision (EU) 2021/1484 of 8 September 2021 on the request for registration of the European citizens' initiative entitled 'Ensuring Common Commercial Policy conformity with EU Treaties and compliance with international law' pursuant to Regulation (EU) 2019/788 of the European Parliament and of the Council, OJ L328.

[39] ibid, Recital 13.

proposal's subject matter and objectives fall within the scope of the common commercial policy. Both competence dimensions are examined below. An illustration of the recent EU Anti-Coercion Instrument further supports the analysis.[40]

1. *Subject Matter*

A measure falls within the subject matter scope of the common commercial policy when it specifically relates to international trade.[41] As explained in chapter three, the notion of 'international trade' undoubtedly includes trade in goods between the EU and a third country. The Court of Justice confirmed this in *Opinion 1/94*. It ruled that 'the Community has sole competence pursuant to Article 113 of the EC Treaty to conclude an external agreement of a general nature, that is to say, encompassing all types of goods'.[42]

This conclusion remains valid under Article 207 TFEU today. Article 207(1) explicitly refers to trade in goods, albeit specifically in the context of agreements. Confirming the obvious, the Court recently noted again that 'the import of goods into the Union falls within the sphere of trade relations between the Union and third countries or international organisations; relations which are governed by the common commercial policy in accordance with Article 207(1) TFEU'.[43] A measure that concerns international trade in goods thus falls within the CCP's subject matter scope.

That includes the Commission's proposal. As the explanatory memorandum emphasised, the import ban is an '[international] trade measure'.[44] It specifically relates to trade in a good – namely, gas – between the EU and Russia. The Commission's proposed phase-out of Russian gas imports into the EU thus falls within the subject matter scope of the common commercial policy. So far, the analysis is straightforward.

2. *Objectives*

The analysis is slightly more complex for the CCP's objectives dimension. However, it reaches a similar conclusion. The Commission's proposal also falls within the objectives scope of the CCP competence. Again, chapter three has already laid the foundations for this conclusion. It showed that the Union does not merely have competence to liberalise international trade; more widely, it may

[40] Regulation (EU) 2023/2675 of the European Parliament and of the Council of 22 November 2023 on the protection of the Union and its Member States from economic coercion by third countries, OJ L 2023/2675.

[41] Case C-414/11 *Daiichi Sankyo and Sanofi-Aventis Deutschland* [2013] ECLI:EU:C:2013:520, para 51.

[42] Opinion 1/94 *Accords annexés à l'accord OMC* [1994] ECR I-5267 ECLI:EU:C:1994:384, para 27.

[43] Case C-399/22 *Confédération paysanne (Melons et tomates du Sahara occidental)* [2024] ECLI:EU:C:2024:839, para 42.

[44] Import ban proposal, COM(2025)828 final/2, 7.

also 'govern' trade.[45] The CCP competence thus allows the EU to pursue objectives other than trade liberalisation.[46]

That is also what the proposed import ban does. It clearly does not seek to liberalise trade. Instead, it governs trade to achieve a security objective. The proposal notes that Russia has 'consistently used gas trade as a weapon to achieve policy instead of trade goals'.[47] The full-scale invasion of Ukraine demonstrated how Russia 'weaponise[s] reductions of gas supplies' and 'manipulat[es] … markets through intentional disruptions of gas flows'.[48]

These Russian actions undermine the EU's economic and energy security and independence. Moreover, Russia could use revenues from its energy trade 'to finance further economic attacks against the Union, undermining economic security', or 'to finance the war of aggression against the Ukraine which constitutes a major threat to political and economic stability in Europe'.[49] For these reasons, the Commission proposes to ban the import of Russian gas. The aim is to protect the EU's security and independence against Russia's weaponisation of energy. The proposal thus pursues a foreign policy and security objective.

From a competence perspective, that is permissible. The CJEU already confirmed this several decades ago in *Werner*.[50] It ruled that a German rule requiring a licence for the export of a vacuum induction oven to Libya, on public security grounds, fell within the scope of the CCP competence. After all, a measure 'cannot be treated as falling outside the scope of the common commercial policy on the ground that it has foreign policy and security objectives'.[51]

There is no reason to reach a different conclusion today. On the contrary, Article 207 now explicitly states that the CCP 'shall be conducted in the context of the principles and objectives of the Union's external action'.[52] Article 21 TEU lists these objectives. They include the 'safeguard[ing] [of the Union's] … values, fundamental interests, security, independence and integrity'.[53] A measure that governs trade in the pursuit of such objectives would thus fall within the scope of the CCP competence. That includes the Commission's proposal.

3. *Subject Matter, Objectives, and the Anti-Coercion Instrument*

The EU legislator recently reached similar conclusions in the context of the Anti-Coercion Instrument. This instrument introduces a framework to deter and

[45] Case C-137/12 *Commission v Council* [2013] ECLI:EU:C:2013:675, para 57.

[46] C Kaddous, 'The Transformation of the EU Common Commercial Policy' in P Eeckhout and M Lopez-Escudero (eds), *The European Union's External Action in Times of Crisis* (Hart Publishing, 2016) 451.

[47] Import ban proposal, COM(2025)828 final/2, Recital 7.

[48] ibid, Recital 4.

[49] ibid, Recital 6.

[50] Case C-70/94 *Werner v Bundesrepublik Deutschland* [1995] ECR I-03189 ECLI:EU:C:1995:328.

[51] ibid, para 10; N Emiliou, 'Strategic Export Controls, National Security and the Common Commercial Policy' (1996) 1 *European Foreign Affairs Review* 55, 67.

[52] Article 207(1) TFEU.

[53] Article 21(2)(a) TEU (Lisbon).

address economic coercion by a third country.[54] Economic coercion exists when a third country adopts or threatens to adopt a trade or investment measure to influence EU or Member State decision-making.[55] The Council determines whether a third country has engaged in economic coercion following a Commission examination.[56] The Commission may then adopt Union response measures to address the economic coercion.[57] Annex I to the Anti-Coercion Instrument contains a list of potential response measures.

The Council and the Parliament adopted the Anti-Coercion Instrument based on Article 207(2) TFEU. They thus presented it as a common commercial policy measure. The Commission had done the same in its proposal. However, the Commission's explanation behind this choice of legal basis was not entirely convincing. The proposal mentioned that it was 'concerned with foreign countries' measures that take the form of measures affecting trade or investment towards the Union', and provided 'a response, in the area of the common commercial policy but also in other areas, to foreign countries' measures of economic coercion'.[58]

This reference to other areas suggested that the proposal went beyond the subject matter scope of the CCP competence. The Council Legal Service agreed: in its legal basis Opinion, it noted that a CCP measure must specifically relate to international trade.[59] For certain potential response measures listed in the proposed Annex I, this specific link with international trade was not sufficiently present. Response measures suspending tariff concessions for goods or restricting trade in services, for instance, clearly fell within the CCP's subject matter scope.[60]

Other response measures fell outside the CCP's scope. The Council Legal Service notably found no sufficient link between international trade and restricting access to Union-funded research programmes.[61] It also expressed doubts on the inclusion of measures against natural or legal persons linked to third-country governments. Such measures could be permissible, but only if the persons concerned were economic operators.[62] Otherwise, a sufficient trade link was again absent.

The Council Legal Service thus suggested amendments to the proposed act to ensure that it fully fell within the CCP's subject matter scope. The Council and Parliament followed its advice on both points. The adopted Anti-Coercion Instrument

[54] Article 1 of the Anti-Coercion Instrument, Regulation (EU) 2023/2675.
[55] ibid, Article 2.
[56] ibid, Articles 4 and 5.
[57] ibid, Article 8.
[58] Commission, Proposal for a Regulation of the European Parliament and of the Council on the protection of the Union and its Member States from economic coercion by third countries, COM/2021/775 final, 2.
[59] Council Legal Service, Opinion on the Anti-Coercion Instrument (legal basis and institutional aspects), 11943/22, para 20.
[60] ibid, para 22.
[61] ibid, para 30.
[62] ibid, para 39.

no longer foresees research-related response measures.[63] Measures against natural and legal persons remain possible if these persons 'engage or might engage in activities falling under Article 207 TFEU and are connected or linked to the government of the third country'.[64]

In its Opinion, the Council Legal Service also addressed the proposal's objectives. It noted that, 'in regulating trade, ...]the common commercial policy [is not] limited to measures that pursue purely commercial objectives: on the contrary, it may take account of wider objectives of the Union's external action'.[65] The proposal reflected two sets of objectives: first, safeguarding the EU's values, fundamental interests, security, independence, and integrity; second, consolidating and supporting the rule of law and the principles of international law. Both sets of objectives fell under the external action objectives as listed in Article 21 TEU.[66] The proposed act, therefore, also fell within the CCP competence's objectives scope.

Thus, the Council Legal Service analysed both dimensions of the common commercial policy competence. Its conclusions are convincing. They can be applied, by analogy, to the Commission's recent proposal to ban the import of Russian gas. Of course, differences exist between this proposal and the Anti-Coercion Instrument;[67] but they fall within the scope of the CCP competence for the same reason. Both the proposed import ban and the Anti-Coercion Instrument pursue security-related objectives under Article 21 TEU. And both pursue these objectives through measures that are specifically linked to international trade. The CCP competence, therefore, covers both.

B. Power

So far, the analysis has focused on competence; it now moves to power. The second question is whether the Parliament and the Council also enjoy the power to adopt the proposed import ban within the CCP. At first sight, the answer is affirmative. Article 207(2) empowers the Council, by a qualified majority (voting majority), and the Parliament (empowered institutions), to adopt regulations (type of legal act). These regulations must define the framework for implementing the common commercial policy (legal instrument). To a large extent, the Commission's proposal reflects these power dimensions and modalities.

[63] Recital 25 of the Anti-Coercion Instrument instead mentions that the Commission may adopt anti-coercion measures under other legal acts, including to limit access to funding or participation in research programmes.

[64] ibid, Article 8(3)(b).

[65] Council Legal Service, Opinion on the Anti-Coercion Instrument, 11943/22, paras 18–19.

[66] ibid, para 21.

[67] Including the fact that the proposed import ban targets a single third country, while the Anti-Coercion Instrument provides a framework against economic coercion by third countries in general. Section III of this chapter examines this difference in more detail.

The proposal presents the import ban as a regulation to be adopted by the Parliament and (by qualified majority) the Council. An import ban is also a trade instrument. The Court recently confirmed this when France banned the import of products violating certain EU consumer information rules.[68] The French import ban was a trade measure that fell within the scope of the CCP.[69] By analogy, the proposed import ban is a legal power instrument to govern international trade within the scope of the CCP. Advocate General Ćapeta also explicitly pointed this out in the same case. She stressed that 'Article 207 TFEU may always serve as a legal basis to introduce an EU measure to suspend trade with a third State or territory.'[70]

Yet there may still be an issue. As mentioned in section I above, Article 207(2) includes an additional power instrument limitation. It only applies to 'measures defining the framework for the implementation of the CCP'. Many scholars argue that the framework requirement prevents the Council and the Parliament from adopting internal CCP measures that target a specific country, good, or service:[71] such measures would not qualify as a 'framework' for implementing the CCP; they could, therefore, not be based on Article 207(2).

If correct, this interpretation would exclude the Council and Parliament's power to ban the import of Russian gas based on Article 207(2). The reality, however, seems more nuanced. The following analysis first revisits the framework requirement's puzzling origins. It then explains how the requirement could be interpreted more or less broadly.

1. *Framework Requirement: Origins*

The framework requirement's origins lie in the draft Constitutional Treaty. They are puzzling. On the one hand, preparatory documents show that the introduction of the framework requirement was a conscious choice.[72] It was widely debated and discussed. On the other hand, these documents also suggest that the requirement emerged as an unconvincing response to (partially) ill-founded concerns.

[68] Case C-399/22, *Confédération paysanne (Melons et tomates du Sahara occidental)* [2024] ECLI:EU:C:2024:839.

[69] ibid, para 48.

[70] Opinion in Case C-399/22, *Confédération paysanne (Melons et tomates du Sahara occidental)* [2024] ECLI:EU:C:2024:262, para 30, fn 30.

[71] C Herrmann, 'Die Gemeinsame Handelspolitik (GHP)' in R Streinz, C Ohler, and C Herrmann (eds), *Der Vertrag von Lissabon zur Reform der EU* (Beck, 2010) 152; M Krajewski, 'New Functions and New Powers for the European Parliament: Assessing the Changes of the Common Commercial Policy from the Perspective of Democratic Legitimacy' in M Bungenberg and C Herrmann (eds), *Common Commercial Policy after Lisbon* (Springer, 2013) 70–71; H-G Dederer, 'The Common Commercial Policy Under the Influence of Commission, Council, High Representative and European External Action Service' in M Bungenberg and C Herrmann, *Common Commercial Policy after Lisbon* (eds) (Springer, 2013) 89; R Schütze, *European Constitutional Law* (CUP, 2012) 248.

[72] E Brok, 'Die neue Macht des Europäischen Parlaments nach "Lissabon" im Bereich der gemeinsamen Handelspolitik' (2010) 3 *Integration* 209, 216.

Before the Lisbon Treaty, the Council enjoyed broad powers to adopt internal CCP measures. Article 133(2) TEC stated that '[t]he Commission shall submit proposals to the Council for implementing the common commercial policy'.[73] The Parliament was not formally involved. During the preparations for a Constitutional Treaty, this became a major discussion point.[74] To enhance democratic legitimacy, the drafters wanted to involve the Parliament as co-legislator for internal CCP measures.[75] An early draft thus generally empowered the Parliament and the Council to adopt measures 'required to implement the common commercial policy'.[76]

However, some drafters feared that this wording did not make it sufficiently clear that the Council could adopt implementing measures without involving the Parliament.[77] In practice, the Council had often used Article 133(2) to lay down general rules that could be implemented further in individual cases.[78] The Anti-Dumping Regulations, for instance, defined the framework for anti-dumping duties on third-country goods.[79] They also empowered the Commission and the Council to impose duties on specific imported goods subject to dumping. Preparatory documents suggest that the drafters wanted to avoid that the Parliament's new powers would undermine this long-standing practice.[80] Thus, one proposed amendment expressly allowed the Council and the Parliament to delegate powers to the Council or the Commission.[81]

The Council Legal Service suggested a different solution. During the intergovernmental conference, its legal experts recommended including the framework requirement.[82] This would

> make it clear that [measures based on the current Article 207(2) TFEU] will, in accordance with [the Treaty provisions on delegated and implementing acts – currently

[73] See also Article 113(2) TEEC and Article 113(2) TEC.

[74] M Krajewski, 'External trade law and the Constitution Treaty: Towards a federal and more democratic common commercial policy?' (2005) 44 *Common Market Law Review* 91.

[75] Convention Secretariat, Final report of Working Group VII on External Action, CONV 459/02, 7; EPP Convention Group, Suggestion for amendment of Article: III-212, CONV 2002–2003.

[76] IGC Secretariat, Draft Treaty establishing a Constitution for Europe, 850/03, 166.

[77] D de Villepin, Suggestion for amendment of Article: 24, CONV 2002–2003; Presidency, Non-institutional issues; including amendments in the economic and financial field, CIG 37/03, 12.

[78] T Müller-Ibold, 'Common Commercial Policy After Lisbon: The European Union's Dependence on Secondary Legislation' in M Bungenberg and C Herrmann (eds), *Common Commercial Policy after Lisbon* (Springer, 2013) 158.

[79] Originally Regulation (EEC) No 459/68 of the Council of 5 April 1968 on protection against dumping or the granting of bounties or subsidies by countries which are not members of the European Economic Community, OJ L93.

[80] D de Villepin, Suggestion for amendment of Article: 24, CONV 2002–2003; Presidency, Non-institutional issues; including amendments in the economic and financial field, CIG 37/03, 12. See also J Bering Liisberg, 'The EU Constitutional Treaty and its distinction between legislative and non-legislative acts – Oranges into apples?' (2006) Jean Monnet Working Paper 01/06, 30–31; and Müller-Ibold (n 78) 159.

[81] D de Villepin, Suggestion for amendment of Article: 24, CONV 2002–2003.

[82] IGC Secretariat, Editorial and legal comments on the draft Treaty establishing a Constitution for Europe – Basic document, CIG 4/03, 380–81; J-C Piris, *The Constitution for Europe – A Legal Analysis* (CUP, 2006) 51.

Articles 290 and 291 TFEU], need to provide for delegation to the Council or the Commission for these urgent cases.[83]

Arguably, the concern of the drafters and the Council Legal Service was ill-founded. Generally empowering the Parliament and the Council to implement the CCP would not have undermined the long-standing practice of Council and/or Commission implementing measures. The explicit reference to the possibility of delegated and implementing acts in both the draft Constitutional Treaty and the Lisbon Treaty supported this.[84]

That may explain why the larger working party of legal experts representing the different Member States and institutions omitted the requirement from their final drafting recommendations.[85] In a later Presidency compromise proposal, however, the requirement resurfaced.[86] Interestingly, the rationale was now slightly different. The document no longer expressly mentioned the need to preserve implementation outside the Parliament. Instead, the drafters wanted 'to clarify that urgent unilateral trade protection measures be adopted under a lighter procedure than the legislative one'.[87]

This reflected a valid concern. Involving the Parliament would indeed slow down the decision-making process.[88] However, at least in urgent ad hoc cases, the framework requirement was an unconvincing solution. In such cases, a broad framework requirement would lead to delays, to the extent that it first required the Council and the Parliament to lay down a general rule that must be implemented further in individual cases.

The drafters could have chosen a different solution. They could have empowered the Council to act alone in certain cases. Such an approach was taken in the field of the common agricultural policy.[89] One legal basis generally empowered the Council and the Parliament to establish the common organisation of agricultural markets.[90] Another empowered the Council to adopt specific measures, such as quantitative limitations.[91] It is unclear why the drafters did not take a similar approach in the CCP.

The final draft Constitutional Treaty thus empowered the Council and the Parliament to adopt 'the measures defining the framework for implementing the

[83] IGC Secretariat, Editorial and legal comments on the draft Treaty establishing a Constitution for Europe – Basic document, CIG 4/03, 381.

[84] Articles I-36 and I-37 of the Draft Treaty establishing a Constitution for Europe (2003) OJ C169; Articles 290 and 191 TFEU.

[85] IGC Secretariat, Draft Treaty establishing a Constitution for Europe (following editorial and legal adjustments by the Working Party of IGC Legal Experts), CIG 50/03, 186.

[86] IGC Secretariat, Addendum to the Presidency proposal, CIG 60/03 Add1, 67.

[87] Presidency, Naples Ministerial Conclave: Presidency proposal, CIG 52/1/03 Rev1, 12.

[88] T Tiilikainen, A Peltomäki, M Vanhanen, R Korhonen, Suggestion for amendment of Article: 24, CONV 2002–2003.

[89] A Dashwood, 'EU Acts and Member State Acts in the Negotiation, Conclusion, and Implementation of International Agreements' in M Cremona and C Kilpatrick, *EU Legal Acts: Challenges and Transformations* (OUP, 2018) 225–26.

[90] Article III-231(2) of the draft Constitutional Treaty; Article 43(2) TFEU.

[91] Article III-231(3) of the draft Constitutional Treaty; Article 43(3) TFEU.

common commercial policy'.[92] Today, Article 207(2) includes the same wording. It only provides a legal basis for the adoption of internal CCP *framework* measures.[93] The rationale behind this requirement is puzzling, but its introduction was a conscious choice. Disregarding it would violate the principle of conferral of powers.[94]

2. *Framework Requirement: Interpretation*

What exactly qualifies as a framework measure, however, remains unclear.[95] The drafters did not explain this; neither has the Court.[96] Many cases are straightforward. The recent Anti-Coercion Instrument, for instance, lays down the framework for EU action against economic coercion. It also confers powers upon the Council and the Commission to identify and respond to economic coercion in individual cases.[97] As the Council Legal Service noted in its legal basis opinion, the Anti-Coercion Instrument thus lays down a framework for implementing the CCP.[98]

The Council Legal Service reached a similar conclusion in 2018 when it examined the Commission's proposal for a Foreign Direct Investments Regulation.[99] The proposal laid down a framework for the screening of foreign direct investments in the EU.[100] Member States could choose to introduce such screening. In some situations, the proposal also foresaw screening by the Commission. Again, the Council Legal Service (briefly) noted that the proposed measure laid down the framework for implementing the CCP.[101] That the final Regulation only provides for screening by the Member States and not directly by the Commission does not invalidate this conclusion.[102]

[92] Article III-315(2) of the Draft Treaty establishing a Constitution for Europe.

[93] Brok (n 72) 216.

[94] M Chamon, *The European Parliament and Delegated Legislation – An Institutional Balance Perspective* (Hart Publishing, 2022) 158.

[95] J-C Piris, *The Lisbon Treaty – A Legal and Political Analysis* (CUP, 2010) 283; G Gosalbo Bono, 'The organisation of the external relations of the European Union in the Treaty of Lisbon' in P Koutrakos (ed), *The European Union's external relations a year after Lisbon* (CLEER Working Papers 2011/3) 18.

[96] Advocate General Emiliou briefly noted that the Anti-Dumping Regulation, 'which in turn empowers the Commission to adopt certain anti-circumvention measures, is unquestionably one of the measures defining the framework for implementing the common commercial policy referred to in Article 207 TFEU'. See Opinion in Case C-517/22 P, *Eurobolt and Others v Commission and Stafa Group* [2023] ECLI:EU:C:2023:649, para 46.

[97] Articles 4 and 5 of the Anti-Coercion Instrument, Regulation (EU) 2023/2675.

[98] Council Legal Service, Opinion on the Anti-Coercion Instrument, 11943/22, para 44.

[99] Council Legal Service, Proposal for a Regulation establishing a framework for screening of foreigndirect investments into the EU – legal basis, 7334/18 Cor1.

[100] Commission, Proposal for a Regulation of the European Parliament and of the Council establishing a framework for screening of foreign direct investments into the European Union, COM/2017/0487.

[101] Council Legal Service, Proposal for a Regulation establishing a framework for screening of foreigndirect investments into the EU – legal basis, 7334/18 Cor1, para 21.

[102] Regulation (EU) 2019/452 of the European Parliament and of the Council of 19 March 2019 establishing a framework for the screening of foreign direct investments into the Union, OJ L 79I.

Measures that introduce specific rules on trade with an individual country, good, or service are less straightforward. This includes the proposed import ban. The question arises whether such measures may also qualify as framework measures. As mentioned, the literature often applies a narrow reading of Article 207(2). This would limit its scope to measures that lay down general rules which then need to be implemented further in individual cases. A more lenient reading is possible too.[103] Article 207(2) could empower the Council and the Parliament to adopt rules on trade with an individual country, good, or service – as long as they delegate the more concrete implementation of these rules to the Commission, the Council, and/or the Member States.

Under this more lenient interpretation, the proposed import ban could qualify as a framework measure. It would lay down a clear, detailed, and specific rule – importing Russian gas into the Union would be prohibited. At the same time, it would lay down a framework for the Commission to 'monitor the development of the Union's energy market' and to 'authorise one or more Member States to temporarily suspend the application of [the import ban]' in the event of serious security-of-supply threats.[104]

Other Article 207(2) measures did something similar. In 2014, the Council and the Parliament froze the level of customs duties on Ecuadorian goods, based on Article 207(2).[105] This was done to facilitate trade in the anticipation of Ecuador's accession to a trade agreement between the Union and countries of the Andes Community. The freezing was conditional.[106] The Council and the Parliament empowered the Commission to verify Ecuador's compliance with these conditions.[107] In the event of a failure to comply, the Commission could temporarily suspend the freezing.

Arguably, the 2014 Regulation qualified as a framework measure. It defined a detailed rule (the freezing) and created a framework for the Commission to suspend the rule if necessary. More recently, the Council and the Parliament applied the same logic in the context of Russia's war against Ukraine. They adopted conditional trade concessions in favour of Ukraine and empowered the Commission to temporarily suspend the concessions in the event of a failure to comply with the conditions.[108] And increased custom duties apply on Russian and

[103] See also Dimopoulos, who notes that 'the addition of the words "defining the framework" in the Lisbon Treaty does not imply that the Union is only competent to define the general framework for achieving its policy goals': A Dimopoulos, The Common Commercial Policy after Lisbon: Establishing Parallelism Between Internal and External Economic Relations?' (2008) 4 *Croatian Yearbook of European Law and Policy* 101, 107.

[104] Import ban proposal, COM(2025)828 final/2, Article 15.

[105] Article 2 of Regulation (EU) No 1384/2014 of the European Parliament and of the Council of 18 December 2014 on the tariff treatment for goods originating in Ecuador, OJ L372.

[106] ibid, Article 3.

[107] ibid.

[108] Regulation (EU) 2023/1077 of the European Parliament and of the Council of 31 May 2023 on temporary trade-liberalisation measures supplementing trade concessions applicable to Ukrainian

Belarusian fertilisers, but the Commission may adopt appropriate remedial action in the event of significant price increases.[109]

Of course, the previous decision-making practice has no precedent value.[110] It remains to be seen how the Court interprets the framework requirement. In the meantime, however, a lenient interpretation is reasonable. Despite the Commission's inadequate justification, Article 207(2) may thus indeed offer a legal basis for the proposed import ban.

III. Sanctions

The 'elephants in the room' are Articles 29 and 215. Based on these provisions, the Council has already adopted a number of import bans. For instance, it has prohibited petroleum imports from North Korea and Syria.[111] Importing Russian seaborne crude oil and liquefied natural gas is also prohibited.[112] It would seem reasonable to think that a ban on the import of Russian natural gas should have the same legal bases. The following parts show that the proposed import ban indeed (also) falls within the scope of the CFSP competence and the powers under Articles 29 and 215.

A. Competence

First, the proposed import ban (also) falls within the scope of the common foreign and security policy competence. The CFSP's subject matter scope is very wide: it covers 'all areas of foreign policy and all questions relating to the Union's security'.[113] Article 29 TEU specifically applies to 'a particular matter of a

products under the Association Agreement between the European Union and the European Atomic Energy Community and their Member States, of the one part, and Ukraine, of the other part, OJ L 144.

[109] Regulation (EU) 2025/1227 of the European Parliament and of the Council of 17 June 2025 on the modification of customs duties applicable to imports of certain goods originating in or exported from the Russian Federation and the Republic of Belarus, OJ L 2025/1227.

[110] Case C-370/07, *Commission v Council* [2009] ECLI:EU:C:2009:590, para 54.

[111] See Council Decision (CFSP) 2016/849 of 27 May 2016 concerning restrictive measures against the Democratic People's Republic of Korea and repealing Decision 2013/183/CFSP, OJ L141; Council Regulation (EU) 2017/1509 of 30 August 2017 concerning restrictive measures against the Democratic People's Republic of Korea and repealing Regulation (EC) No 329/2007, OJ L224; Council Decision 2013/255/CFSP of 31 May 2013 concerning restrictive measures against Syria, OJ L147; Council Regulation (EU) No 36/2012 of 18 January 2012 concerning restrictive measures in view of the situation in Syria and repealing Regulation (EU) No 442/2011, OJ L16.

[112] Council Decision 2014/119/CFSP of 5 March 2014 concerning restrictive measures directed against certain persons, entities and bodies in view of the situation in Ukraine, OJ L66 (amended); Council Regulation (EU) No 833/2014 of 31 July 2014 concerning restrictive measures in view of Russia's actions destabilising the situation in Ukraine, OJ L299 (amended).

[113] Article 24(1) TEU (Lisbon).

geographical or thematic nature'.[114] This includes the matter of Russia's weaponisation of its energy resources.

In terms of objectives, the Lisbon Treaty does not formally identify CFSP-specific objectives. However, as explained in section I of this chapter, the CFSP competence's objectives scope undoubtedly extends to the protection of the EU's security and independence.[115] This follows from Article 21(2)(a) TEU. Thus, for instance, the Council has adopted restrictive CFSP measures to protect the Union against Russian actions and policies that 'undermine or threaten democracy, the rule of law, stability or security'.[116] By analogy, the CFSP competence also extends to measures that aim to protect the Union against Russia's energy weaponisation.

Admittedly, the Court has declared that Article 215 measures do 'not fall within the scope of the CFSP'.[117] That reasoning dates back to the pre-Lisbon pillar structure.[118] The CFSP provisions, including Article 29's predecessor, were part of the more intergovernmental CFSP pillar. Article 215's predecessor was part of the Community pillar, with legislative procedures and Court of Justice scrutiny instead. That old pillar structure explained why Article 215 could not be part of the CFSP.

Today, excluding Article 215 from the CFSP competence is no longer convincing.[119] As the Court expressly acknowledged, Article 215 measures implement a prior CFSP decision.[120] They thus pursue the same CFSP objectives. Their specific subject matter scope – economic relations with third countries – also fits within the CFSP's wider subject matter scope as described above. These measures should, therefore, be considered to fall within the CFSP competence, despite Article 215's location in the TFEU rather than the TEU. However, this precise competence classification is not decisive here. Even if Article 215 is (wrongly) considered part of a non-CFSP competence, its objectives and subject matter scope in any event also extend to the proposed import ban.

[114] Article 29 TEU (Lisbon).

[115] P Koutrakos, *The EU Common Security and Defence Policy* (OUP, 2013) 35; A Dashwood, 'The Law and Practice of CFSP Joint Actions' in M Cremona and B de Witte (eds), *EU Foreign Relations Law: Constitutional Fundamentals* (Hart Publishing, 2008) 65–67.

[116] Article 1 of Council Decision (CFSP) 2024/2643 of 8 October 2024 concerning restrictive measures in view of Russia's destabilising activities, OJ L 2024/2643; Council Regulation (EU) 2024/2642 of 8 October 2024 concerning restrictive measures in view of Russia's destabilizing activities, OJ L 2024/2642.

[117] Case C-134/19 P *Bank Refah Kargaran v Council* [2020] ECLI:EU:C:2020:793, para 28.

[118] See Lenaerts, Van Nuffel, and Corthaut (n 6) 28–32.

[119] Although there seems to be no clear scholarly support for this position. The literature, rather, focuses on the question whether the EU has an exclusive sanctions competence for sanctions. As the CFSP competence is certainly not an exclusive competence, this implies a view that Article 215 is not part of the CFSP. See R Schütze, *Foreign Affairs and the EU Constitution – Selected Essays* (CUP, 2014) 64 and fn 83; C Eckes, 'Controlling the Most Dangerous Branch from Afar: Multilayered Counter-Terrorist Policies and the European Judiciary' (2011) 4 *European Journal of Risk Regulation* 505, 515.

[120] Case C-134/19 P *Bank Refah Kargaran v Council*, para 28.

B. Power

Second, Articles 29 TEU and 215 TFEU provide the necessary powers to adopt an import ban within the scope of the CFSP competence.

Article 29 broadly empowers the Council to adopt a decision to 'define the approach of the Union' to Russia's energy weaponisation.[121] The approach may include a decision to restrict trade, as a power instrument to achieve a CFSP objective. Based on Article 215, the Council may then adopt necessary regulations to implement this decision by partially or fully interrupting or reducing economic relations with a third country. A Russian gas import ban qualifies as a reduction of economic relations with a third country. Moreover, as explained in section I, neither Article 29 not Article 215 limit the Council's powers to temporary measures.

Thus, the Council may also ban the import of Russian gas under Articles 29 and 215. There may be a practical issue here. Article 29 requires unanimity in the Council.[122] This may be difficult to achieve in practice. But that does not affect the applicability of Articles 29 and 215, as such.

IV. Sanctions and Trade

Section II explained that the proposed import ban falls within the scope of the CCP competence and the Council and Parliament's powers under Article 207(2). Section III showed that the same applies to the CFSP competence and Articles 29 and 215. It is now time to examine the relationship between these legal bases. Does the existence of Article 215 exclude the power to restrict trade with a third country for foreign and security reasons under Article 207(2)?[123]

One option would be to apply a *lex specialis* rule. Scholars have advocated for such a rule where a measure's aim and content reflect both a CFSP and a non-CFSP legal basis.[124] For international trade restrictions with a foreign policy and security objective, however, it does not offer a straightforward solution. To some

[121] Article 29 TEU (Lisbon).

[122] Article 31(1) TEU (Lisbon).

[123] P Koutrakos, *Trade, Foreign Policy and Defence in EU Constitutional Law – The Legal Regulation of Sanctions, Exports of Dual-use Goods and Armaments* (Hart Publishing, 2001) 78–79; R Schütze, *Foreign Affairs and the EU Constitution* (n 119), 64–65. For an affirmative answer, see, eg K Lenaerts and E De Smijter, 'The United Nations and The European Union: Living Apart Together' in K Wellens, *International Law: Theory and practice: Essays in honour of Eric Suy* (Nijhoff, 1998) 449; L Defalque and D Luff, 'L'embargo et l'Union européenne' in *L'Embargo, Actes de la journée d'étude du 1er décembre 1995 organisée par l'Association européenne pour le droit bancaire et financier* (Bruylant, 1996) 106.

[124] M Cremona, 'Defining Competence in EU External Relations: Lessons From the Treaty Reform Process' in A Dashwood and M Maresceau (eds), *Law and Practice of EU External Relations* (CUP, 2008) 46; P Eeckhout, 'The EU's Common Foreign and Security Policy after Lisbon: From Pillar Talk to Constitutionalism' in A Biondi, P Eeckhout, and S Ripley (eds), *EU Law after Lisbon* (OUP, 2012) 274.

extent, Article 215 is more specific: its power instrument is the restriction of economic relations with third countries. But the reverse is also true: in terms of subject matter competence, the CCP specifically relates to international trade and the CFSP does not.

Another option would be to give the CCP legal basis priority over the CFSP legal bases for democratic reasons: Article 207(2) includes the Parliament as co-decision-maker; Articles 29 and 215 do not.[125] This approach is not convincing either. As the Court emphasised, a difference between a CFSP legal basis and a non-CFSP legal basis,

> so far as the Parliament's involvement is concerned, is the result of the choice made by the framers of the Treaty of Lisbon conferring a more limited role on the Parliament with regard to the Union's action under the CFSP.[126]

Article 207(2) should, therefore, not take priority over Articles 29 and 215 merely because the former involves the Parliament.

This chapter proposes a different option: Articles 29 and 215 and Article 207 simply exist as alternative legal bases. The following parts explain why. First, Article 215's origins suggest that the drafters did not aim to restrict the powers under the CCP when they added the specific sanctions legal basis to the Treaties. Second, Article 40 TEU excludes such a restriction.

A. Origins

In the 1960s, the white settler regime of Southern Rhodesia proclaimed independence from the United Kingdom. The UN Security Council responded with sanctions. UN members notably had to prohibit certain imports from Southern Rhodesia.[127] Such import bans specifically related to international trade. The EEC Member States, however, were reluctant to accept that measures with a foreign policy and security aim could fall within the scope of the CCP.[128] They therefore insisted on implementing the sanctions nationally.[129]

[125] On such a democratic approach in general, see S Garben, 'The Principle of Legality and the EU's Legitimacy as a Constitutional Democracy: A Research Agenda' in S Garben, I Govaere, and P Nemitz (eds), *Critical Reflections on Constitutional Democracy in the European Union* (Hart Publishing, 2019), 385–417.

[126] Case C-130/10 *Parliament v Council* [2012] ECLI:EU:C:2012:472, para 82.

[127] UN Security Council Resolution 232 of 16 December 1966 (Southern Rhodesia).

[128] Koutrakos, *Trade, Foreign Policy and Defence in EU Constitutional Law* (n 123), 58–59. See also PJ Kuyper, 'Sanctions against Rhodesia, The EEC and the Implementation of General International Legal Rules' (1975) 12 *Common Market Law Review* 231.

[129] C-D Ehlermann, 'Communautés européennes et sanctions internationals – Une réponse à J. Verhoeven' (1984–1985) 1 *Revue Belge de Droit International*, 96. To justify this, they relied on Article 224 TEEC. This provision allowed Member States to take measures 'to carry out obligations [they] ha[d] accepted for the purpose of maintaining peace and international security'.

This solution was not entirely satisfactory. Disparate implementations could hinder the common market.[130] In the 1980s, the Council therefore started to adopt trade-related sanctions in the context of the CCP.[131] A two-step structure emerged. The Member States first supported sanctions in the context of the European political co-operation (EPC) – the CFSP's more informal precursor. The Council then adopted the concrete sanctions based on Article 113 TEEC.[132]

The Maastricht Treaty formalised this. It introduced a European Union based on three pillars: a 'Community' pillar, a CFSP pillar, and a justice and home affairs pillar.[133] Maastricht thus introduced the CFSP. Within the Community pillar, it also introduced Article 228a TEC. Inspired by the pre-Maastricht two-step structure, this provision empowered the Council to take urgent measures to interrupt or reduce economic relations with a third country if needed to implement a decision under the CFSP.[134]

The new Article 228a cast doubts on the continued applicability of Article 113. Advocate General Jacobs summarised the problem in *Centro-Com*: 'there is now a specific legal basis in Article 228a of the EC Treaty for the adoption of embargo measures … Those amendments may have removed embargo measures from the scope of Article 113 of the Treaty.'[135]

Arguably, however, the drafters did not intend to limit Article 113's scope; rather, they added Article 228a to guarantee a sufficient legal basis to adopt economic sanctions.[136] Before Maastricht, two issues existed: the CCP's objectives scope was uncertain; and its subject matter scope was, in any case, not wide enough to cover all economic sanctions.

First, the Council was reluctant to accept that CCP measures could pursue foreign policy and security objectives.[137] It argued that CCP measures had to pursue a trade-related objective instead.[138] Although the two-step structure offered a practical compromise, scepticism remained. The first sanction based on Article 113 TEEC illustrates this. When the Polish communist regime suppressed

[130] C Schmitter, 'Article 228a' in V Constantinesco, R Kovar, and D Simon (eds), *Traité sur l'Union européenne, signé à Maastricht le 7 février 1992 – Commentaire article par article* (Economica, 1995) 758.

[131] Defalque and Luff (n 123) 101–02; S Bohr, 'Sanctions by the United Nations Security Council and the European Community' (1993) 4 *European Journal of International Law* 256, 266.

[132] Article 113 empowered the Council to 'implement … the common commercial policy'.

[133] Lenaerts, Van Nuffel, and Corthaut (n 6) 28–32. This pillar structure existed until the Lisbon Treaty. The 'Community' pillar comprised the European Community, the European Coal and Steel Community, and Euratom. Decisions generally happened via legislative procedures and were subject to Court of Justice scrutiny. The second and third pillars on common foreign and security policy and cooperation in the fields of justice and home affairs were different: they operated on an intergovernmental basis.

[134] Article 228a TEC thus formed a bridge between the Community pillar and the CFSP pillar. See Joined Cases C-402/05 P and C-415/05 P, *Kadi and Al Barakaat*, para 197.

[135] Opinion in Case C-124/95 *The Queen, ex parte Centro-Com v HM Treasury and Bank of England* [1996] ECLI:EU:C:1996:345, para 42. See also Schmitter (n 130) 763.

[136] Lenaerts and De Smijter (n 123) 449.

[137] Schmitter (n 130) 759.

[138] Answer of the Council of 17 March 1976 to Written Question No 526/75, OJ C 89/7.

Solidarność protests under Soviet threats, the Council noted, in the context of EPC, that 'a very large majority was in favour of a reduction in the Community's imports from the Soviet Union, to be carried out on the basis of Article 113'.[139] The Commission thus proposed the first trade-related sanction under a CCP legal basis.[140]

The sanction restricted Soviet Union imports into the EEC. It clearly pursued a foreign policy and security objective. However, it scarcely addressed this objective.[141] Its preamble merely noted that 'the interests of the Community require that imports from the USSR be reduced'.[142] This illustrates the Council's reluctance to refer to foreign policy and security objectives in a CCP measure. Denmark, in particular, criticised the CCP legal basis.[143] *Werner* later confirmed that these objectives concerns were ill-founded.[144] Nonetheless, they help explain why the drafters chose to introduce Article 228a.

Second, and more convincingly, the CCP competence's subject matter scope was too narrow to accommodate certain sanctions. This proved problematic when the Community tried to implement UN Security Council sanctions against Iraq and Kuwait.[145] The sanctions included bans on trade in certain services. But services – in particular, transport services – arguably fell outside the CCP's subject matter scope. The Council thus considered adding Articles 84 (transport) and 235 (flexibility clause) TEEC as legal bases.[146] However, this would have meant consulting the Parliament.[147] For urgency reasons, the Council ultimately based the measure on Article 113 alone.[148] But the Council also stressed that the use of Article 113 was not meant as a precedent for including services in the CCP.[149]

[139] EC Activities in February 1982, Bull. EC 2-1982, 49.

[140] Council Regulation (EEC) No 596/82 of 15 March 1982 amending the import arrangements for certain products originating in the USSR, OJ L72.

[141] Koutrakos, *Trade, Foreign Policy and Defence in EU Constitutional Law* (n 123) 60.

[142] Preamble of Council Regulation (EEC) No 596/82.

[143] E Stein and L Henkin, 'Towards a European Foreign Policy? The European Foreign Affairs System from the Perspective of the United States Constitution' in M Cappelletti, M Seccombe, and J Weiler (eds), *Integration Through Law: Europe and the American Federal Experience, vol 1, Book 3* (De Gruyter, 1986) 75.

[144] This also means that the two-step structure was not legally necessary or effective. The Community could have adopted trade sanctions under Article 113 regardless of prior EPC support. And if Article 113 had genuinely excluded trade measures with foreign policy and security aims, the EPC procedure could not have changed this. Under the principle of conferral, Member States could not simply invite the Community to act in the absence of 'competence'.

[145] UN Security Council Resolution 661 of 6 August 1990 (Iraq and Kuwait).

[146] General Secretariat, Project de compte rendu sommaire de la 1446ème reunion (Coreper), 8858/90, para 22.

[147] ibid, para 22.

[148] Council Regulation (EEC) No 3155/90 of 29 October 1990 extending and amending Regulation (EEC) No 2340/90 preventing trade by the Community as regards Iraq and Kuwait, OJ L304; General Secretariat, Mesures à l'égard de l'Iraq et du Koweït, 9221/90, 2. Member States also questioned whether the proposed measure pursued a Community objective for which the Council could invoke Article 235.

[149] General Secretariat, Note "Point A" – Adoption d'un Règlement empêchant les échanges concernant l'Iraq et le Koweït, 9505/90, Annex; General Secretariat, 9221/90, 1–2. The Commission issued a

This political solution was legally flawed. With or without a Council statement, the measure went beyond Article 113's subject matter scope, and thus infringed the principle of conferral. In this context, it is telling that Article 228a referred to 'economic relations'.[150] This was broader than the CCP concept of international trade. The Maastricht Treaty could have expanded the CCP's scope. As explained in chapter three, the drafters did indeed consider adding trade in services to Article 113, but chose not to. But Article 228a empowered the Council to adopt economic sanctions beyond the CCP's strict subject matter scope.[151] It provided a legal route for measures that had been adopted unlawfully before. That, rather than a limitation of Article 113, seems to have been the drafters' aim.

The Maastricht Treaty's preparatory documents support this. In April 1991, the Luxembourg Presidency presented a draft version of Article 228a.[152] It empowered the Council to restrict economic relations with third countries if necessary to honour international commitments or to safeguard important Union interests. Interestingly, this power would have existed 'in derogation from the provisions relating to the European Communities' – including Article 113.[153] The drafters did not adopt this wording; this suggests that they did not intend to limit Article 113's scope by introducing Article 228a.

The Council and the Commission shared this view.[154] When the Danes rejected the Maastricht Treaty, the Council explored possible solutions in a White Paper. One option involved excluding Denmark from the CFSP. Denmark could then not participate in economic sanctions based on Article 228a; however, it 'might be able to join in economic sanctions on the basis of Article 113'.[155] Similarly, the Commission mentioned in a 1993 GATT submission that the new Article 228a foresaw the adoption of economic sanctions '[i]n addition to the existing possibility of adopting such measures in the context of the common commercial policy'.[156]

Thus, the drafters introduced Article 228a as an explicit legal basis for the adoption of economic sanctions in the context of the new CFSP. But they arguably did not aim to limit the Council's powers under Article 113. That conclusion remains valid for Article 207.

similar statement when the Council adopted Council Regulation (EEC) No 2340/90 of 8 August 1990 preventing trade by the Community as regards Iraq and Kuwait, OJ L213.

[150] J Cloos, G Reinesch, D Vignes, and J Weyland, *Le traité de Maastricht: genèse, analyse, commentaires* (Bruylant, 1993) 361.

[151] Commission, Rapport sur le Fonctionnement du Traité sur l'Union européenne, SEC(95)731, 56.

[152] R Corbett, *The Treaty of Maastricht* (Longman Group, 1993) 267–88.

[153] Luxembourg Presidency, Non-paper – Draft Treaty articles with a view to achieving political union, 12 April 1991.

[154] Defalque and Luff (n 123) 106; Lenaerts and De Smijter (n 118) 449.

[155] Council, White Paper on Denmark and the Maastricht Treaty (1992) 191.

[156] GATT Trade Policy Review Mechanism, submission of the European Communities of 26 April 1993, C/RM/G/36, 17.

B. Article 40 TEU

There is a second reason why the import ban proposal may (also) be based on Article 207(2). That reason lies in Article 40 TEU:

> The implementation of the common foreign and security policy shall not affect the application of the procedures and the extent of the powers of the institutions laid down by the Treaties for the exercise of the Union competences referred to in Articles 3 to 6 of the Treaty on the Functioning of the European Union.
>
> Similarly, the implementation of the policies listed in those Articles shall not affect the application of the procedures and the extent of the powers of the institutions laid down by the Treaties for the exercise of the Union competences under this [CFSP] Chapter.[157]

This provision applies to the relationship between Article 207(2), on the one hand, and Articles 29 and 215, on the other hand. It means that the import ban proposal could be adopted under either the former or the latter. The following sections explain why.

1. *Applicability*

Article 40 is not entirely new. The Maastricht Treaty had already introduced a safeguarding clause that protected Community competences and powers from interference by the new Treaty on European Union.[158] Article M TEU stated that 'nothing in this Treaty shall affect the Treaties establishing the European Communities'.[159] The original safeguarding clause was, therefore, one-directional: it only protected Community competences and powers, not Union competences and powers.

The current Article 40 works both ways.[160] At first sight, this suggests that the CCP is now more vulnerable to CFSP interference than before. Yet, for the relationship between Articles 207 and 215, Article 40 has the opposite effect. Before, it remained unclear whether Article M also protected the Community's CCP competence and powers against interference by Article 228a. Article M applied to interference by the TEU; Article 228a, however, was placed in the TEC.

[157] Article 40 TEU (Lisbon).

[158] A Dashwood, 'External Relations Provisions of the Amsterdam Treaty' in D O'Keeffe and P Twomey (eds), *Legal Issues of the Amsterdam Treaty* (Hart Publishing, 1999) 221; DT Murphy, 'The European Union's Common Foreign and Security Policy: It is Not Far From Maastricht to Amsterdam' (1998) 31 *Vanderbilt Journal of Transnational Law* 871, 894–95.

[159] Article M TEU (Maastricht).

[160] T Konstadinides, 'EU Foreign Policy under the Doctrine of Implied Powers: Codification Drawbacks and Constitutional Limitations' (2014) 39 *European Law Review* 511, 524; RA Wessel, 'Resisting Legal Facts: Are CFSP Norms as Soft as They Seem?' (2015) 20 *European Foreign Affairs Review* 123, 139; T Lock, 'The not so free choice of EU member states in international dispute settlement' in M Cremona, A Thies, and RA Wessel (eds), *The European Union and International Dispute Settlement* (Hart Publishing, 2017) 124.

Today, Article 40 no longer refers to the TEU. Instead, it ensures that the implementation of the CFSP does not affect the application of the procedures and the extent of the powers under the CCP.[161] That implementation includes Article 215. As the Court of Justice confirmed, Article 215 implements the CFSP.[162] Thus, Article 40 also protects Article 207 against interference from Article 215, and vice versa.

Admittedly, the Court has not explicitly confirmed this. On the contrary, it has implied that Article 215 falls under the 'competences referred to in Articles 3 to 6 of the Treaty on the Functioning of the European Union' rather than the CFSP.[163] *Rosneft* concerned sanctions imposed on Russia for its aggression against Ukraine in 2014.[164] Again, there was an Article 29 Decision and an Article 215 Regulation. The Russian oil company argued that the Decision violated Article 40 because it set out the sanctions in detail.[165] In Rosneft's view, the details had to be laid down in the Regulation instead.

The Court rejected the claim. It found that the Decision did not exceed the boundaries of Article 29.[166] However, the Court did not rule out the application of Article 40 to the relationship between Articles 29 and 215, as such. That is regrettable. As mentioned, despite its place in the TFEU, Article 215 implements the CFSP. Article 29 clearly also implements the CFSP. This means that Article 40 does not apply to the relationship between these provisions. Of course, that does not mean that an Article 29 measure cannot be unlawful on the ground that it should have been based on Article 215. However, this would not entail an infringement of Article 40. Article 40 protects both Articles 29 and 215 against non-CFSP legal bases – and vice versa. These non-CFSP legal bases include Article 207. Article 40 is, therefore, relevant to the proposed import ban.

2. *Meaning*

This raises the question of what exactly Article 40 does.[167] In most cases, its impact is limited. The CJEU has interpreted Article 40 as a confirmation of the normal choice-of-legal basis rules.[168] A violation of Article 40 exists when the aim and content of an alleged CFSP measure points to a non-CFSP legal basis instead. The same applies when an alleged non-CFSP measure could (at least partially) have been adopted based on a CFSP legal basis.

[161] B Van Vooren, *EU External Relations Law and the European Neighbourhood Policy – A paradigm for coherence* (Routledge, 2012) 170.

[162] Case C-134/19 P *Bank Refah Kargaran v Council*, para 28.

[163] Article 40 TEU (Lisbon).

[164] Case C-72/15 *Rosneft* [2017] ECLI:EU:C:2017:236.

[165] ibid, para 84.

[166] ibid, paras 89–90.

[167] See also Wessel, 'Resisting Legal Facts: Are CFSP Norms as Soft as They Seem?' (n 160) 139.

[168] T Ramopoulos, 'The Institutional Structure' in R Schütze and T Tridimas (eds), *Oxford Principles Of European Union Law: The European Union Legal Order: Volume I* (OUP, 2018) 1076.

Tanzania illustrates this.[169] It concerned an EU–Tanzania Agreement on the transfer of suspected pirates. The Parliament claimed that the Council had wrongly concluded the Agreement under a sole CFSP legal basis. According to the Parliament, the Agreement also fell within the scope of the area of freedom, security, and justice competence. This was because it laid down obligations on cross-border judicial co-operation. However, the Parliament did not explicitly invoke Article 40.[170]

The CJEU did. It recalled the need to ensure compliance with Article 40. Crucially, it also linked this to the rules on the choice of legal basis.[171] Applying these rules, the Court found that the Agreement essentially aimed to protect international security.[172] Although the Agreement did contain obligations on cross-border judicial co-operation these obligations were an instrument to achieve that CFSP objective.[173] Thus, the normal rules on the choice of legal basis confirmed the Council's approach. This also excluded a violation of Article 40.

That the non-affectation clause often merely requires a correct application of the choice-of-legal-basis rules may explain why the CJEU does not always address the clause explicitly. *Al Qaeda* offers an illustration.[174] It concerned the legal basis for the EU implementation of UN Security Council sanctions on the al-Qaeda terrorist group. This notably included freezing funds. The Council adopted these sanctions on the basis of a CFSP Decision and an Article 215 TFEU Regulation.[175]

Supported by its Legal Service, the Parliament argued that the sanctions should have been based on Article 75 TFEU instead.[176] This provision empowered the Council and the Parliament to freeze funds to prevent and combat terrorism. The CJEU rejected this. Unlike Advocate General Bot, the judges remained silent on Article 40 TEU.[177] Arguably, however, their reasoning again boiled down to an application of the choice-of-legal-basis rules.

[169] Case C-263/14 *Parliament v Council* [2016] ECLI:EU:C:2016:435.

[170] See Advocate General Kokott's remark in Opinion in Case C-263/14, *Parliament v Council* [2015] ECLI:EU:C:2015:729, para 43: 'Even though, regrettably, the Parliament does not at any point refer expressly to Article 40 TEU, it clearly has in mind, from a substantive point of view, the problem addressed therein of the demarcation between the CFSP on the one hand and the "communitarised" policies on the other.'

[171] Case C-263/14 *Parliament v Council*, para 42.

[172] ibid, paras 48–53.

[173] ibid, para 54. Moreover, as Advocate General Kokott noted in her Opinion, the subject matter scope of the area of freedom, security and justice is geographically limited to the EU itself. This means that measures on cross-border judicial co-operation that aim to enhance security may only fall within the scope of the area of freedom, security and justice to the extent that they aim to enhance security within the Union. The Court only vaguely hinted at this with its reference to 'international security'. See Opinion in Case C-263/14 *Parliament v Council*, paras 63–66.

[174] Case C-130/10 *Parliament v Council*.

[175] Article 215(2) TFEU provides a legal basis for economic and financial sanctions against natural or legal persons and groups or non-State entities.

[176] Parliament Legal Service, Legal Opinion – Proposals for Council Regulations on restrictive measures, SJ-0592/09, D(2009)68509.

[177] Opinion in Case C-130/10 *Parliament v Council* [2012] ECLI:EU:C:2012:50, para 67.

The Court focused on objectives. It stressed that the fight against 'international terrorism' fell within the scope of the CFSP objectives. By contrast, Article 75's objectives, 'although complementary, do not have the same scope'. The judgment lacks clarity here. However, it appears that the judges accepted the Council's view that Article 75 applies to internal as opposed to international terrorism.

This approach is open to criticism. What exactly counts as internal terrorism remains unclear. Overlaps would, in any case, lead to difficulties in practice. Yet the ruling may be defensible from a competence perspective. Although the Court focused on objectives, it is better explained in terms of subject matter. The subject matter scope of the area of freedom, security and justice competence is geographically limited to the EU.[178] By contrast, the CFSP logically has a foreign dimension. From that perspective, distinguishing between internal and international terrorism makes sense. It again reflects the normal choice-of-legal-basis rules.

Legal scholars have noted that these rules may not always lead to an obvious solution.[179] This is especially because the Lisbon Treaty does not define specific objectives for the CFSP competence.[180] That hinders its delimitation with non-CFSP competences. However, a particular problem exists for the relationship between Articles 207 and (29 and) 215 in the context of trade restrictions with foreign policy and security objectives. Section II explained that the proposed import ban falls – fully – within the scope of the CCP competence and the power of Article 207(2). Section III pointed out that it also falls – fully – within the scope of the CFSP competence and the powers of Articles 29 and 215. The overlap is thus complete.

Here, Article 40 should play a more significant role. The normal choice-of-legal-basis rules do not offer a solution, because two equally applicable legal routes exist. Arguably, non-affectation should mean that both the CCP and the CFSP routes must be preserved. Articles 29 and 215 empower the Council to ban, in two steps, the import of Russian gas for foreign policy and security objectives. Article 207(2) empowers the Council and the Parliament to do the same. The EU institutions thus face a choice. They could take the CFSP route; they could also take the CCP route. The non-affectation clause is only meaningful if it preserves that choice.

[178] M Cremona, 'External Competences And The Principle Of Conferral' in R Schütze and T Tridimas (n 161) 1118; A Engel, *The Choice of Legal Basis for Acts of the European Union: Competence Overlaps, Institutional Preferences, and Legal Basis Litigation* (Springer, 2018) 39. See also Advocate General Kokott's Opinion in Case C-263/14 *Parliament v Council*, described in n 173 above.

[179] P Van Elsuwege, 'EU External Action after the Collapse of the Pillar Structure: In search of a New Balance between Delimitation and Consistency' (2010) 47 *Common Market Law Review* 987, 1004–08; A Dashwood, 'Article 47 TEU and the relationship between first and second pillar competences' in A Dashwood and M Maresceau (eds), *Law and Practice of EU External Relations* (CUP, 2008) 74–75 and 102; C Hillion, 'A Powerless Court? The European Court of Justice and the EU Common Foreign and Security Policy' in A Thies and M Cremona (eds), *The European Court of Justice and External Relations Law: Constitutional Challenges* (Hart Publishing, 2014) 60.

[180] See Article 21 TEU (Lisbon).

Combining both routes, by contrast, would contravene Article 40. Once the Council has imposed a trade restriction within the scope of the CFSP, that restriction must be implemented based on Article 215. Using Article 207(2) instead would encroach upon the implementation of the CFSP and violate Article 40. Conversely, requiring a CFSP Decision before the use of Article 207(2) would undermine the latter's power modalities. Of course, Article 40 also confirms that Article 207(2) should not take priority over Articles 29 and 215 simply because the former involves the Parliament as co-decision-maker.

It is true that the Court has not yet spoken on this issue. Perhaps it will reach a different conclusion. Arguably, however, Article 40 recognises Article 207(2) and Articles 29 and 215 as equally valid alternatives. In the absence of an Article 29 Decision, Article 40 protects the Council and the Parliament's powers to restrict trade based on Article 207(2). For Russian gas imports, that is precisely what the Commission proposes.

V. Conclusion

Thus, distinguishing between the different concepts of 'competence' leads to a more precise and nuanced analysis of whether the Council and the Parliament may ban the import of Russian gas, based on Article 207(2) TFEU. Arguably, the answer is affirmative. An import ban that pursues a foreign policy and security objective falls within the scope of the CCP competence. To the extent that it lays down a framework for the implementation of the CCP, it also reflects a 207(2) power.

The difficulty is that the same applies to the CFSP and Articles 29 TEU and 215 TFEU. An import ban that pursues a foreign policy and security objective also falls within the scope of the CFSP competence and the powers under Article 29 and 215. However, that does not undermine the applicability of Article 207(2). Article 215's origins suggest that the drafters did not intend to limit the scope of the CCP legal basis. Moreover, Article 40 TEU mutually protects Article 207(2) and Articles 29 and 215 from encroachment. Thus, the EU may arguably choose to adopt import bans with a foreign policy and security objective either under the former or the latter.

Some caveats apply. The exact meaning of Article 207(2)'s framework requirement is not yet clear. Neither is the Court's interpretation of Article 40. However, the concepts of 'competence' already provided a more precise and nuanced 'competence' analysis of international trade restrictions with a foreign policy and security objective. This is relevant to the proposal to ban the import of Russian gas. It also matters for any future trade restrictions on third countries that violate international law or threaten the EU's security.

PART 4

A Note of 'Competence' Optimism

The final part of this book – Part 4 – brings a note of 'competence' optimism. Chapter 1 explained how Article 95(1) served to fill the gaps in the ECSC's system of 'competence'. A similar, yet distinct, provision exists today. Through another set of legal disputes, the following Chapter 7 studies its history. It starts with the Rome Treaty and concludes with the Lisbon Treaty.

Like the chapters of Part 3, its approach is evaluative. It points out where the 'competence' analysis went wrong. The scope of the original flexibility clause was (too) open to interpretation and the Community institutions failed to adequately motivate their recourse to it. Yet this Part does more than addressing flaws in the legal 'competence' reasoning; it also shows that that legal reasoning improved over time. The flexibility clause gained precision. The institutions better justified the recourse to it. And a clearer (yet still imperfect) distinction between competence and power was part of the improvement. This Part thus brings a note of optimism. The EU's 'competence' analysis must become more rigorous and precise. The example of the flexibility clause shows that it can.

The chapter makes another important point. In its analysis of the flexibility clause's scope after the Maastricht Treaty, it examines the impact of Article 3b TEC. That provision introduced the first explicit principle of conferred competences in the Treaties. The conclusion of the examination is worth emphasising. Substantively, the new Article 3b did not bring any change. Chapter 1 already explained that the principles of conferred competences and of conferred powers both applied in the ECSC, even without explicit reference to the former. The history of Article 3b TEC confirms this for the EEC; 'competence' always mattered.

7

Filling the Gaps of the Treaty: The Encouraging Road to Article 352

After two critical chapters, this chapter shows how 'competence' reasoning can, indeed, improve. In the early days of the European Economic Community, the flexibility clause was so scarcely used that some feared it was 'destined to remain a dead letter'.[1] A few years later, its widespread use raised concerns instead.[2] But even when the introduction of alternative Treaty legal bases reduced recourse to the clause, critical voices continued to be heard.[3] Not all measures seemed to respect the boundaries of Community (and Union) 'competence'. There was also the more fundamental question whether the flexibility clause was at all compatible with the principle of conferral, and with national constitutional law.[4] Thus, the flexibility clause remained controversial. If clarity of scope and thorough motivation were crucial anywhere, it was here.

Yet both have been problematic in the history of the flexibility clause. Firstly, its scope was long unclear and remains somewhat undefined today. From Article 235 TEEC to Article 352 TFEU, the flexibility clause has served to fill gaps in the Treaty. It has provided necessary flexibility where Community or Union action is needed yet not specifically foreseen in the Treaties.[5] But precisely which gaps may be filled is less straightforward. Does the clause only grant means of action within existing policy fields, or does it enable action within new policy fields too? Arguably, that question is best answered in terms of competence and power.

[1] P Pescatore, *Le droit de l'intégration* (AW Sijthoff, 1972) 3.

[2] See, eg P Lachmann, 'Some Danish Reflections on the Use of Article 235 of the Rome Treaty' (1981) 18 *Common Market Law Review* 447, 448; JA Usher, 'The Gradual Widening of European Community Policy on the Basis of Articles 100 and 235 of the EEC Treaty' in HG Schermers and J Schwarze (eds), *Structure and Dimensions of European Community Policy* (Nomos, 1988) 25; P Pescatore in Institut d'études juridiques européennes (ed), *De l'union douanière à l'union économique: Actes du quatrième colloque sur la fusion des Communautés européennes, organisé à Liège les 23, 24 et 25 avril 1969* (Université de Liège, 1970) 256.

[3] See, eg R Schütze, 'Organized Change towards an "Ever Closer Union": Article 308 EC and the Limits to the Community's Legislative Competence' (2003) 22 *Yearbook of European Law* 79; A Dashwood, 'Article 308 EC as the Outer Limit of Expressly Conferred Community Competence' in C Barnard and O Odudu (eds), *The Outer Limits of European Union Law* (Hart Publishing, 2009) 39; S Weatherill, 'Competence Creep and Competence Control' (2004) 23 *Yearbook of European Law* 1.

[4] A von Bogdandy and J Bast, 'The European Union's vertical order of competences: the current law and proposals for its reform' (2002) 39 *Common Market Law Review* 227, 233; Cases 2 BvE 2/08 ea [2009] BVerfG; Cases 2 BvR 2134/92 ea [1993] BVerfG.

[5] Opinion in Case C-1/99 *Kofisa Italia* [2000] ECR I-00207 ECLI:EU:C:2000:498, para 34.

There has also been an issue of motivation. The flexibility clause's broad use often received criticism. Several measures did not appear to satisfy Article 235's conditions.[6] The Council, driven by political consensus, adopted them anyway. That, at least, was a common view. The reality may have been different. Often, Article 235 was not applied too widely; it simply was rather wide itself. Clearly setting out why could have eased some concerns. But the Community institutions frequently failed to do so. Perhaps more than the substance of the measures, their inadequate motivation was problematic.

Combined, these were serious flaws. That Article 235 could be interpreted as rather narrow or very wide was not ideal.[7] This could raise legal certainty issues.[8] Then again, the law simply is not always perfectly defined.[9] A more serious problem lay in the combination with inadequate motivation. In a Treaty system based on conferral, leaving undefined what has been conferred is one thing. It is quite another to fail to motivate why, within the scope of possibilities, a certain interpretation is followed. What is at stake here is the legitimacy of the EU legislator and, especially, the Court. 'Courts create their own legitimacy by the quality of their decisions.'[10] Repeatedly failing to explicitly address a major condition of one of the Treaty's more contentious legal bases is not, however, a sign of quality.

There is a bright side to this story. Over time, the flaws of textual unclarity and inadequate motivation lessened. This chapter follows the flexibility clause through three case studies. They cover the clause's evolution from Rome until Maastricht *(Birds)*, and from Maastricht until Lisbon *(Human Rights and Asset Freezing)*. The chapter concludes with the situation as it is now. In the Rome era, the clause was vague, and its application was insufficiently motivated. Post-Maastricht, the Court reshaped the understanding of the flexibility clause. It also paid renewed attention to the clause's conditions for application. The Lisbon Treaty, finally, consolidated the Court's understanding.

As always, there remains scope for criticism and improvement. Nonetheless, the clause's evolution is important. It offers constructive thinking. This book began with the German Constitutional Court's 'competence' anxieties. It argued that thinking in clearer conceptual terms offers a way to solving those anxieties. By recognising that 'competence' is about more than competence alone, this book proposes a more nuanced and precise analysis of whether the Union may act. The story of the flexibility clause shows that such improvements are not merely theoretical; they have already shaped an important part of the EU legal system as it exists today.

[6] eg Regulation (EEC) No 907/73 of the Council of 3 April 1973 establishing a European Monetary Cooperation Fund OJ L89; Council Directive 76/160/EEC of 8 December 1975 concerning the quality of bathing water OJ L31.

[7] JHH Weiler, 'Supranational Law and the Supranational System: Legal Structure and Political Process in the European Community' (Doctoral thesis, European University Institute 1982) 356.

[8] ML Dabin in Institut d'études juridiques européennes (n 2) 148.

[9] T Endicott, *Vagueness in Law* (OUP, 2000) 190.

[10] U Everling, 'The Court of Justice as a Decisionmaking Authority' (1984) 82 *Michigan Law Review* 1294, 1308.

I. Birds

'It is a creation of the law; it is a source of law; and it is a legal system.'[11] In those words, the Commission's first President described the EEC. The European Economic Community was a Community of law, no less than the European Coal and Steel Community was.[12] No more than the ECSC could the EEC act when the Treaty had not given it the competences and powers to do so.

In summary, the Rome Treaty established a customs union[13] with a common market[14] based on four freedoms[15] (goods, services, workers/persons, and capital) and approximation[16] of national laws. It also introduced common policies on agriculture[17] and transport,[18] as well as a common commercial policy.[19] Member States would co-operate in fields of social[20] and economic policy.[21] The EEC's competences and powers were thus generally limited to the economic sphere. Yet the Council adopted legislation on the conservation of wild birds.[22]

Today, the Birds Directive is a textbook example of overreaching Community action.[23] To adopt it, the Council relied on the flexibility clause:

> If action by the Community should prove necessary to attain, in the course of the operation of the common market, one of the objectives of the Community and this Treaty has not provided the necessary powers, the Council shall, acting unanimously on a proposal from the Commission and after consulting the Assembly, take the appropriate measures.[24]

The problems with the Community legislator's approach seemed obvious. Environmental concerns were nowhere to be seen in the Treaty, let alone as explicit

[11] W Hallstein, *Europe in the Making* (George Allen and Unwin, 1972) 30.
[12] See Chapter 1.
[13] Article 9 TEEC.
[14] Articles 2 and 8 TEEC.
[15] Pt 2, Titles I and III TEEC.
[16] Article 100 TEEC.
[17] Pt 2, Title II TEEC.
[18] Pt 2, Title IV TEEC.
[19] Pt 3, Title II, ch 3 TEEC.
[20] Pt 3, Title III TEEC.
[21] Pt 3, Title II TEEC.
[22] Council Directive 79/409/EEC of 2 April 1979 on the conservation of wild birds, OJ L130.
[23] See, eg D Chalmers, 'Inhabitants in the Field of Environmental Law' in P Craig and G De Búrca (eds), *The Evolution of EU Law* (OUP, 1999) 661; R Schütze, *From Dual to Cooperative Federalism: The Changing Structure of European Law* (OUP, 2017) 139 fn 38. Not all criticism of the Directive was recent. See the concise, but unsympathetic, mentions in AJ Easson, 'EEC Directives for the Harmonisation of Laws: Some Problems of Validity, Implementation and Legal Effects' (1981) 1 *Yearbook of European Law* 1, 7; PH Teitgen and J Mégret, 'La fumée de la cigarette dans la "zone grise" des compétences de la C.E.E' (1981) 17 *Revue trimestrielle de droit européen* 68, 73; and D Vandermeersch, 'The Single European Act and the Environmental Policy of the European Economic Community' (1987) 12 *European Law Review* 407, 411. See also JH Kaiser, 'Grenzen der EG-Zuständigkeit' (1980) 15 *Europarecht* 97, criticising Article 235's vagueness without explicitly mentioning the Birds Directive; and J Touscoz, 'L'action des communautés européennes en matière d'environnement' (1973) 9 *Revue trimestrielle de droit européen* 3, emphasising Article 235's limits as an environmental legal basis.
[24] Article 235 TEEC.

objectives.[25] And to situate the Directive in the sphere of the common market, the Council appeared to be 'clutching at economic straws'.[26] Scholars did not hesitate to criticise this illustration of a 'process of "creeping" centralisation'.[27] It was, to sum up, an era of 'radical law-making by consensus'.[28]

In reality, the Birds Directive tells a more complex story. There is no doubt that the legal basis justifications in its preamble are unsatisfactory. The preparatory works, however, suggest that this may not have been a problem of 'competence'. They show how the Commission and the Council did recognise the importance of a valid legal basis. Contrary to what the final result may reflect, both institutions' legal services were actively involved in the proceedings. Their discussions pierce the idea that the Directive was nothing more than a political project devoid of legal foundation.

This, in itself, is not surprising. Although the Rome Treaty did not explicitly state that the Community only enjoyed conferred competences and powers, the principle of conferral undoubtedly applied. Seeing it reflected in the legislative process was, therefore, unremarkable. Perhaps more unexpectedly, plausible arguments to identify the necessary competence and power to adopt the Directive were made. None of them ended up in the Directive's text, yet these arguments existed. That puts the Birds Directive in a different perspective. Its 'competence' justifications were indeed unsatisfactory. But its preparatory works suggest that this may have been a problem of motivation more than of substance.

The following analysis explores that idea. It first explains how the wording of the flexibility clause invited diverse interpretation. The clause's scope could be rather narrow, or very wide. Second, it examines where the Birds Directive was oriented in that range of legal possibilities. The Directive reflected a wider interpretation of Article 235. Yet it did not, arguably, cross the margins of what was lawful. Finally, the analysis looks at the inadequate motivation which gave the Birds Directive, and the flexibility clause in general, its notoriety.

A. The Many Faces of Article 235

Until the 1970s, the Council largely restricted its Article 235 measures to agriculture and the customs union.[29] This early hesitance gave way to a more enthusiastic approach. Article 235 provided a legal basis in areas ranging from monetary policy to environmental protection, often without explicit Community competence in

[25] S Weatherill, *Law and Integration in the European Union* (Clarendon Press, 1995) 51–52.

[26] Easson (n 23) 7.

[27] S Weatherill, 'Supply of and demand for internal market regulation: strategies, preferences and interpretation' in NN Shiubhne (ed), *Regulating the Internal Market* (Edward Elgar Publishing, 2006) 33; Schütze, *From Dual to Cooperative Federalism* (n 23), 139 fn 38.

[28] D Wyatt, 'The Growing Competence of the European Community' (2005) 16 *European Business Law Review* 483, 484.

[29] H Lesguillons, 'L'extension des compétences de la Communauté économique européenne par l'article 235 du Traité de Rome' (1974) 20 *Annuaire français de droit international* 886, 887.

those areas.[30] Although the flexibility clause only applied to the pursuit of the Community's objectives in the course of the functioning of the common market, political consensus in the Council seemed to overcome those limitations.[31]

Perhaps the reality was less straightforward. Article 235 did not authorise the Community to do whatever it desired.[32] In addition to several procedural requirements, four substantive conditions applied: the proposed act had to pursue a Community objective, in the course of the common market, and be necessary to attain that objective; finally, the Treaty could not include specific powers to enact it. Only if it satisfied all four conditions could the Council act.

The fourth condition proved most contentious in Luxembourg. The Court frequently dealt with claims that the legislator should,[33] or should not,[34] have chosen Article 235 as the legal basis instead of a specific Treaty provision. These cases concerned the basis for Community action. The clause's objectives and common market conditions, however, determined whether the Community could act at all. The present analysis thus focuses on these.

1. *Community Objectives*

Under Article 235, the Community could only act to attain 'one of the objectives of the Community'.[35] The difficulty lay, of course, in identifying what precisely constituted a Community objective.[36] The Treaty did not give a clear answer.[37]

Different commentators suggested different solutions. Some suggested a narrow view:[38] the objectives of the Community were those mentioned in the list of activities of Article 3 TEEC alone; Article 235 then only applied to fields for which a specific Treaty policy existed. Others read the condition more widely and also included the objectives mentioned in Article 2 TEEC.[39] After all, Article 3

[30] Working Group V (complementary competencies), Note by Mrs Lena Hjelm-Wallen on The Residual Competence: Basic Statistics on Legislation with a Legal Basis in Article 308 EC (CONV 2002–2003); A Tizzano, 'The Powers of the Community' in Commission (ed), *Thirty Years of Community Law* (Office for Official Publications of the EC, 1983) 60–63.

[31] von Bogdandy and Bast (n 4) 237; Weatherill, *Law and Integration in the European Union* (n 25) 51.

[32] V Constantinesco, 'Who's Afraid of Subsidiarity?' (1991) 11 *Yearbook of European Law* 33, 44; G Marenco, 'Les conditions d'application de l'article 235 du Traité CEE' (1970) 12 *Revue du marché commun* 147, 148.

[33] Case C-62/88 *Greece v Council* [1990] ECR I-01527 ECLI:EU:C:1990:153; Case C-350/92 *Spain v Council* [1995] ECR I-01985 ECLI:EU:C:1995:237.

[34] Case 8/73 *Hauptzollamt Bremerhaven v Massey-Ferguson* [1973] ECR-00897 ECLI:EU:C:1973:90; Case 45/86 *Commission v Council* [1987] ECR-01493 ECLI:EU:C:1987:163; Case 242/87 *Commission v Council* [1989] ECR-01425 ECLI:EU:C:1989:217.

[35] Article 235 TEEC.

[36] Weiler (n 7) 356.

[37] Schütze, 'Organized Change towards an 'Ever Closer Union' (n 3) 85; F Behrens, 'Die Umweltpolitik der Europäischen Gemeinschaften und Art. 235 EWGV' (1978) *Deutsches Verwaltungsblatt* 462, 465.

[38] Schütze, 'Organized Change towards an 'Ever Closer Union' (n 3) 84; Weiler (n 7) 357.

[39] T Hartley, *The Foundations of European Community Law* (OUP, 1981) 87; RH Lauwaars, *Lawfulness and legal force of community decisions* (AW Sijthoff, 1973) 85; Tizzano, 'The Powers of the Community' (n 30) 53.

referred to the purposes of Article 2.[40] A third view included objectives mentioned elsewhere in the Treaty, possibly even in the preamble.[41] Marenco, however, rightly remarked that preamble objectives should only serve to reinforce the objectives contained in the Treaty itself.[42]

1.1. Articles 2 and 3

To understand Article 235, therefore, first means to understand Articles 2 and 3. Article 2 entrusted the Community with the task to promote 'a harmonious development of economic activities, a continuous and balanced expansion, an increase in stability, an accelerated raising of the standard of living and closer relations between the States belonging to it'.[43] It also laid down two means to fulfil that task: the establishment of a common market and the progressive approximation of the economic policies of the Member States.[44]

Article 3 elaborated these means by setting out the Community's activities.[45] These activities ranged from 'the elimination, as between Member States, of customs duties and of quantitative restrictions on the import and export of goods, and of all other measures having equivalent effect'[46] to 'the association of the overseas countries and territories in order to increase trade and to promote jointly economic and social development'.[47]

Neither Article 2 nor Article 3 expressly mentioned 'objectives'.[48] However, the Court did not hesitate to read the objectives of the Community into both provisions. It clarified that the 'aims of the Community' were 'set out in Article 2 and enlarged upon in Article 3 of the Treaty'[49] and referred to the 'principles … and objectives set out in Articles 2 and 3'.[50] Although the Court sometimes distinguished between the objectives of Article 2 and the activities of Article 3,[51] it undoubtedly allowed the pursuit of the latter under Article 235. In *Massey-Ferguson*, the establishment of a customs union under Articles 3(a) and (b) qualified as a Community objective.[52]

[40] Weiler (n 7) 357.

[41] M Dony and J-V Louis, *Commentaire J. Mégret: le droit de la CE et de l'Union européenne – Relations extérieures* (Editions de l'Université de Bruxelles, 2005) 137.

[42] Marenco (n 32) 149.

[43] Article 2 TEEC.

[44] ibid; P-H Teitgen in Institut d'études juridiques européennes (n 2) 273.

[45] H von Boeckh, 'Grundsätze' in H von der Groeben and H von Boeckh (eds), *Kommentar zum EWG Vertrag I* (Verlag August Lutzeyer, 1958) 6.

[46] Article 3(a) TEEC.

[47] Article 3(k) TEEC.

[48] Article 3 does refer to the 'purposes' of Article 2.

[49] Case 249/81 *Commission v Ireland* [1982] ECR-04005 ECLI:EU:C:1982:402, para 28.

[50] Case 6/72 *Europemballage Corporation and Continental Can Company v Commission* [1973] ECR-00215 ECLI:EU:C:1973:22, 25.

[51] Case 270/80 *Polydor ea v Harlequin ea* [1982] ECR-00329 ECLI:EU:C:1982:43, para 16.

[52] Schütze, 'Organized Change towards an 'Ever Closer Union' (n 3) 85.

1.2. And Elsewhere?

Both Articles 2 and 3 thus laid down Community objectives. The question then arose whether the Community could also use Article 235 to pursue objectives found elsewhere in the Treaty. The answer seemed confirmatory. Two arguments supported a wider objectives view.

A first argument invoked the rationale behind Article 235. Like the Paris Treaty, the Rome Treaty established a Community with specific conferred competences and powers.[53] It also introduced Article 235 to fill the gaps in this specific system of conferral.[54] In the absence of specific powers (and competences), it provided the necessary flexibility to pursue the Community's objectives without requiring a cumbersome Treaty change.[55] In view of this flexibility function, it would have been be surprising if Article 235 had only filled the gaps of the more general Treaty objectives and not those arising in the context of the more specific objectives connected to a specific policy field.

A second argument stemmed from the Treaty's preparation. Article 235 resembled Article 95(1) TECSC, yet differences existed. One difference concerned objectives. The ECSC flexibility clause only applied in the pursuit of the objectives specified in Articles 2 to 4 TESCS;[56] the Rome version did not include such a restriction. Importantly, the preparatory documents confirm that the drafters considered Article 95 when designing Article 235.[57] The Common Market Group that introduced Article 235 instructed the jurists in the Drafting Group to fine-tune its wording based on Article 95.[58] It was, therefore, difficult to view the absence of a similar limitation in Article 235 as a mere accident. The 'objectives of the Community' stretched beyond Articles 2 and 3.

[53] M Lagrange, 'Les pouvoirs de la Haute Autorité et l'application du Traité de Paris' (1961) 79 *Revue du droit public et de la science politique* 40, 45; Marenco (n 32) 147; P Reuter, *Organisations européennes* (Presses Universitaires de France, 1970) 216, G Nicolaysen, 'Zur Theorie von den implied powers in den europäischen Gemeinschaften' (1966) 1 *Europarecht* 129, 129.

[54] GJP Kapteyn, 'Article 235' in P Herzog and H Smit (eds), *The Law of the European Economic Community, A Commentary on the EEC Treaty* (M Bender, 1976) 296 and 315; Weiler (n 7) 357.

[55] Dashwood (n 3) 36; G Barrett, 'Creation's Final Laws: The Impact of the Treaty of Lisbon on the "Final Provisions" of Earlier Treaties' (2008) 27 Yearbook of European Law 3, 39; V Engström, 'How to tame the elusive: Lessons from the Revision of the EU Flexibility Clause' (2010) 7 *International Organizations Law Review* 343, 345; P Gori, *Les clauses de sauvegarde des traités CECA et CEE* (UGA, 1967) 249; Tizzano, 'The Powers of the Community' (n 30) 51.

[56] P Gori, 'Art.95(1)–(2)' in R Quadri, R Monaco, and A Trabucchi (eds), *Trattato istitutivo della CECA: commentario* (Giuffrè, 1970) 1339; Gori, *Les clauses de sauvegarde des traités CECA et CEE* (n 55) 252.

[57] Tizzano, 'The Powers of the Community' (n 30) 60; Hartley (n 39) 87; Lesguillons (n 29) 894; Marenco (n 32) 149.

[58] Projet de rédaction des articles concernant la politique de conjoncture et les difficultés dans l'approvisionnement, CM3 153 MAE 424, 4; Rédaction approuvée par les chefs de délégation en ce qui concerne la politique de conjuncture, CM3 266 MAE 521, 4; P Pescatore, 'Les travaux du "groupe juridique" dans la négociation des traités de Rome' (1981) 34 *Studia Diplomatica* 159, 172.

2. The Common Market

An Article 235 measure not only had to pursue a Community objective;[59] it also needed to pursue this objective 'in the course of the operation of the common market'.[60] This second condition could be interpreted very widely or rather narrowly. Much depended on the meaning of the 'common market'.[61]

2.1. Market versus Economy

A narrower reading of Article 235 saw the common market as one of two means to pursue the Community's objectives.[62] Article 2 identified the Community's task as being to pursue its objectives 'by establishing a common market and progressively approximating the economic policies of Member States'.[63] From that duality seemed to follow that the flexibility clause could not apply to economic policy; it only applied in the framework of the common market.

What the 'common market' meant and which Treaty parts fell under its scope, however, remained unclear. The Treaty did not define it. Neither did, in exhaustive terms, the Court. Undoubtedly, the common market included the four freedoms and the rules on competition; the Court repeatedly confirmed that.[64] For some scholars, Article 235, therefore, only authorised measures ensuring the free movement of goods, services, capital, and workers/persons, and undistorted competition.[65] The progressive approximation of economic policies, by contrast, covered economic policy in the strict sense as well as agricultural, transport, commercial, and social policies.[66] These fell outside the clause's scope.

More often, the common market received a wider interpretation;[67] not only free movement and competition, but also many common policies fell within its

[59] A Tizzano, 'Quelques Observations sur le Développement des Compétences Communautaires' (1998) 48 Pouvoirs 81, 82.

[60] Article 235 TEEC.

[61] Scholars also debated what it meant to pursue an objective 'in the course of the operation of the common market', 'dans le fonctionnement du marché commun', or 'nel funzionamento del mercato commune' versus 'im Rahmen des Gemeinsamen Marktes' or 'in het kader van de gemeenschappelijke markt'. Some scholars saw the latter as wider than the former. The Commission read a framework notion in both, and this interpretation seems most convincing. See Commission, Communication relative à la mise en oeuvre du financement des aides aux EAMA, COM(67)107, 4; Marenco (n 32) 149.

[62] Marenco (n 32) 149; Tizzano, 'The Powers of the Community' (n 30) 53; Schütze, 'Organized Change towards an 'Ever Closer Union' (n 3) 88; Dashwood (n 3) 36; U Everling, 'Die allgemeine Ermächtigung der Europäischen Gemeinschaft zur Zielverwirklichung nach Art 235 EWGV' (1976) 11 *Europarecht* 2, 10.

[63] Article 2 TEEC.

[64] See, for instance, Case 32/65 *Italy v Council and Commission* [1966] ECR-00563 ECLI:EU:C:1966:42, 405; Case 78/70 *Deutsche Grammophon v Metro SB* [1971] ECR-00487 ECLI:EU:C:1971:59, para 8; Case 15/81 Schul [1982] ECR-01409 ECLI:EU:C:1982:135, para 33.

[65] H Ehring, 'Allgemeine und Schlußbestimmungen (Art.235)' in H von der Groeben and H von Boeckh (eds), *Kommentar zum EWG Vertrag II* (Verlag August Lutzeyer, 1958) 448.

[66] T Oppermann in Institut d'études juridiques européennes (n 2) 213.

[67] Dashwood (n 3) 36–37; A Giardina, 'The Rule of Law and Implied Powers in the European Communities' (1975) 1 *Italian Yearbook of International Law* 99, 106; Weiler (n 7) 361.

scope. These were the common agricultural policy (CAP), the common transport policy, and the common commercial policy with the common customs tariff. The Commission Legal Service supported this view. The Rome Treaty entrusted the realisation of its objectives to two '*grandes actions*'.[68] One of these was the establishment of the common market.[69] This consisted of the four freedoms, the competition policy, and the three accompanying common policies.[70] The second was the progressive approximation of the economic policies of the Member States.

This interpretation of Article 2 had clear consequences for the flexibility clause. It meant that Article 235 not only granted powers in the framework of the four freedoms and competition rules, but also in that of the common policies mentioned. But for economic policy, it did not apply.[71] Thus, the Council could not have lawfully relied on the clause to enact, for instance, some of its measures aimed at the creation of an economic and monetary union.[72]

2.2. An Alternative Perspective

The dichotomy between common market and economic policy could also be explained differently. To understand this, it is necessary to return to the Rome Treaty's origins. In April 1956, Belgian foreign minister Paul Henri Spaak presented a report, to the governments of the six ECSC Member States,[73] which would shape the future of the European project. The Spaak Report made a palette of suggestions for further economic integration.[74] Surpassing expectations, all its major themes entered the Treaty negotiations.[75] Although the eventual Rome Treaty, of course, differed from the Spaak Report, the latter's content thus remains worth revisiting.

Essentially, the Report proposed the creation of 'a large area committed to a common economic policy'.[76] This 'European common market'[77] required three types of action:[78] first, the abolition of restrictions on trade between the Member States; second, common rules to ensure undistorted competition, and concerted action to mitigate balance of payment difficulties; and third, measures to encourage

[68] Service Juridique de la Commission, Note sur la Cohésion économique et sociale UE(85) 137 (II), 1.
[69] ibid.
[70] ibid.
[71] RH Lauwaars, 'Artikel 235 als Grundlage für die flankierenden Politiken im Rahmen der Wirtschafts und Währungsunion' (1976) 11 *Europarecht* 100, 125.
[72] Giardina (n 67) 106.
[73] Rapport des chefs de délégation aux Ministres des Affaires Etrangères (1956) ('Spaak Report').
[74] P Bourguignon, 'De l'entrée en vigueur du traité de Paris à celle des traités de Rome' (1981) 34 *Studia Diplomatica* 293, 312.
[75] ibid, 313; J Mertens de Wilmars, 'La contribution des juristes belges à l'intégration européenne' (1981) 34 *Studia Diplomatica* 137, 148.
[76] Spaak Report (n 73) 8.
[77] ibid.
[78] ibid, 9–10.

development within the common market. All three were 'conditions for the establishment and operation of a common market'.[79]

The Report's logic was not one of common market versus economic policy. Rather, it focused on the common market and the action needed to establish it. Abolishing national restrictions alone would not suffice. '[A] common market [was] inconceivable without common rules, a common policy and common supervisory institutions.'[80] Thus, the Report proposed rules on competition,[81] harmonisation of national laws,[82] common policies for transport,[83] and balance-of-payment measures.[84] Agriculture fell under the heading of the first line of action, but the same logic applied. Alongside the abolition of barriers, a common agricultural market necessitated a common policy.[85]

To a large extent, this structure remained visible in the Rome Treaty. The final version did not maintain the threefold categorisation; instead, the Treaty distinguished between '[t]he foundations of the Community'[86] and the '[p]olicy of the Community'.[87] Under the former came, notably, the fundamental freedoms. The latter included competition rules, harmonisation of laws, and economic and social policy. The common transport and agricultural policies combined free movement and market intervention aspects,[88] but ended up in Part Two.

This all seems very technical. Yet it mattered for Article 235. For some, the Article 2 duality between common market and economic policy determined the scope of the flexibility clause. But the logic underlying that duality may not have been one of common market integration versus economic policies left to the Member States. Article 2 may not have referred to economic policies in a strict sense,[89] but to the common rules and co-operation needed for the common market in general. The Spaak Report distinguished between the abolition of national barriers to trade and the intervention on the market. Arguably, Article 2 followed the same logic.

Indeed, the drafters did not consider economic policy as a subject matter strictly separate from the common market. They emphasised that the common market would require some economic policy interventions.[90] That interrelation

[79] ibid, 16.
[80] ibid, 9.
[81] ibid, 43.
[82] ibid, 49.
[83] ibid, 55.
[84] ibid, 59.
[85] ibid, 37.
[86] Pt 2 of the TEEC.
[87] Pt 3 of the TEEC.
[88] Article 61(1) TEEC.
[89] As opposed to what would today constitute the Economic Policy under Chapter 1 of Title VIII of the TFEU.
[90] Document de travail N°6 – les institutions, CM3 30 MAE 530, 1; Directive N°1 à la Commission du Marché Commun, des investissements et des problèmes sociaux, CM3 23 MAE 68, 1.

was why the Commission later promoted the idea of an economic and monetary union. With the common market's progressive development, it argued, the need for further integration in the general economic sphere increased.[91] Of course, the Community institutions did not enjoy the same powers in economic policy as in the Treaty's common policies. Economic policy largely remained the province of the Member States.[92] But that did not mean that Article 2 divided two substantive fields of action based on their Community or Member State dominance. It could equally have set out the two means available for the creation and operation of the common market.

Article 235's origins support that alternative perspective. The Spaak Report did not propose a flexibility clause; only near the end of the Treaty negotiations did the Belgian delegation propose its introduction.[93] And they did so during the discussions on conjunctural policy;[94] that is, a part of economic policy. The preparatory documents do not reveal the content of those discussions. They do note that the delegations unanimously recognised the possibility of using the flexibility clause for the instalment of financial mechanisms.[95] They also show how the delegations invited the legal experts to include the clause in the Treaty's general provisions.[96] This suggests that Article 235 originated in the context of economic policy and only later developed into a more general clause.

Article 235's origins thus undermined the restrictive interpretation of the common market condition. Nevertheless, the conclusion of a vague provision inviting diverse interpretation still stands. Indeed, the preparatory documents contradicted the view that excluded economic measures from the clause's scope. However, nothing in the Treaty's wording reflected these origins. Only that wording had authentic legal value; Pescatore, who participated in the Rome Treaty negotiations, underlined that 'no credit at all' was to be attached to its preparatory documents.[97] These documents, therefore, cannot exclude the interpretative flexibility offered by the wording of the Treaty itself.

[91] Commission, A Plan for the Phases Establishment of an Economic and Monetary Union (1970); F Amtenbrink, 'Denationalizing Monetary Policy: Reflections on 60 Years of European Monetary Integration' in NN Shiubhne and LW Gormley (eds), *From Single Market to Economic Union* (OUP, 2012) 18–19.

[92] Spaak Report (n 73) 17; Dabin in *De l'union douanière à l'union économique* (n 2) 187.

[93] J Van Tichelen, 'Souvenirs de la négociation du Traité de Rome' (1981) 34 Studia Diplomatica 327, 342.

[94] Projet de rédaction des articles concernant la politique de conjoncture et les difficultés dans l'approvisionnement, CM3 153 MAE 424, 4; Projet d'articles concernant la politique conjoncturelle et les cas de pénurie, CM3 262 MAE 242.

[95] Projet de rédaction des articles concernant la politique de conjoncture et les difficultés dans l'approvisionnement, CM3 153 MAE 424, 4.

[96] ibid; Rédaction approuvée par les chefs de délégation en ce qui concerne la politique de conjoncture, CM3 266 MAE 521, 4.

[97] Pescatore, 'Les travaux du "groupe juridique" dans la négociation des traités de Rome' (n 58) 167. See also Bourguignon (n 74) 320–21.

B. The Birds Directive

In 1979, the Birds Directive came into existence. As its title suggested, it aimed to ensure the conservation of wild birds.[98] It obliged Member States to maintain bird populations at certain levels based on a balance between economic and other requirements.[99] To achieve those levels, the Directive notably prohibited most killing and marketing of birds.[100] For some species, however, exemptions existed. The Directive also allowed derogations for a number of reasons, and as a last resort.[101] Member States could, for instance, authorise the killing of birds 'to prevent serious damage to crops, livestock, forests, fisheries and water'.[102] Finally, there were also provisions on habitat protection.[103]

1. Legal Basis and Context

The Directive was not adopted to further economic objectives. It was an environmental protection measure which partially covered some elements of economic activity. Yet the Council adopted it under Article 235. This drew criticism.[104] Firstly, the Treaty did not yet expressly include environmental protection among its objectives.[105] Furthermore, the Council seemed to be 'clutching at economic straws' when it based its Directive on a provision that depended on a common market connection.[106]

The provisions on exploitation and marketing did indeed fall within the framework of the common market. Convincing arguments to include rules on bird hunting or natural habitats in this framework, however, were simply absent.[107] That the birds concerned formed an 'integral part of the heritage of the peoples of Europe' could not change that.[108] Neither could the fact that their protection constituted a typical 'transfrontier environment problem entailing common responsibilities for the Member States'.[109]

Nonetheless, the Directive did not come as a surprise.[110] In the 1972 Paris Summit, the Member States had declared that 'it was advisable to use as widely as possible all the provisions of the Treaties, including Article 235 of the EEC

[98] Article 1 of the Birds Directive, 79/409/EEC. See also JT Lang, 'The European Community Directive on Bird Conservation' (1982) 22 *Biological Conservation* 11.
[99] Article 2 of the Birds Directive, 79/409/EEC.
[100] ibid, Articles 5–9.
[101] ibid, Article 9.
[102] ibid, Article 9(1)(a), second indent.
[103] ibid, Articles 3 and 4.
[104] Usher (n 2) 32–33; Teitgen and Mégret (n 23) 73; Vandermeersch (n 23) 11.
[105] Weatherill, *Law and Integration in the European Union* (n 25) 52.
[106] Easson (n 23) 7.
[107] Schütze, *From Dual to Cooperative Federalism* (n 23) 139 fn 38.
[108] Preamble of the Birds Directive, 79/409/EEC.
[109] ibid.
[110] Tizzano, 'The Powers of the Community' (n 30) 60.

Treaty'.[111] A year later, the first Community Environmental Action Plan (EAP) was announced.[112] From then on, the use of Article 235 significantly increased and grew into a cornerstone of the EEC's environmental policy.[113]

Formally, the Paris Summit Declaration and the EAP respected the principle of conferral. The Declaration called for a wide use of Article 235, but only within the limits of the law.[114] The EAP underlined that it 'should in some cases be carried out at Community level, and in others be carried out by the Member States'.[115] The perception, however, differed. A consensus among Member States and institutions on the need for action seemed to overcome the Treaty's limits. The Birds Directive, in particular, strengthened these concerns. On the one hand, it followed the political line of the 1973 EAP; on the other hand, it reflected citizens' strong emotions triggered by bird documentaries.[116] If any context could facilitate measures adopted on the basis of political and popular considerations, this was it.

The Court never ruled on the validity of the Birds Directive, but the French Conseil d'Etat did. With clear conviction, it rejected any suggestion that the Directive could not be adopted under Article 235.[117] Behind this conviction may have hidden a desire to avoid a preliminary reference to the Court. Or perhaps the Conseil d'Etat genuinely believed that the Directive could be based on the flexibility clause. Its preparatory documents suggest that this option is not so implausible after all.

2. *Birds and the Common Market*

One striking feature of the Bird Directive's preparations is how much legal reasoning they contained. Regardless of the lawfulness of the eventual measure, extensive 'competence' discussions did take place. Both the Commission and Council legal

[111] Solemn Declaration of the Heads of State and Governments of the Member States of the enlarged Community (1972) Bull EC Supplement 10/72, point 15.

[112] Council and Representatives of the Governments of the Member States, Declaration of 22 November 1973 on the programme of action of the European Communities on the environment, OJ C112.

[113] T Konstadinides, 'Drawing the line between Circumvention and Gap-Filling: An Exploration of the Conceptual Limits of the Treaty's Flexibility Clause' (2012) 31 *Yearbook of European Law* 227, 232; J Van Zeben, 'Subsidiarity in European Environmental Law: a competence allocation approach' (2014) 38 *Harvard Environmental Law Review* 415, 425; L Azoulai, 'Introduction' in L Azoulai (ed), *The Question of Competence in the European Union* (OUP, 2014) 6.

[114] Solemn Declaration of the Heads of State and Governments of the Member States of the enlarged Community (1972) Bull EC Supplement 10/72, point 15.

[115] Council and Representatives of the Governments of the Member States, Declaration of 22 November 1973 on the programme of action of the European Communities on the environment, OJ C112.

[116] Chalmers (n 23) 661; European Parliament, Written Questions 321/73, OJ C160, 666/73 OJ C49, and 412/74, OJ C156.

[117] Cases 94359-94936 *Ministre délégué chargé de l'environnement et Fédération Rhône-Alpes de protection de la nature v Fédération départementale des chasseurs de l'Isère et autres* [1990] Receuil des décisions du Conseil d'Etat, 133; WPJ Wils, 'The Birds Directive 15 Years Later: A Survey of the Case Law and a Comparison with the Habitats Directive' (1994) 6 *Journal of Environmental Law* 219, 224.

services worked to ensure that the measure did not go without valid legal basis. This attention to competence and power should, of course, be self-evident; conferral applied. Nonetheless, it is reassuring to see it confirmed in a Directive known as a core illustration of 'competence creep'.[118]

The Commission initially proposed the Directive based on Articles 100 (common market harmonisation) and 235.[119] The Parliament requested the addition of Article 43 (CAP).[120] In a partial response, the Commission changed the proposed legal bases to Articles 43 and 235.[121] The Council finally only used the flexibility clause. Not all Member States agreed. Germany regretted the absence of Article 100 and doubted whether Article 235 sufficed as legal basis.[122] Denmark questioned the general applicability of Article 235.[123] Both Member States also denied the Directive any precedent role.[124]

Before the Directive's adoption, in-depth legal discussions took place. The legal services of the Commission and the Council advised on its legal basis.[125] The former argued in favour of Articles 43 and 235; the latter defended Article 235 as sole legal basis.

2.1. The Council Legal Service

The Council Legal Service first rejected Article 100 as legal basis for the Directive's marketing parts. The Service noted that the Directive prohibited trade in all but some wild birds.[126] Such a ban, it argued, did not constitute harmonisation; it also signalled an environmental protection rather than a common market objective. Article 100, therefore, did not apply.[127]

Second, the Service studied Article 235. It omitted to independently verify whether the proposed Directive pursued a Community objective. Instead, the Service was satisfied that 'the Council [had] already given its own answer', in several

[118] S Garben, 'Restating the Problem of Competence Creep, Tackling Harmonisation by Stealth and Reinstating the Legislator' in S Garben and I Govaere (eds), *The Division of Competences between the EU and the Member States: Reflections on the Past, the Present and the Future* (Hart Publishing, 2017) 300.

[119] Commission, Proposal for a Council Directive on bird conservation, COM(76)676.

[120] Parliament, Resolution on the Proposal for a Directive on bird conservation (1977) OJ C24, point 2.

[121] Commission, Modifications of a proposal for a Council Directive on bird conservation, COM(77)379.

[122] Council, Introductory note on the Adoption of the Council Directive on the conservation of wild birds, 4643/79.

[123] ibid.

[124] ibid.

[125] Council Legal Service, Note on the Proposal for a Council Directive on bird conservation, R/1867/77; Services de la Commission, Document de travail (Analyse juridique) sur la Proposition de directive concernant la conservation des oiseaux, SEC(77)3035.

[126] ibid, 3–4.

[127] Note the contrast with later internal market harmonisation measures: see, eg Case C-210/03 *Swedish Match* [2004] ECR I-11893 ECLI:EU:C:2004:802 and Case C-154/04 *Alliance for Natural Health and others* [2005] ECR I-06451 ECLI:EU:C:2004:848.

EAPs, that bird protection fell under Article 2 of the Treaty.[128] Next, it found that no other Treaty provision granted the necessary powers to act.[129] Finally, it argued that it was for the Council to decide whether the measure was necessary.[130]

Remarkably, the Council Legal Service did not explain how the proposed Directive fulfilled the common market condition. Compliance with that condition did not even feature in the Opinion. The Service thus ignored one of the core conditions for the application of the flexibility clause; a condition which, at least at first sight, was not fulfilled.

2.2. The Commission Legal Service

The Commission Legal Service reached a different conclusion; it proposed a dual legal basis of Articles 43 and 235. Summarised, Article 43 applied to the Directive's marketing aspects. Wild birds fell within the subject matter scope of the common agricultural policy.[131] Article 43 could not, however, carry the entire Directive. The Service thus proposed Article 235 as joint legal basis. Importantly, its Opinion did (implicitly) explain how the objectives and the common market conditions were satisfied.

First, on objectives, the Commission Legal Service referred to Article 2's reference to 'the harmonious development of economic activities' and 'an accelerated raising of the standard of living'.[132] It proposed an evolutive reading. As a 'consequence of industrial development', the importance of environmental problems had been progressively revealed.[133] In those circumstances, protecting birds as part of a qualitative improvement of living conditions fell under the Article 2 objectives.[134]

Undeniably, that was a very wide interpretation of the Article 235 objectives condition. But it was not an impossible one. Although the Treaty did indeed remain silent on environmental objectives, it was plausible to argue that a healthy environment contributed to improved living conditions, and that a harmonious economic activity required some environmental standards.

Second, the question arose whether the proposed Directive pursued these objectives within the course of the functioning of the common market. While the Commission Legal Service did not address this condition expressly, it did so implicitly. It again connected the Birds Directive with the CAP. On the one hand, birds aided agriculture by controlling insects.[135] If that biological balance

[128] Council Legal Service, Note on the Proposal for a Council Directive on bird conservation, R/1867/77, 5.
[129] ibid, 7.
[130] ibid.
[131] Services de la Commission, Document de travail (Analyse juridique) sur la Proposition de directive concernant la conservation des oiseaux, SEC(77)3035, 3–4.
[132] Article 2 TEEC.
[133] Services de la Commission, Document de travail (Analyse juridique) sur la Proposition de directive concernant la conservation des oiseaux, SEC(77)3035, 4.
[134] ibid.
[135] ibid, 3.

got upset, farmers would need to use environmentally harmful pesticides instead. Those pesticides would, in turn, detrimentally affect birds. On the other hand, the Service pointed to the link between agriculturally cultivated land and bird habitats.[136]

The Commission Legal Service thus implied that Article 235 could be used when the operation of the common market jeopardised the attainment of a Community objective. That explained the connections made between birds and agriculture. Studies commissioned by the Commission had shown that agriculture negatively affected bird habitats.[137] A common market activity thus negatively affected a Community objective. Article 235 could be used to mitigate this.

This logic was not new. A few years earlier, the Council had adopted a Regulation establishing a Regional Development Fund, based on Article 235.[138] A well-functioning common market required a Community regional policy.[139] But there was a second justification. Although the Regulation only vaguely referred to it,[140] the Commission proposal was more explicit; it identified 'the tendency for companies to locate themselves in already highly developed regions'.[141] Importantly, it acknowledged that '[t]he achievement of the common market [was] in itself likely to strengthen this tendency'.[142] The flexibility clause thus also served to offset negative consequences of the common market.

3. *Inadequate Motivation*

The Council Legal Service won the debate. The Council adopted the Birds Directive under Article 235 alone. Regrettably, it did not include the more sophisticated reasoning of the Commission Legal Service. To many critics, the Directive's provisions on general species and habitat protection seemed far removed from market concerns. The preamble offered little to prove them wrong. However, the problem was not that no plausible arguments for the flexibility clause existed; it was, rather, that the Council saw no need to show that all its conditions had been fulfilled.

To make matters worse, this was not an isolated issue. The Court showed the same apparent lack of interest in the common market condition. None of its judgments on Article 235 explicitly examined compliance with that condition. In *Massey-Ferguson*, for instance, the Court confirmed Article 235 as legal basis for

[136] ibid.

[137] S Cramp, *Bird Conservation in Europe* (HMSO, 1977); B Grzimek, European Commission study entrusted to the Zoologischen Gesellschaft von 1858 (1974).

[138] Regulation (EEC) No 724/75 of the Council of 18 March 1975 establishing a European Regional Development Fund, OJ L73.

[139] J-V Louis, 'Le Fonds européen de coopération monétaire' (1973) 3 *Cahiers de droit européen* 255, 289.

[140] Preamble of Regulation (EEC) No 724/75 of the Council of 18 March 1975 establishing a European Regional Development Fund, OJ L73.

[141] Commission, Proposal for a Council Regulation establishing a Regional Development Fund, COM(73)1170, 1.

[142] ibid.

a Council Regulation on the valuation of goods for customs purposes. The judges only explicitly verified whether the Regulation pursued a Community objective and whether no specific customs union powers applied.[143] They ignored the common market condition.

In another case, the Court briefly explained why the European Centre for the Development of Vocational Training had been lawfully established by an Article 235 measure.[144] Again, the Court mentioned objectives. The Centre would 'contribute, by its activity, to achieving the objectives of the Communities and in particular to the harmonious development of economic activities'.[145] Again, however, the Court did not explicitly address the common market condition.

The Court also condoned the Council's inadequate motivation. In *Erasmus*, the Commission challenged the Council's use of Article 235 for the research aspects of a student mobility scheme.[146] In its view, the relevant recital was 'drawn up in vague and imprecise terms which shed no light on the reasons that led the Council to have recourse to Article 235 as a legal basis'.[147] That recital explained that the vocational policy legal basis was insufficient, that the action contributed to the harmonious development of economic activities, and that it was 'necessary to attain, in the course of the operation of the common market, one of the objectives of the Community'.[148] Once again, there was no common market motivation. Yet the Court dismissed the claim. It found that the Council had 'unequivocally' expressed its conviction that 'the Treaty had not provided the necessary powers within the meaning of Article 235'.[149] Motivating the fulfilment of the common market condition was, apparently, not needed.

In reality, these measures did pursue their objectives in the course of the functioning of the common market. *Massey-Ferguson* concerned the customs union. The Centre promoted the development of vocational training relating to access to economic activity on the common market. The *Erasmus* decision promoted research as a motor for economic growth and encouraged mobility in the common market.[150] 'Competence' was, therefore, not an obvious problem. But the Court did not show that. By ignoring the common market condition, it gave the flawed impression that the Council could use Article 235 whenever it found a Community objective and no specific competences and powers to attain it.

The same problem existed for the Birds Directive. There was a plausible justification for the use of Article 235, but the Council ignored it. That was why the Directive became so notorious. But it was also why the Commission Legal Service,

[143] Case 8/73 *Massey-Ferguson*, 3–4.
[144] Case 16/81 *Alaimo v Commission* [1982] ECR-01559 ECLI:EU:C:1982:154, 12.
[145] ibid.
[146] Case 242/87 *Commission v Council* [1989] ECR-01425 ECLI:EU:C:1989:217.
[147] ibid, para 38.
[148] Preamble of Council Decision 87/327/EEC of 15 June 1987 adopting the European Community Action Scheme for the Mobility of University Students (Erasmus), OJ L166.
[149] Case 242/87 *Commission v Council*, para 39.
[150] V Mitzner, *European Union Research Policy: Contested Origins* (Springer, 2020) 63.

after recognising that 'efforts had to be undertaken to better show the existence [...] of incontestable economic elements and to explain [the] direct or indirect connections with a subject-matter governed by the Treaty', emphasised that that was 'perfectly possible' for the Birds Directive.[151]

II. Human Rights and Asset Freezing

From birds, the analysis now turns to human rights and asset freezing. With the Maastricht Treaty, both flexibility clause problems – its unclear scope and the inadequateness of the motivation for its application – evolved. Without changing the clause's wording, the Treaty gave Article 235 (now TEC) a new meaning. Moreover, the Court finally addressed the common market condition.

First, *Opinion 2/94* announced a change in Article 235's scope. The Court famously ruled that the Community had 'no competence' to accede to the European Convention for the Protection of Human Rights and Fundamental Freedoms (ECHR).[152] For the first time, the judges stressed the limits of the flexibility clause in the light of the principle of conferral.[153] Article 235 only applied within the general framework of the Community's tasks and activities.[154]

This was a turning point. It is best explained through the lens of competence and power. In the Rome years, Article 235 TEEC enabled the Community to legislate in new fields, such as the environment. It thus granted both powers to act in existing fields of competence and competences to enter new fields. Maastricht altered that. Article 235 TEC only granted powers within existing fields of competence. The Council could no longer use the flexibility clause to act in new fields.

Second, *Kadi* brought change to Article 235's motivation.[155] In this complex case on suspected terrorism support, asset freezing, and international obligations, the Court for the first time explicitly verified whether an Article 235 (then 308) measure pursued a Community objective 'in the course of the functioning of the common market'.[156] This was a fundamental step. Even if the common market condition was a lenient one, the lack of attention to it was problematic. By explicitly addressing the condition in *Kadi*, the Court moved towards a better statement of reasons.

[151] Service Juridique de la Commission, Note sur les Difficultés soulevées par le Danemark à l'égard de certaines applications de l'Article 235 du Traité CEE, SEC(80)403/3, 11.

[152] Opinion 2/94 *Adhésion de la Communauté à la CEDH* [1996] ECR I-01759 ECLI:EU:C:1996:140, para 36.

[153] Director-General of the Commission Legal Service, Note on Opinion 2/94 (1996); Schütze, 'Organized Change towards an 'Ever Closer Union' (n 3) 93.

[154] Opinion 2/94, para 30.

[155] Case T-315/01 *Kadi v Council and Commission* [2005] ECR II-03649 ECLI:EU:T:2005:332; Joined Cases C-402/05 P and C-415/05 P *Kadi and Al Barakaat International Foundation v Council and Commission* [2008] ECR I-6351 ECLI:EU:C:2008:461.

[156] Article 308 TEC (Amsterdam and Nice). See also Articles 235 TE(E)C.

A. Human Rights

Would the accession of the European Community to the Convention for the Protection of Human Rights and Fundamental Freedoms … be compatible with the Treaty establishing the European Community?'[157] – that was the fundamental question in *Opinion 2/94*. The Court answered negatively. What follows is an exploration of the ruling itself, the modifications to the scope of the flexibility clause signalled in it, and the foundations behind those modifications.

1. *Power, not Competence:* Opinion 2/94

'[A]s Community law now stands, the Community has no competence to accede to the Convention':[158] the Court thus disappointed those who hoped that the Community could rely on Article 235 to join the ECHR. Central in its ruling stood the Maastricht Treaty's new Article 3b. For the first time, that provision explicitly stated that '[t]he Community shall act within the limits of the powers conferred upon it by this Treaty and of the objectives assigned to it therein'.[159] The Court emphasised that this principle of conferral 'must be respected', both internally and in the Community's international action.[160]

After ruling out a specific legal basis, the Court examined whether Article 235 applied.[161] This was not the case. The Court famously ruled as follows:

> Article 235 is designed to fill the gap where no specific provisions of the Treaty confer on the Community institutions express or implied powers to act, if such powers appear none the less to be necessary to enable the Community to carry out its functions with a view to attaining one of the objectives laid down by the Treaty.
>
> That provision, being an integral part of an institutional system based on the principle of conferred powers, cannot serve as a basis for widening the scope of Community powers beyond the general framework created by the provisions of the Treaty as a whole and, in particular, by those that define the tasks and the activities of the Community. On any view, Article 235 cannot be used as a basis for the adoption of provisions whose effect would, in substance, be to amend the Treaty without following the procedure which it provides for that purpose.[162]

The ECHR accession would not meet these requirements. Although fundamental rights formed 'an integral part of the general principles of law whose observance the Court ensures',[163] and their respect was 'a condition for the lawfulness of

[157] Commission, Request for an Opinion pursuant to 228 TEC [1994] OJ C174.
[158] Opinion 2/94, para 36.
[159] Article 3b TEC (Maastricht).
[160] Opinion 2/94, para 24.
[161] ibid, para 28.
[162] ibid, paras 29–30.
[163] ibid, para 33.

Community acts',[164] the constitutional implications of accession were too significant to be brought outside a Treaty amendment.[165] The Community thus lacked 'competence' to accede to the ECHR.[166]

Actually, the Opinion did not seem to be about competence at all.[167] The Court never examined whether the flexibility clause covered human rights as a field of competence.[168] Instead, it focused on the implications of accession for the Community legal order. These implications were predominantly institutional.[169] An accession to the ECHR would encroach upon the Court's monopoly of jurisdiction over Community law.[170] It would upset the balance of powers in the Community legal order. Even more fundamentally, accepting jurisdiction of the ECHR Court would reduce the autonomy of the Community legal order.[171]

None of this was about competence. What the Court really said was that Article 235 could not authorise a certain type of measure – a measure that modified the Community legal order and judicial system of human rights protection.[172] Since ECHR accession constituted such a measure, the Court did not need to examine the question of competence. Even if the flexibility clause included an unspecified competence in the field of human rights, it could not grant a power to change the Community system as a whole.

2. *Power, not Competence: Article 235*

So, *Opinion 2/94* reflected concerns of power. It did not say so much about the Community's competence in the field of human rights. Even if there had been a human rights competence, it could never have come with a power to change the Community's legal set-up. Nonetheless, the Court's wider ruling did indicate a fundamental competence-related shift. Article 235 could not 'serve as a basis for widening the scope of Community powers beyond the general framework created

[164] ibid, para 34.
[165] ibid, paras 34–35.
[166] ibid, para 36.
[167] J Odermatt, 'The Principle of Autonomy: An Adolescent Disease of EU External Relations Law?' in M Cremona (ed), *Structural Principles in EU External Relations Law* (Hart Publishing, 2018) 312.
[168] J Kokott and F Hoffmeister, 'Opinion 2/94, Accession of the Community to the European Convention for the Protection of Human Rights and Fundamental Freedoms' (1996) 90 *American Journal of International Law* 664, 666–67; G Gaja, 'Opinion 2/94, accession by the Community to the European Convention for the Protection of Human Rights and Fundamental Freedoms' (1996) 33 *Common Market Law Review* 973, 984; Konstadinides (n 113) 235.
[169] Opinion 2/94, paras 35–36.
[170] Articles 164 and 219 TEC.
[171] Case 26/62 *Van Gend en Loos* [1963] ECR-00003 ECLI:EU:C:1963:1, 12; Case 6/64 *Costa v E.N.E.L.* [1964] ECR-01141 ECLI:EU:C:1964:66, 593; Opinion 1/09 *Accord sur la création d'un système unifié de règlement des litiges en matière de brevets* [2011] ECR I-01137 ECLI:EU:C:2011:123, para 65; Konstadinides (n 113) 236.
[172] S Peers, 'Case C-268/94, Portugal v. Council, (development policy)' (1998) 35 *Common Market Law Review* 539, 543.

by the provisions … that define the tasks and the activities of the Community'.[173] Arguably, this meant that the flexibility clause no longer authorised the Community to act in new competence fields.

The reference to 'activities' is crucial. In the Treaty, the Community's activities were listed in Articles 3 and 3a. These Articles suggested that 'activities' were, rather, policy fields. There was mention of the environment, the internal market, fisheries, etc. The activities thus reflected what are now the Union's competences.[174] Admittedly, Articles 3 and 3a did not exhaustively list all Community activities.[175] But activities, or policy fields, which did not appear either in the specific Treaty provisions or in the Article 3 and 3a lists could not be considered Community activities. Neither, therefore, could Article 235 apply.

The previous section did not emphasise it, but the Rome Treaty situation was different. Just as in the ECSC,[176] the flexibility clause originally granted both competences and powers. As long as a measure pursued a Community objective in the framework of the common market, it could go beyond the Community's existing competences.[177] The Birds Directive illustrated this for the environment. The Maastricht Treaty, as interpreted in *Opinion 2/94*,[178] changed that.

3. *Power, not Competence: The Maastricht Treaty*

It would be tempting to think that Article 3b caused the change. This provision introduced the principle of conferral of Community competence. Until then, the Treaty had only explicitly stipulated that the Community institutions enjoyed powers to the extent that they were conferred upon them. However, it remained silent on the conferral of competence. Article 3b changed that.

Admittedly, the drafters failed to be conceptually consistent. The French, Italian, Greek, and Spanish versions mentioned competence.[179] By contrast, the

[173] Opinion 2/94, para 30.

[174] See Articles 3–6 TFEU.

[175] K Bradley, 'Powers and procedures in the EU constitution: legal bases and the court' in P Craig and G De Búrca (eds), *The Evolution of EU Law* (OUP, 2011) 100.

[176] See Chapter 1.

[177] The preparatory works of the Single European Act confirm this. The drafters considered procedural amendments to Article 235. A (rejected) proposal would have allowed the Council to act by qualified majority in competence fields that already existed in the Treaty or in which the Community had already acted. In new competence fields, Article 235 would continue to require unanimity. See Groupe Union européenne, Extension des possibilités de vote à la majorité au Conceil, UE(85)37/2, 1–4; Groupe Union européenne, Propositions pour renforcer le processus décisionnel de la Communauté, UE(85)81, 3.

[178] Later judgments did not contradict this. None of the Article 235 or 308 measures approved by the Court went beyond the Community's existing competences. See, eg Case C-436/03 *Parliament v Council* [2006] ECR-I 03733 ECLI:EU:C:2006:277; Case C-209/97 *Commission v Council* [1999] ECR-I 08067 ECLI:EU:C:1999:559.

[179] As mentioned in Chapter 2, a distinction between competence and power currently does not exist in the Dutch Treaty versions. The Portuguese version referred to attributions rather than competence or power.

English, German, and Danish versions referred to the limits of the Community's powers. The former were more accurate. Article 3b focused on the Community as a whole; it did not protect the balance of *power* between the institutions, but the balance of *competence* between the Community and the Member States.

In substance, however, Article 3b was not new. 'Competence' had always mattered. Article 3b's drafting history confirms that. It is, therefore, unpersuasive that the introduction of an explicit Community-oriented principle of conferral (of competence) would have triggered Article 235's refined scope. The real reason may instead lie in a few modest changes to the list of Community activities.

3.1. The Road to Maastricht

From the start, the EEC only enjoyed the competences and powers conferred upon it in the Treaty.[180] Much like in the ECSC, however, the Rome Treaty focused on the division of power between the Community institutions. Article 4(1) TEEC only confirmed the principle of conferral of powers to these Community institutions. Intense institutional negotiations explained that focus.[181]

In the ECSC, the institutional emphasis lay on the High Authority.[182] To reflect the shift from '*traité-loi*' to '*traité-cadre*',[183] the Spaak Report proposed a Council of Ministers as the predominant Community institution.[184] The Dutch delegation, however, insisted on a strong role for a supranational Commission.[185] The EEC's eventual institutional design was the compromise result of intensive debates. This explains why the Rome Treaty focused on the powers of the Community institutions and only implicitly confirmed the attribution of competences to the EEC as a whole.

For the first time, the Maastricht Treaty explicitly stated that the Community as a whole had to act within the limits of its powers – or (more accurately) competences. The new Article 3b stated that '[t]he Community shall act within the limits of the powers [French: *compétences*] conferred upon it by this Treaty and of the objectives assigned to it therein'.[186] It was the result of an evolving awareness of the 'competence' question in the Member States.

[180] Tizzano, 'The Powers of the Community' (n 30) 44.

[181] Pescatore, 'Les travaux du "groupe juridique" dans la négociation des traités de Rome' (n 58) 80; P Craig, 'Institutions, Power, and Institutional Balance' in P Craig and G De Búrca (eds), *The Evolution of EU Law* (OUP, 2011) 39.

[182] See Chapter 1.

[183] Reuter, *Organisations européennes* (n 53) 188; M Lagrange, 'L'Europe institutionelle: Réflexions d'un témoin' (1971) *Revue du marché commun* 216, 222; B Beutler, *Die Europäische Gemeinschaft* (Nomos, 1982) 40.

[184] Spaak Report (n 73) 25.

[185] A Boerger-De Smedt, 'Negotiating the Foundations of European Law, 1950–57: The Legal History of the Treaties of Paris and Rome' (2012) 21 *Common European History* 339, 349.

[186] First para of Article 3b TEC (Maastricht).

A few years earlier, in 1986, the signature of the Single European Act had caused a 'watershed' in the Community.[187] It involved the European Parliament in the legislative process. It also replaced unanimous voting with qualified majority voting in important fields of competence. This included the broad internal market harmonisation power.[188] The Single European Act thus sparked fears in the Member States of a European (market) integration process covering ever more and wider fields, to the detriment of their own competences.[189]

Yet the Single European Act still did not include an explicit Community-oriented principle of conferral. Its focus remained on the conferral of power to the Community's institutions. The genuine shift came with Maastricht. The Maastricht Treaty introduced new legislative powers for the Parliament, increased qualified majority voting in the Council, and conferred novel fields of competence on the Community. A deepening of this nature also led to growing worries over the boundaries of Community 'competence'.

3.2. The Principle of Subsidiarity (and Conferral)

Article 3b served to soothe these 'competence' concerns. It did not, however, do so by introducing a Community-oriented principle of conferral of competence; that principle always existed. The real novelty was the principle of subsidiarity. Just like Article 5(3) TEU today, Article 36 TEC designed subsidiarity as a tool to decide whether the Community should act (but not whether it might act).[190]

Although subsidiarity only reached the Treaties as a self-standing principle with Article 3b, its roots date back further. Already, in 1975, the Commission had seen its potential as a counterweight to the increase of Community competences.[191] In 1984, so did the Parliament. Its ambitious new Draft Treaty for a European Union would significantly expand the Community (or Union)'s competences.[192] To balance this, it would also state that: 'The Union shall only act to carry out those tasks which may be undertaken more effectively in common than by the Member States acting separately.'[193] The Parliament's proposal was never adopted.

[187] Craig, 'Institutions, Power, and Institutional Balance' (n 181) 54.

[188] Article 100a TEEC (SEA).

[189] K Van Kersbergen and B Verbeek, 'The Politics of Subsidiarity in the European Union' (1994) 32 *Journal of Common Market Studies* 215, 219.

[190] Presidency, Conclusion on the European Council (Edinburgh, 11–12 December 1992), SN456/1/92 Rev1, 16. The drafters of the Treaty also applied a subsidiarity test when granting new competences to the Community. They only did so if these areas could be better dealt with at the Community level. See Presidency, Conclusions on the European Council (Rome, 27–28 October 1990), SN304/90 Rev2, 3; Presidency, Conclusions on the European Council (Rome, 14–15 December 1990), SN424/1/90 Rev1, 10; Parliament, Resolution on the principle of subsidiarity (1990) OJ C231, 14.

[191] AL Teasdale, 'Subsidiarity in post-Maastricht Europe' (1993) 64 *The Political Quarterly* 187, 189; L Tindemans, Report on European Union (1975) Bull EC supplement 1/76.

[192] Teasdale, 'Subsidiarity in post-Maastricht Europe' (n 191) 188.

[193] Parliament, Draft Treaty establishing the European Union (1984) Article 12(2).

A few years later, however, the Single European Act set the first official subsidiarity step. It introduced the principle in the field of the environment.[194] The Maastricht Treaty added the principle more generally.[195] The Parliament and then Commission President Jacques Delors, in particular, advocated for its inclusion. They expressed federal aspirations for the Community and saw subsidiarity as a reflection – not a contradiction – of these aspirations.[196]

Contemporary legal developments in Germany supported that federalist view. Some foundations of subsidiarity may have been present in the German legal system earlier.[197] In the Basic Law, however, the principle only really gained expression in the Maastricht era.[198] The German unification and accompanying accession of new *Länder* had led to an expression of subsidiarity in Germany's own federal context.[199] It was, therefore, not surprising that those who aspired to deepen the European integration also advocated for the introduction of subsidiarity in the Treaties.

At the same time, the principle clearly suited those who worried about precisely such federal aspirations.[200] Probably the most notorious example was the United Kingdom.[201] Germany, for its part, occupied a middle ground. On the one hand, its Länder cautiously guarded their competences, since the Single European Act had brought regional competences, such as the environment, into the Community sphere.[202] On the other hand, Germany did favour further integration in a federalist style. Subsidiarity suited both those federal aspirations and the desire to limit them. Thus, the principle's greatest asset may have been its ability to please very divergent points of view.

Interestingly, the early subsidiarity drafts showed a significant overlap with the principle of conferral. A first proposal came from the Parliament. It included an idea of conferral as an element of the principle of subsidiarity. Article 3a would have stipulated the following:

> The Community shall act only to fulfil the tasks conferred on it by the Treaties and to achieve the objectives defined therein. Where powers have not been exclusively or

[194] Article 130r(4) SEA.

[195] Article 3b TEC (Maastricht).

[196] J Delors, Speech at the Opening session of the 40th academic year of the College of Europe (1989) Bull EC 10; Conference of European Community Parliaments, Final declaration (Rome, November 1990) 23; Parliament, Resolution on the Intergovernmental Conference in the context of Parliament's strategy for European Union (1990) OJ C96; R Corbett, *The Treaty of Maastricht: From Conception to Ratification: A Comprehensive Reference Guide* (Longman, 1993) 18.

[197] J Isensee, *Subsidiaritätsprinzip und Verfassungsrecht* (Ducker & Humblot, 2001) 35.

[198] J Schwarze, 'Le principe de subsidiarité dans la perspective du droit constitutionnel allemand' (1993) 370 *Revue du marché commun* 615, 617.

[199] Article 72(2) of the Grundgesetz für die Bundesrepublik Deutschland [1994]; G Taylor, 'Germany: The subsidiarity principle' (2006) 4 *International Journal of Constitutional Law* 115, 117. A new Article 23 also mentioned subsidiarity in the Community context.

[200] J Cloos, G Reinesch, D Vignes, and J Weyland, *Le traité de Maastricht: genèse, analyse, commentaires* (Bruylant, 1993) 141.

[201] A Blair, *The UK & the Negotiation of the Maastricht Treaty, 1990–1991* (Doctoral thesis, University of Leicester 1997) 138.

[202] Constantinesco (n 32) 37.

> completely assigned to the Community, it shall, in carrying out its tasks, take action wherever the achievement of these objectives requires it because, by virtue of their magnitude or effects, they transcend the frontiers of the Member States or because they can be undertaken more effectively by the Community than by the Member States acting separately.[203]

The Luxembourg Presidency drew on the Parliament's proposal.[204] In a non-paper, it proposed an updated version that referred to the Community's 'powers' instead of 'tasks'. But, as the Parliament had done earlier, the Presidency presented the idea of conferral as part of the principle of subsidiarity. Its draft Article 3b stated:

> The Community shall act within the limits of the powers conferred upon it by this Treaty and of the objectives assigned to it therein. In the areas which do not fall within its exclusive jurisdiction, the Community shall take action, in accordance with the principle of subsidiarity, if and insofar as those objectives can be better achieved.[205]

The principle of conferral was not only hidden in the text of the draft Treaty; it also remained in the background in the negotiations in general. The drafters did not explicitly distinguish between conferral and subsidiarity in the negotiations. The two concepts were seen as closely interrelated, or even confused.[206] Preparatory documents of the Maastricht Treaty showed only a limited interest – if any – in the principle of conferral as such. A 1991 Commission document discussing the main negotiation topics prominently mentioned subsidiarity; however, it remained silent on conferral.[207]

So did the conclusions of the European Council.[208] They repeatedly referred to subsidiarity. Conferral, by contrast, did not appear as a concept to be added to the Treaty. Only after the signature of the Treaty did the European Council expressly identify the three distinct principles covered by Article 3b (conferral, subsidiarity, and proportionality).[209] If conferral had been an important element of the negotiations, surely the conclusions would have mentioned it more centrally.

Moreover, those Member States who most strongly supported limiting the Union's competences did not emphasise the principle of conferral either. Two months before the Luxembourg non-paper, the United Kingdom proposed a

[203] Parliament, Resolution on the Intergovernmental Conferences in the context of the European Parliament's strategy for European Union (1990) OJ C324.

[204] Presidency, Conclusions on the European Council (Dublin 28 April 1990), SN/46/3/90.

[205] Presidency, Non-paper on the Draft Treaty Articles with a view to achieving Political Union, CONF-UP 1800/91, 12.

[206] Constantinesco (n 32) 49; Parliament, Resolution on a draft constitution for the European Union (1990) OJ C231. Commission, Communication to the Council and the European Parliament on the principle of subsidiarity (1992) Bull EC, 10.

[207] Commission, Programme for 1991, Bull EC supplement 1/91, 23.

[208] Presidency, Conclusions on the European Council (Dublin, 28 April 1990), SN/46/3/90; Presidency, Conclusions on the European Council (Rome, 27–28 October 1990), SN304/90 Rev2; Presidency, Conclusions on the European Council (Rome, 14–15 December 1990), SN424/1/90 Rev1.

[209] Presidency, Conclusion on the European Council (Edinburgh, 11–12 December 1992), SN456/1/92 Rev1, 13–15.

subsidiarity article which was less oriented towards conferral than the non-paper.[210] Although its draft provision did replace the Parliament's reference to 'tasks' with 'powers', it did not even contain a separate sentence on conferral.[211]

Thus, conferral did not occupy a crucial place in the Maastricht negotiations.[212] Its importance, rather, derived from its connection to subsidiarity. Subsidiarity governed the exercise of power within a field of competence. It was logical to then also clarify that power only existed if it had been conferred; or, more accurately, that the Community institutions only enjoyed conferred powers in fields of competence conferred upon the Community. But, as the European Council confirmed in its 1992 Edinburgh Conclusions, that was nothing new.[213]

3.3. Article 3

These origins explained why the Council Legal Service ignored conferral in a post-Maastricht note on Article 3b's impact on the flexibility clause.[214] The Service merely remarked that Article 235's necessity condition was to be interpreted in view of subsidiarity.[215] It remained silent on Article 3b's first paragraph. Conferral was not noteworthy, because it was not new. It therefore could not have changed the scope of the flexibility clause. Even in the absence of Article 3b, *Opinion 2/94* would thus have produced the same outcome.

An alternative explanation for Article 235's changed scope exists. Indeed, Article 3b merely confirmed that the Community only enjoyed conferred competences. Since the Maastricht reforms, however, these competences arguably had to be specifically identified in the Treaty. The flexibility clause could no longer add them. Article 3 TEC explained why. Before Maastricht, this provision listed the Community's activities. All these activities were developed further in other Treaty provisions. After Maastricht, that changed.

The Maastricht Treaty added several activities to the Article 3 list. Crucially, that list included activities which did not reappear elsewhere in the Treaty.[216] The Community could adopt 'measures in the spheres of energy, civil protection and tourism'.[217] Yet there was no specific Treaty competence (and thus power) to do so. During the negotiations, specific legal bases had been considered.[218] They did not

[210] United Kingdom delegation, Note to the IGC on Political Union (subsidiarity), CONF-UP 1721/91 Annex 3.

[211] ibid.

[212] See, eg Permanent Representation of Belgium to the European Communities, Contribution to a joint study of the prospects for political union, 5519/90; Présidence, Non-paper sur les Compétences, UP/7/91.

[213] Presidency, Conclusion on the European Council (Edinburgh 11-12 December 1992), SN456/1/92 Rev1, 14.

[214] Service Juridique du Conseil, Avis sur la relation entre les articles 3B et 235 TCE, 9404/92.

[215] ibid, 5.

[216] K Lenaerts and M Desomer, 'Bricks for a Constitutional Treaty of the European Union: values, objectives and means' (2002) 27 *European Law Review* 377, 386 and 393.

[217] Article 3(t) TEC (Maastricht).

[218] General Secretariat, Note on Political Union – Outcome of the proceedings of the personal representatives of the Ministers for Foreign Affairs, 10356/90, 2; Conference of the Representatives

survive. The Commission, therefore, declared that it would propose Community action in those spheres under the existing Treaty provisions.[219] Article 235 applied. The later negotiations on a Constitutional Treaty supported this interpretation.[220]

Thus, the Maastricht Treaty added three spheres of Community activity to the Treaty, without specific corresponding competence (and power) provisions. Perhaps it was purely a matter of symbolism. A declaration added to the Maastricht Treaty announced the possibility of future specific Treaty titles on energy, tourism, and civil protection.[221] The addition in Article 3 could simply have reflected this endeavour. Arguably, however, its importance was greater than that. By identifying those fields in which the Community could act without a specific legal basis, the drafters cast doubts over the applicability of the flexibility clause to fields which had not reached the Treaty. Under the Rome Treaty, Article 235 conferred unspecified competence in the field of the environment. The Maastricht version, albeit textually identical, no longer permitted this.

B. Asset Freezing

The Maastricht Treaty did not change the text of Article 235. Thus, the common market condition logically continued to apply. In this context, the post-Maastricht era produced a second milestone: *Kadi* concerned a measure adopted under the flexibility clause. Much has been written about the question whether the measure did or did not pursue a Community objective as required under Article 308 TEC.[222] There is, however, a different point to be made. For a long time, the Court seemed to ignore the flexibility clause's common market condition. With *Kadi*, that changed. At last, the judges ruled on a measure's compliance with the condition.

1. Kadi *and the Common Market*

Mr Kadi, a Saudi Arabian resident, successfully challenged his inclusion on a list annexed to Council Regulation (EC) No 881/2002.[223] The Regulation implemented UN Security Council Resolutions on the freezing of assets of persons suspected of terrorism support. They identified Mr Kadi as such a person, although this was

of the Governments of the Member States, Non-paper on Political Union – Powers, CONF-UP 1824/91.

[219] Member States, Declaration on civil protection, energy and tourism (1992) OJ C191.

[220] Convention Praesidium, Note on the Delimitation of competence between the European Union and the Member States, CONV 47/02, 8; Convention Secretariat, Final report of Working Group V, CONV 375/1/02 Rev1, 15.

[221] Member States, Declaration on civil protection, energy and tourism (1992) OJ C191.

[222] See J Kokott and C Sobotta, 'The Kadi Case – Constitutional Core Values and International Law – Finding the Balance?' (2012) 23 *European Journal of International Law* 1015; M Cremona, 'EC Competence, "Smart Sanctions", and the Kadi Case' (2009) 28 *Yearbook of European Law* 559; K Lenaerts, 'The Kadi Saga and the Rule of Law within the EU' (2014) 67 *SMU Law Review* 707.

[223] First instance in Case T-315/01 *Kadi v Council and Commission*; Appeal in Joined Cases C-402/05 P and C-415/05 *P Kadi and Al Barakaat.*

later reversed.[224] Article 2 of the contested Regulation thus imposed the freezing of the assets of, among others, Mr Kadi. After an unsuccessful attempt at the Court of First Instance (CFI), the Court of Justice (ECJ) annulled the Regulation. It did so on grounds unrelated to conferral. Not a lack of 'competence', but a violation of fundamental rights, rendered the measure unlawful.[225]

Nevertheless, *Kadi* was worth discussing from a conferral perspective too. One of the Regulation's legal bases was the flexibility clause. The question arose whether the clause indeed applied. The CFI explicitly rejected Article 308 as sole legal basis.[226] So did, implicitly, the ECJ, on appeal.[227] To understand why, it is necessary to recall the pre-Lisbon pillar structure: the European Community, the common foreign and security policy, and justice and home affairs.[228] The flexibility clause only applied to Community objectives. If the Regulation pursued CFSP objectives, Article 308 could not constitute its sole legal basis.

Article 308 combined with Articles 60 and 301 TEC was a different matter. The latter provisions authorised the Community to take economic measures against third countries (not their nationals) following a CFSP position or action.[229] Both the CFI and the ECJ confirmed the validity of this triple legal basis. However, they did so on different grounds. The CFI argued that Articles 60 and 301 provided a bridge between the Community and Union pillars.[230] These provisions thus 'imported' EU objectives into the EC legal order.[231]

The ECJ's approach was more nuanced. It accepted the existence of a bridge between the economic measures under Articles 60 and 301 and the objectives of the TEU, but refused to extend it to other Community provisions.[232] The Council could not use Article 308 to pursue EU objectives.[233] However, the Regulation did indeed pursue a Community objective.[234] Articles 60 and 301 'provide[d] for Community powers to impose restrictive measures of an economic nature in order to implement actions decided on under the CFSP'.[235] In doing so, these provisions were 'the expression of an implicit underlying objective, namely, that of making it possible to adopt such measures through the efficient use of a Community instrument'.[236] The Regulation aimed to do the same. Thus, it pursued a Community objective and Article 308 applied.

[224] Lenaerts (n 222) 707.
[225] Joined Cases C-402/05 P and C-415/05 P *Kadi and Al Barakaat*, para 371.
[226] Case T-315/01 *Kadi v Council and Commission*, paras 85 and 121.
[227] Joined Cases C-402/05 P and C-415/05 P *Kadi and Al Barakaat*, paras 212–16; Cremona, 'EC Competence, "Smart Sanctions", and the Kadi Case' (n 222) 280.
[228] W Van Gerven, *The European Union: A Polity of States and Peoples* (SUP, 2005) 7.
[229] See Chapter 6.
[230] Case T-315/01 *Kadi v Council and Commission*, 123–25.
[231] Cremona, 'EC Competence, "Smart Sanctions", and the Kadi Case' (n 222) 575.
[232] Joined Cases C-402/05 P and C-415/05 P *Kadi and Al Barakaat*, paras 195–97.
[233] ibid, paras 198–200.
[234] Dashwood (n 3) 40.
[235] Joined Cases C-402/05 P and C-415/05 P *Kadi and Al Barakaat*, para 226.
[236] ibid.

This reasoning drew some criticism that the ECJ had 'confuse[d] means with objectives'.[237] In his Opinion, Advocate General Maduro correctly stressed that Article 308 was 'strictly an enabling provision: it provide[d] the means, but not the objective'.[238] Thus, that provision only applied if the adoption of economic sanctions against individuals constituted an objective of Articles 60 and 301. But if it did, exactly these Articles 60 and 301 already provided a legal basis.[239]

The issue with this criticism is that it failed to distinguish between competence and power. When the Court unveiled the implicit objective behind Articles 60 and 301, it also identified the competence connected to these provisions. The Community enjoyed the competence to implement, in an economic sphere, the decisions taken under the CFSP. Within that field of competence, Articles 60 and 301 empowered the Council to adopt measures against states.[240] Within the same field of competence, Article 308 did the same for measures against individuals.

Much has been written about the question whether the Council Regulation did or did not pursue a Community objective.[241] Most interesting to this analysis, however, was the ECJ's approach to the common market condition. *Opinion 2/94* did not address this requirement. For the first time, the appeal ruling in *Kadi* did.[242] This finally remedied a significant deficiency in the Court's reasoning on the flexibility clause. More than the Community-oriented principle of conferral in Article 3b, that should have reassured those Member States anxious about wide(ning) Community competences.

2. *The Common Market Condition Explained*

Kadi interpreted the common market condition widely. To be 'in the course of the operation of the common market', a link with the common market sufficed.[243] More precisely, the ECJ held that the unilateral imposition of economic restrictions by the Member States

> might well affect the operation of the common market. Such measures could have a particular effect on trade between Member States, especially with regard to the movement of capital and payments, and on the exercise by economic operators of their right of establishment.[244]

[237] T Tridimas, 'Terrorism and the ECJ: Empowerment and Democracy in the EC Legal Order' (2009) 34 *European Law Review* 103, 107; Konstadinides (n 113) 247.

[238] Opinion in Joined Cases C-402/05 P and C-415/05 P *Kadi and Al Barakaat* [2008] ECR I-6351 ECLI:EU:C:2008:11, para 15.

[239] Cremona, 'EC Competence, "Smart Sanctions", and the Kadi Case' (n 222) 585; Tridimas (n 236) 110.

[240] Konstadinides (n 113) 244.

[241] Kokott and Sobotta (n 222) 1015; Cremona, 'EC Competence, "Smart Sanctions", and the Kadi Case' (n 222) 559; Tridimas (n 236) 901.

[242] Joined Cases C-402/05 P and C-415/05 P *Kadi and Al Barakaat*, para 229.

[243] ibid.

[244] ibid, para 230.

This could also distort competition, 'because any differences between the measures unilaterally taken by the Member States could operate to the advantage or disadvantage of the competitive position of certain economic operators although there were no economic reasons for that advantage or disadvantage'.[245] While the internal market's Article 95 excluded 'abstract risks', the flexibility clause was, therefore, much more lenient.[246]

One year later, another judgment confirmed the common market condition's wide interpretation. Discussing the legal basis of a Council Regulation on contributions to the International Fund for Ireland, the Court ruled that the objective 'to bring about economic improvements in disadvantaged areas of two Member States' fell 'within the framework of the common market', 'and thus relate[d] to the functioning of the common market'.[247] The judgment thus confirmed, after 30 years, at least part of the logic behind the creation of the Regional Development Fund.[248]

It is not surprising that the Court decided to explicitly address the common market condition after Maastricht. During the Treaty negotiations, both the Luxembourg and the Dutch Presidencies proposed to replace the condition with a reference to Articles 3 and 3a.[249] The Commission campaigned for 'a new Article 235 freed from its economic purpose'.[250] Neither proposal was accepted. The common market condition was a major negotiation topic and the drafters decided to retain it.[251] That made it even more difficult for the Court to ignore.

III. Conclusion: Lisbon

The story began with birds. Today, scholars often see the Birds Directive as a triumph of political consensus over legal reality. Its preparatory documents show a more nuanced picture. The flexibility clause could be interpreted widely or narrowly. Under the former, the Directive was defensible. However, the Council failed to adequately motivate why it could adopt the Directive. In its rulings on Article 235, the Court did the same.

Maastricht brought two changes. First, as clarified by *Opinion 2/94*, Article 235 no longer granted competences. It only provided the means (powers) to act within an existing field of competence. This followed from changes to Article 3 TEC.

[245] ibid.

[246] Case C-58/08 *Vodafone and others* [2010] ECR I-04999 ECLI:EU:C:2010:321, para 30.

[247] Case C-166/07 Parliament v Council [2010] ECR I-07135 ECLI:EU:C:2009:499, para 67.

[248] See section I.B.2.2. in this chapter.

[249] Presidency, Non-paper on the Draft Treaty Articles with a view to achieving Political Union CONF-UP 1800/91, 71; Presidency, Draft Treaty on the Union, CONF-UP 1845/91, 104.

[250] General Secretariat, Note on Political Union – Outcome of the proceedings of the personal representatives of the Ministers for Foreign Affairs, 10356/90, 6.

[251] Council Legal Service, Comments on draft Article 235, SEC(91)2144; Cloos, Reinesch, Vignes, and Weyland (n 200) 135–36.

Second, the Court in *Kadi* ended the unfortunate silence on the common market condition.

For now, the story ends with Lisbon. The Lisbon Treaty introduced the current flexibility clause. It copied the text of the draft Constitutional Treaty.[252] The clause's inclusion in that draft Treaty was not a given. In 2001, the European Council announced that it was time 'to clarify, simplify and adjust the division of competence between the Union and the Member States in the light of the new challenges facing the Union'.[253] This also influenced the debates on the flexibility clause.[254] Some drafters saw the clause as a threat to conferral and proposed to scrap it.[255] Others wanted to repurpose it to a clause which both conferred powers upon the Community and returned them to the Member States.[256] Overall, however, there was a broad acceptance that flexibility had to be maintained;[257] and so it was.

Article 352 TFEU is the clause's first amended version since the Rome Treaty. Instead of the common market condition, it refers to the framework of the Union's policies. This consolidates *Opinion 2/94*. It is now clearer that Article 352 grants power, but not competence.[258] At the same time, it removes the need to tie a measure to economic activity. Falling within the framework of a Union policy, whether economically linked or not, suffices. Other changes include a harmonisation ban in certain cases and a stronger role for national parliaments in the context of subsidiarity. Responding to *Kadi*, the clause also excludes measures with a CFSP objective.

Jurisprudence on Article 352 has been scarce so far. It remains to be seen whether the Court indeed sees the flexibility clause as a power-only provision, and whether it explicitly verifies compliance with the policies' condition. At least one ruling suggests that it will. In *Costantini*, the General Court examined the Commission's refusal to register a European Citizens Initiative.[259] The Commission had identified no power to propose the measure concerned. The ECI organisers

[252] Committee on Constitutional Affairs, Report on the Treaty of Lisbon, A6-0013/2008, 15 and 19; Presidency, Conclusions on the European Council (Brussels, 21–22 June 2007), 11177/1/07 Rev1, Annex 1; Presidency, Report on Pursuing the treaty reform process, 10659/07, 3; K Lenaerts, P Van Nuffel, and T Corthaut, *EU Constitutional Law* (OUP, 2021) 39.

[253] European Council, Laeken Declaration on the Future of the European Union, SN 300/1/01 Rev1, Annex 1.

[254] Convention Secretariat, Cover note on the Report of the Select Committee on the European Union of the House of Lords presented by Lord Tomlinson and Lord Maclennan, CONV 598/03, 25.

[255] Convention Secretariat, Cover note on the Reactions to draft Articles 1 to 16 of the Constitutional Treaty, CONV 574/1/03 Rev1, 104.

[256] European Convention, Working document 28 of Working group V 'Paper on priority issues regarding complementary competence' (CONV 2002-2003) 5; Committee on Constitutional Affairs, Report on the division of competences between the European Union and the Member States, A5-0133/2002, 13 and 23.

[257] Convention Secretariat, Note on the Summary of the meeting on 6 September 2002, CONV 251/02, 3.

[258] L Michel, K De Gucht, E Di Rupo, A Van Lancker, P Chevalier, and M Nagy, Proposition d'amendement à l'Article 16 (CONV 2002–2003); Convention Praesidium, Note on the Draft of Articles 1 to 16 of the Constitutional Treaty, CONV 528/03, 8.

[259] Case T-44/14 *Costantini ea v Commission* [2016] ECLI:EU:T:2016:223.

notably reproached the Commission for not having considered Article 352 as a legal basis.

The Court did not engage with Article 352's conditions. That was not needed, because the proposed ECI had failed to substantiate why the flexibility clause would apply. But by emphasising conferral, hinting at the distinction between fields (competences) and powers, and stressing the need to fulfil Article 352's conditions, the Court showed cause for optimism:

> The objective of democratic participation of Union citizens underlying the ECI mechanism cannot frustrate the principle of conferred powers and authorise the European Union to legislate in a field for which no power has been accorded to it, so that the conditions set out in Article 352 EC must also be complied with in the context of a proposed ECI.[260]

Of course, Article 352 is not perfect. The motivations of the institutions invoking or interpreting it will not be either. But that is not the point. The flexibility clause has long been controversial, and remains under scrutiny today. This chapter examined where it went right: by implicitly adopting a power-competence logic, its scope became clearer; and by explicitly addressing all its conditions, its motivation improved. That positive evolution is important. This book proposes a way forward. It argues for a more detailed and precise 'competence' analysis based on the distinct concepts of competence and power. The story of the flexibility clause shows that this is feasible.

[260] ibid, para 53.

Conclusion

It is now time to conclude. This book's core argument is twofold. First, the question of 'competence' always was a legal question. Ever since the Coal and Steel Community, the principle of conferral governed Community and Union action. Second, 'competence' is about more than competence alone. Whether the EU might act depends on a wider range of concepts. Their roots lie in the Treaties, the institutional practice, and the case law. However, they have never been applied with consistency. That should change.

In essence, 'competence' consists of competence and power. Competence is the field in which the EU may act. Power is the EU institutions' actual authorisation to act. To fall within a certain field of competence, a measure must pursue the objective(s) of that competence and relate to its subject matter. Those are the two dimensions of competence. Power, too, has two dimensions. It determines which legal instrument may be adopted through which type of legal act. There are also power modalities. They relate to the procedural side of the exercise of power: which EU institution(s) may act and through which voting majority.

Today, a paradox exists. 'Competence' is a crucial concept of EU law. In a legal system based on the principle of conferral, the Union may only act if it has competence and power to do so. It is important to review compliance with this principle. A rich set of legal scholarship does precisely that. It argues that a certain EU measure does or does not remain within the scope of EU 'competence'. Often, it also identifies a tendency to creep beyond that scope.[1] Without a doubt, such critical 'competence' debates are important. Yet there is an issue: a real shared conceptual understanding of 'competence' itself is missing. Legal scholars' different interpretations of the relationship between competence and power illustrate this.

The concepts of 'competence' are helpful, because they provide such a shared understanding. They also reflect that questions of 'competence' arise in a variety of forms. This book's many legal disputes illustrate that. The Tobacco Advertising Directives, for instance, raised questions on the pursuit of public health objectives in the internal market competence. *Opinion 1/94* addressed the subject matter scope of the CCP competence. And a set of intellectual property measures illustrated the different dimensions and modalities of power. The concepts of

[1] S Weatherill, 'Competence Creep and Competence Control' (2004) 23 *Yearbook of European Law* 1, 1; S Garben, 'Restating the Problem of Competence Creep, Tackling Harmonisation by Stealth and Reinstating the Legislator' in S Garben and I Govaere (eds), *The Division of Competences between the EU and the Member States: Reflections on the Past, the Present and the Future* (Hart Publishing, 2017) 300.

'competence' provide nuance and precision to answer these questions. This always matters. However, as the legal disputes on posted workers and an import ban for Russian gas showed, it is especially important in sensitive areas where the stakes are high and the opinions divided.

Two final legal disputes illustrate these benefits. The first is very recent. It concerns a legal challenge to the Minimum Wage Directive.[2] Despite its name, the Directive does not set an EU minimum wage. Instead, it requires all Member States to promote collective bargaining on wage-setting.[3] It also obliges those Member States with statutory minimum wages to establish procedures for determining adequate statutory minimum wages.[4] Such procedures must be 'guided' by criteria that 'are set to contribute to [the statutory minimum wages'] adequacy' and, at least, include the four elements defined in the Directive.[5] Moreover, any automatic indexation may 'not lead to a decrease of the statutory minimum wage'.[6]

The Directive's legal bases are Articles 153(1)(b) and 153(2)(b) TFEU. These provisions empower the Council, by qualified majority, and the Parliament, to introduce minimum requirements to improve working conditions.[7] Denmark voted against the Directive and challenged its legal bases in Court.[8] Two of its arguments are noteworthy here.[9] First, Article 153(5) explicitly states that Article 153 'shall not apply to pay'.[10] Yet the Directive clearly relates to pay. Second, Articles 153(1)(f) and 153(2)(b) specifically empower the Council, unanimously, to adopt minimum requirements to promote the collective defence of the interests of workers. Yet the Directive requires Member States to promote collective wage bargaining.

In *Minimum Wage*, Advocate General Emiliou advised that the Directive should be annulled in full.[11] The Court of Justice disagreed.[12] It only annulled

[2] Directive (EU) 2022/2041 of the European Parliament and of the Council of 19 October 2022 on adequate minimum wages in the European Union, OJ L 275.

[3] ibid, Article 4.

[4] ibid, Article 5.

[5] ibid, Article 5(1)–(2). Those elements are: (1) the purchasing power of statutory minimum wages, taking into account the cost of living; (2) the general level of wages and their distribution; (3) the growth rate of wages; and (4) long-term national productivity levels and developments.

[6] Directive (EU) 2022/2041, Article 5(3).

[7] See the objectives listed in Article 151 TFEU.

[8] Action brought on 18 January 2023 – *Kingdom of Denmark v European Parliament and Council of the European Union* (Case C-19/23); Denmark opposed the Directive as a matter of principle, to respect national competence and preserve the autonomy of the social partners for the determination of wages. See Council Secretariat, Draft Directive on adequate minimum wages in the European Union – Statements, 12616/22 Add1 Rev2, 2.

[9] Similar arguments were raised during the legislative proceedings. See Council Secretariat, Proposal on adequate minimum wages in the European Union – Evaluation of the Impact Assessment, Compilations of answers of Member states, 14934/20; European Economic and Social Committee, Opinion on Proposal for a directive of the European Parliament and of the Council on adequate minimum wages in the European Union (2021) SOC/664, 15–16.

[10] Article 153(5) TFEU.

[11] Opinion in Case C-19/23 *Denmark v Parliament and Council* [2025] ECLI:EU:C:2025:11.

[12] Case C-19/23 *Denmark v Parliament and Council* [2025] ECLI:EU:C:2025:865.

the provisions that laid down four elements to be considered when determining minimum wages, and a ban on automatic indexations that decrease statutory minimum wages. The main difference between the Advocate General's and the Court's reasoning lay in the interpretation of Article 153(5)'s pay exemption. And, interestingly, that difference is best explained through the concepts of 'competence'.

In previous case law, the Court had interpreted the pay exemption as a test of direct interference.[13] Article 153(5) did not exclude measures merely because they were somehow linked to pay; it only excluded measures that directly interfered with pay. In *Minimum Wage*, the judges clarified that this test of direct interference relates to the type of power instrument used. To the extent that the Minimum Wage Directive introduces non-binding, vague, and/or merely procedural rules, it does not directly interfere with pay.[14] That includes the requirement for Member States with statutory minimum wages to establish procedures for determining adequate statutory minimum wages: it is broadly worded, 'based on a procedural approach', 'leaves a significant margin of discretion to the Member States to define [adequacy]', and 'does not confer a right to an adequate statutory minimum wage'.[15] By contrast, the four elements harmonised an aspect of statutory minimum wages.[16] So did the ban on decreasing indexations.[17] These provisions directly interfered with pay, and the Court annulled them.

Advocate General Emiliou had reached a different conclusion. In his view, the test of direct interference did not relate to power. Rather, it rather served 'to differentiate instruments whose object is to regulate/harmonise pay from those whose object is to regulate a matter other than pay'.[18] Put differently, the test related to competence. Regardless of the power instrument used, 'there is no EU competence whatsoever for the matters covered by Article 153(5) TFEU'.[19] The Minimum Wage Directive thus went beyond the EU's competence under Article 153(1)(b). While the Directive did indeed aim to improve working conditions, it regulated a category of working conditions that falls outside Article 153(1)(b)'s subject matter scope.[20] The drafters explicitly excluded pay from that subject matter scope.[21] Even

[13] See, notably, Case C-268/06 *Impact* [2008] ECR I-02483 EU:C:2008:223, para 124; Case C-262/20 *Glavna direktsia 'Pozharna bezopasnost i zashthe na naselenieto'* [2022] EU:C:2022:117, para 30.

[14] This approach aligned with the positions taken by the Council Legal Service and Parliament's Legal Service and Committee on Legal Affairs during the Directive's legislative process. They had found no violation of Article 153(5) because vague procedural obligations only indirectly interfered with the determination of pay. See Council Legal Service, Commission proposal for a Directive of the European Parliament and of the Council on adequate minimum wages in the European Union – Legal basis, 6817/21; and Committee on Legal Affairs, Opinion on the legal basis of the of the proposal for a Directive of the European Parliament and of the Council on adequate minimum wages in the European Union (2021) PE699.235.

[15] Case C-19/23 *Denmark v Parliament and Council*, paras 88–91.

[16] ibid, paras 94–96.

[17] ibid, paras 97–98.

[18] Opinion in Case C-19/23 *Denmark v Parliament and Council*, para 60.

[19] ibid, para 65.

[20] ibid, para 95.

[21] ibid, para 65.

to the extent that the Directive only imposed vaguely worded and/or procedural requirements for the determination of minimum wages, it regulated pay, and therefore breached Article 153(5).[22]

However, the Court and the Advocate General also agreed on some aspects of the case. Again, the distinction between competence and power clarifies the analysis. Both the judgment and the Opinion rejected Denmark's subsidiary claim that the Directive fell under Article 153(1)(f)'s subject matter scope to the extent that it promotes collective wage bargaining.[23] That competence classification would have had important power modality consequences. The Council would have had to act alone and by unanimity. However, promoting collective wage bargaining is not a self-standing objective of the Directive; it is a power instrument to achieve a wide coverage of adequate statutory minimum wages.[24] In other words, to the extent that the pay exemption does not apply, the Minimum Wage Directive does indeed fall within the subject matter scope of Article 153(1)(b). But, of course, the Court and the Advocate General each gave a different response to that crucial qualification.

Arguably, the Opinion is more convincing than the judgment. Nothing in Article 153(5) suggests that this provision only limits the EU legislator's powers. On the contrary, the pay exemption clearly applies to the subject matter competences defined in Article 153(1). However, there is no need to choose a definite side here. Regardless of its exact legal flaws, the Minimum Wage Directive already illustrates how the concepts of 'competence' can contribute to a more precise and nuanced 'competence' analysis.

The second legal dispute illustrates how the concepts of 'competence' can contribute to a shared legal language. This book began with German 'competence' concerns. In *Weiss*, the Constitutional Court highlighted that the question whether the Union might act requires solid legal reasoning. As mentioned above, that is where the concepts of 'competence' come in. They contribute to a more nuanced and precise 'competence' analysis. Together, they can form the shared legal language which is currently missing in the 'competence' debate. A final return to Germany for another dispute between the Constitutional Court and the CJEU shows why this has real practical importance.

In 2013, after the economic and financial crisis, the Council adopted the SSM Regulation.[25] This Regulation entrusted the European Central Bank with the prudential oversight of the credit institutions established in the Member States.[26] The ECB would carry out these tasks 'within a single supervisory mechanism

[22] ibid, paras 51–66 and 86.

[23] Opinion in Case C-19/23 *Denmark v Parliament and Council*, para 120; Case C-19/23 *Denmark v Parliament and Council*, para 139.

[24] Opinion in Case C-19/23 *Denmark v Parliament and Council*, para 119; Case C-19/23 *Denmark v Parliament and Council*, para 136.

[25] Council Regulation (EU) No 1024/2013 of 15 October 2013 conferring specific tasks on the European Central Bank concerning policies relating to the prudential supervision of credit institutions, OJ L287.

[26] ibid, Article 4.

composed of the ECB and national competent authorities'.[27] Whether the ECB itself or the relevant national competent authority carried out the prudential review depended on the 'significance' of the credit institution concerned.[28] This significance depended, among other things, on the institution's size and economic importance in the Member State.[29] For significant credit institutions, the ECB was primarily responsible.[30]

A few months after the adoption of the SSM Regulation, the ECB classified the German Landeskreditbank Baden-Württemberg (Förderbank) as such a significant institution.[31] The German bank disagreed with this decision and requested its annulment.[32] There is no need to examine the case's details here; a closer look at one part of the judgment suffices. The General Court ruled that the ECB enjoyed exclusive competence over the supervision of both significant and less significant credit institutions.[33] Articles 4 and 6 of the SSM Regulation did not share competence between the ECB and the national competent authorities.[34] The latter only exercised decentralised supervision 'as a mechanism of assistance to the ECB rather than the exercise of autonomous competence'.[35] On appeal, the Court of Justice confirmed this reasoning.[36]

The German Federal Constitutional Court did not agree.[37] It ruled on the SSM Regulation when several applicants argued that aspects of the EU's Banking Union were ultra vires.[38] These aspects included the Regulation. Ultimately, the Constitutional Court rejected the claims.[39] It did, however, contradict the Union Courts on the nature of the ECB's competence. The German judges did not accept that the SSM Regulation granted an exclusive competence in prudential oversight to the ECB.[40]

Unlike the General Court and the Court of Justice, the Constitutional Court first examined Article 127(6) TFEU. This provision was the Regulation's legal basis. It authorised the Council to 'confer specific tasks upon the European Central Bank concerning policies institutions'.[41] Crucially, Article 127(6) did not appear to fall within the Union's exclusive monetary competence. The competence's objectives

[27] ibid, Article 6(1).
[28] ibid, Article 6(5).
[29] ibid.
[30] R Cranston, E Avgouleas, K van Zwieten, C Hare, and T van Sante, *Principles of Banking Law* (OUP, 2018) 163.
[31] ECB Decision ECB/SSM/15/1 of 5 January 2015.
[32] Case T-122/15 *Landeskreditbank Baden-Württemberg v ECB* [2017] ECLI:EU:T:2017:337.
[33] ibid, para 22.
[34] ibid, para 54.
[35] ibid, paras 58 and 63.
[36] Case C-450/17 P *Landeskreditbank Baden-Württemberg/ECB* [2019] ECLI:EU:C:2019:372, paras 37–49.
[37] Case 2 BvR 1685/14 [2019] BVerfG; P Schammo, 'Institutional Change in the Banking Union: The Case of the Single Supervisory Mechanism' (2021) 40 *Yearbook of European Law* 265, 299.
[38] T Tuominen, The Euro Crisis and Constitutional Pluralism: Financial Stability but Constitutional Inequality (Edward Elgar, 2021) 100.
[39] Case 2 BvR 1685/14 [2019] BVerfG.
[40] Schammo (n 37) 298.
[41] Article 127(6) TFEU.

dimension explained why: Article 127(6) did not aim to ensure price stability.[42] Also supported by the fact that national authorities had long performed the supervision tasks now entrusted to the ECB, the Constitutional Court ruled that Article 127(6) did not confer an exclusive competence upon the ECB.[43]

Then, the Constitutional Court turned to the SSM Regulation itself. The German judges did not share the EU Courts' interpretation of Articles 4 and 6 either.[44] They ruled that the ECB did not enjoy exclusive competence for all tasks listed in Article 4 in general. Instead, that provision had to be read through the lens of Article 6, which distinguished between significant and less significant credit institutions.[45] According to the Constitutional Court, the national competent authorities, therefore, acted by virtue of their own national competence.

It thus seemed that Luxembourg and Karlsruhe were miles apart. The EU Courts said that the ECB enjoyed an exclusive competence; the German Court denied this. Yet a compromise view might exist. The tension between the EU and national courts might have stemmed from a misunderstanding of the concepts of 'competence'. It appears that the German Court was right to dismiss the claim of exclusive ECB *competence*. The field of prudential supervision indeed remains open to both the ECB and the national authorities. After all, the SSM Regulation only conferred nine specific tasks upon the ECB.[46] Other supervision tasks remain for the national authorities. But with respect to these specific tasks, the ECB does enjoy exclusive *power*. Only the ECB may exercise the supervision listed in Article 4 for significant institutions. And, for less significant institutions, the national authorities may only act in a framework of decentralisation of exclusive ECB powers.

Thus, the concepts of 'competence' could help to reconcile the EU Courts' rulings with the 'competence' objections of the German Constitutional Court. Their value is not, however, limited to judicial disputes between EU and Member State courts. Conferral is a foundational stone of the European Union's legal order. Questions of 'competence' arise whenever the Union prepares to act. It is important that they can be answered with nuance and precision, and in a legal language which is understood by all participants in the debate. Today, Montesquieu's standard has not yet been met. 'Competence' does not awaken the same ideas in all men.[47] The concepts of 'competence' could change that.

[42] A de Gregorio Merino, 'Institutional Report' in G Bándi, P Darák, and K Debisso (eds), *European Banking Union, FIDE Congress Proceedings (Vol 1)* (Kluwer, 2016) 169; T Tridimas, 'The constitutional dimension of Banking Union' in S Grundmann and H-W Micklitz (eds), *The European Banking Union and Constitution: Beacon for Advanced Integration or Death-Knell for Democracy* (Hart Publishing, 2019) 36.

[43] Case 2 BvR 1685/14 [2019] BVerfG, paras 166–69.

[44] Schammo (n 37) 299.

[45] ibid.

[46] Article 4 of Council Regulation (EU) 1024/2013; Opinion in Case C-450/17 P *Landeskreditbank Baden-Württemberg/ECB* [2018] ECLI:EU:C:2018:982, para 50.

[47] After Montesquieu, *De l'Esprit des Lois* (Librairie de Firmin Didot, 1862) 490.

BIBLIOGRAPHY

Books

Adams Z, Barnard C, Deakin S, and Butlin SF, *Deakin and Morris' Labour Law* (Hart Publishing, 2021) 1186
Alexander K and Andenas MT, *The World Trade Organization and Trade in Services* (Brill, 2008) 1010
Auby JM and Fromont M, *Les recours contre les actes administratifs dans les pays de la CEE* (Dalloz, 1971) 473
Barnard C, *The Substantive Law of the EU* (OUP, 2016) 626
Basedow J, *The Law of Open Societies – Private Ordering and Public Regulation in the Conflict of Laws* (Brill, 2015) 634
Bell M, *Anti-discrimination Law and the European Union* (OUP, 2002) 296
Berthélémy L, *Traité élémentaire de droit administratif* (Rousseau, 1910) 996
Beutler B, *Die Europäische Gemeinschaft* (Nomos, 1982) 537
Bonnard R, *Précis de Droit Administratif* (LGDJ, 1943) 786
Buttgenbach A, *Manuel de droit administratif* (Larcier, 1966) 751
Chamon M, *The European Parliament and Delegated Legislation – An Institutional Balance Perspective* (Hart Publishing, 2022) 232
Cloos J, Reinesch G, Vignes D, and Weyland J, *Le traité de Maastricht: genèse, analyse, commentaires* (Bruylant, 1993) 804
Cockfield FA, *The European Union: Creating the Single Market* (Wiley 1994) 185
Corbett R, *The Treaty of Maastricht* (Longman Group, 1993) 512
Craig P, *EU Administrative Law* (OUP, 2012) 777
——, *The Lisbon Treaty: Law, Politics and Treaty Reform* (OUP, 2013) 529
Craig P and De Búrca G, *EU Law: Text, Cases and Materials* (OUP, 2008) 1148
——, *EU law: Text, Cases, and Materials* (OUP, 2020) 1264
Cranston R, Avgouleas E, van Zwieten K, Hare C, and van Sante T, *Principles of Banking Law* (OUP, 2018) 632
De Ruyt J, *L'Acte Unique Européen* (Editions de l'Université de Bruxelles, 1989) 408
de Soto J, *La Communauté européenne du charbon et de l'acier* (Presses universitaires de France, 1958) 124
Dony M and Louis J-V, *Commentaire J. Mégret: le droit de la CE et de l'Union européenne – Relations extérieures* (Editions de l'Université de Bruxelles, 2005) 648
Ecke C, Leino-Sandberg P, and Ghavanini AW (eds), *The Dynamics of Powers in the European Union* (Hart Publishing, 2024) 352
Eeckhout P, *EU External Relations Law* (OUP, 2011) 644
Endicott T, *Vagueness in Law* (OUP, 2000) 226
Engel A, *The Choice of Legal Basis for Acts of the European Union: Competence Overlaps, Institutional Preferences, and Legal Basis Litigation* (Springer, 2018) 142
Engström V, *Constructing the Powers of International Institutions* (Brill, 2012) 214
Garben S and Govaere I (eds), *The Division of Competences between the EU and the Member States: Reflections on the Past, the Present and the Future* (Hart Publishing, 2017) 274
Gil Ibáñez A, *The Administrative Supervision and Enforcement of EC Law: Powers, Procedures and Limits* (Hart Publishing, 1999) 404

Goldman B, *European Commercial Law* (Stevens, 1973) 452
Gori P, *Les clauses de sauvegarde des traités CECA et CEE* (UGA, 1967) 348
Haas EB, *The Uniting of Europe: Political, Social, and Economic Forces* (SUP, 1958) 552
Hallstein W, *Europe in the Making* (George Allen and Unwin, 1972) 343
——, *Die Europäische Gemeinschaft* (Econ Verlag, 1974) 421
Hartley T, *The Foundations of European Community Law* (OUP, 1981) 551
Hatzopoulos V, *Regulating Services in the European Union* (OUP, 2012) 417
Ilardi A, *The New European Patent* (Hart Publishing, 2015) 150
Ipsen H, *Europäisches Gemeinschaftsrecht* (JCB Mohr, 1972) 1092
Isensee J, *Subsidiaritätsprinzip und Verfassungsrecht* (Ducker & Humblot, 2001) 391
Kapteyn PJG, Barents R, and VerLoren van Themaat P, *Inleiding tot het recht van de Europese Gemeenschappen: na Maastricht* (Kluwer, 1995) 935
Konstadinides T, *Division of Powers in European Union Law – The Delimitation of Internal Competence Between the EU and the Member States* (Wolters Kluwer, 2009) 333
Koutrakos P, *Trade, Foreign Policy and Defence in EU Constitutional Law – The Legal Regulation of Sanctions, Exports of Dual-use Goods and Armaments* (Hart Publishing, 2001) 243
——, *The EU Common Security and Defence Policy* (OUP, 2013) 370
Kovar R, *Le pouvoir réglementaire de la Communauté européenne du charbon et de l'acier* (LGDJ, 1964) 348
Kuijpers J-J, *EU Law and Private International Law – The Interrelationship in Contractual Obligations* (Brill, 2011) 371
Kur A, Dreier T, and Luginbuehl S, *European Intellectual Property Law: Text, Cases and Materials* (Edward Elgar, 2013) 548
Lasok D, *The Trade and Customs Law of the European Union* (Kluwer, 1998) 470
Lauwaars RH, *Lawfulness and legal force of Community decisions* (AW Sijthoff, 1973) 355
Lenaerts K, *Le Juge et la Constitution aux Etats-Unis d'Amérique et dans l'ordre juridique européen* (Bruylant, 1988) 817
——, *European Union Law* (Sweet & Maxwell, 2011) 1083
Lenaerts K, Van Nuffel P, and Corthaut T, *EU Constitutional Law* (OUP, 2021) 1024
Lindberg L, *The Political Dynamics of European Economic Integration* (UC Berkeley, 1962) 367
Lindseth P, *Power and Legitimacy: Reconciling Europe and the Nation-State* (OUP, 2011) 339
Martinsen DS, *An Ever More Powerful Court? The Political Constraints of Legal Integration in the European Union* (OUP, 2014) 256
Mitzner V, *European Union Research Policy: Contested Origins* (Springer, 2020) 282
Monnet J, *Mémoires* (Fayard, 1976) 642
Montesquieu, *De l'Esprit des Lois* (Librairie de Firmin Didot, 1862) 490
Oliver P, *Free Movement of Goods in the E.E.C.: Under Articles 30 to 36 of the Rome Treaty* (European Law Centre, 1988) 407
Pescatore P, *Le droit de l'intégration* (AW Sijthoff, 1972) 99
——, *L'ordre juridique des Communautés européennes – Etude des sources du droit communautaire* (Presses universitaires de Liège, 1975) 316
Petersmann E-U, *International and European Trade and Environmental Law After the Uruguay Round* (Springer, 1995) 168
Pila J and Torremans P, *European Intellectual Property Law* (OUP, 2019) 712
Piris J-C, *The Constitution for Europe – A Legal Analysis* (CUP, 2006) 267
——, *The Lisbon Treaty – A Legal and Political Analysis* (CUP, 2010) 462
Poidevin R and Spierenburg D, *The History of the High Authority of the European Coal and Steel Community* (Weidenfeld & Nicolson, 1994) 711
Rabe HJ, *Das Verordnungsrecht der Europäischen Wirtschaftsgemeinschaft* (Kommissionsverlag Appel, 1963) 215
Reich N, *Understanding EU Law – Objectives, Principles and Methods of Community Law* (Intersentia, 2003) 400

Reuter P, *La Communauté européenne du charbon et de l'acier* (LGDJ, 1953) 320
——, *Organisations européennes* (Presses Universitaires de France, 1970) 451
Šarčević S, *Language and Culture in EU Law: Multidisciplinary Perspectives* (Routledge, 2015) 270
Schmidt M, *Das Arbeitsrecht der Europäischen Gemeinschaft* (Nomos, 2001) 368
Schuman R, *Pour l'Europe* (Nagel, 1963) 156
Schütze R, *European Constitutional Law* (CUP, 2012) 484
——, *Foreign Affairs and the EU Constitution – Selected Essays* (CUP, 2014) 522
——, *European Union Law* (CUP, 2015) 946
——, *From International to Federal Market: The Changing Structure of European Law* (OUP, 2017) 378
——, *European Constitutional Law* (OUP, 2021) 608
——, *European Union Law* (OUP, 2021) 1006
Tuominen T, *The Euro Crisis and Constitutional Pluralism: Financial Stability but Constitutional Inequality* (Edward Elgar, 2021) 272
Van Der Mei P, *Free Movement of Persons within the European Community* (Hart Publishing, 2003) 528
Van Gerven W, *The European Union: A Polity of States and Peoples* (SUP, 2005) 397
Van Vooren B, *EU External Relations Law and the European Neighbourhood Policy – A Paradigm for Coherence* (Routledge, 2012) 384
Weatherill S, *EC Law* (Penguin, 1993) 846
——, *Law and Integration in the European Union* (Clarendon Press, 1995) 306
——, *EU Consumer Law and Policy* (Edward Elgar, 2014) 334
——, *Cases and Materials on EU Law* (OUP, 2016) 720
——, *The Internal Market as a Legal Concept* (OUP, 2017) 240
Wouters J, Hoffmeister F, De Baere G, and Ramopoulos T, *The Law of EU External Relations* (OUP, 2013) 1160

Book Chapters

Amtenbrink F, 'Denationalizing Monetary Policy: Reflections on 60 Years of European Monetary Integration' in Shiubhne NN and Gormley LW (eds), *From Single Market to Economic Union* (OUP, 2012) 13–32
Azoulai L, 'Introduction' in Azoulai L (ed), *The Question of Competence in the European Union* (OUP, 2014) 1–16
Barnard C, 'Fifty Years of Avoiding Social Dumping?' in Dougan M and Currie S (eds), *50 Years of the European Treaties: Looking Back and Thinking Forward* (Hart Publishing, 2009) 311–42
——, 'The Protection of Fundamental Social Rights in Europe after Lisbon: a Question of Conflicts of Interests' in de Vries S, Bernitz U, and Weatherill S (eds), *The Protection of Fundamental Rights in the EU After Lisbon* (Hart Publishing, 2013) 37–58
——, 'The Day the Clock Stopped: EU Citizenship and the Single Market' in Koutrakos P and Snell J (eds), *Research Handbook on the Law of the EU's Internal Market* (Edward Elgar Publishing, 2017) 102–14
Beaud O, 'The Allocation of Competences in a Federation – A General Introduction' in Azoulai L (ed), *The Question of Competence in the European Union* (OUP, 2014) 19–38
Bradley K, 'Powers and procedures in the EU constitution: legal bases and the court' in Craig P and De Búrca G (eds), *The Evolution of EU Law* (OUP, 2011) 85–110
Brinckhorst LJ, in Melchior M (ed), *Les relations extérieures de la communauté européenne unifiée: actes du troisième Colloque sur la fusion des Communautés européennes* (Institut d'études juridiques européennes de la Faculté de droit de l'Université de Liège, 1967) 310
Chalmers D, 'Inhabitants in the Field of Environmental Law' in Craig P and De Búrca G (eds), *The Evolution of EU Law* (OUP, 1999) 653–92

Countouris N and Engblom S, 'Civilising the European Posted Workers Directive' in Freedland M and Prassl J (eds), *Viking, Laval and Beyond* (Hart Publishing, 2014) 279–94
Craig P, 'The Evolution of the Single Market' in Barnard C and Scott J (eds), *The Law of the Single European Market: Unpacking the Premises* (Hart Publishing, 2002) 1–40
——, 'Institutions, Power, and Institutional Balance' in Craig P and De Búrca G (eds), *The Evolution of EU Law* (OUP, 2011) 41–84
——, 'Integration, Democracy, and Legitimacy' in Craig P and De Búrca G (eds), *The Evolution of EU Law* (OUP, 2011) 13–40
Cremona M, 'The External Dimension of the Single Market: Building (on) the Foundations' in Barnard C and Scott J (eds), *The Law of the Single European Market: Unpacking the Premises* (Hart Publishing, 2002) 351–94
——, 'Defining Competence in EU External Relations: Lessons From the Treaty Reform Process' in Dashwood A and Maresceau M (eds), *Law and Practice of EU External Relations* (CUP, 2008) 47–70
——, 'EC External Commercial Policy after Amsterdam: Authority and Interpretation with Interconnected Legal Orders' in Weiler JHH (ed), *The EU, the WTO, and the NAFTA: Towards a Common Law of International Trade?* (OUP, 2010) 5–34
——, 'External Competences And The Principle Of Conferral' in Schütze R and Tridimas T (eds), *Oxford Principles of European Union Law: Volume I* (OUP, 2018) 1110–40
——, 'External Relations of the European Union: The Constitutional Framework for International Action' in Craig P and De Búrca G (eds), *The Evolution of EU Law* (OUP, 2021) 431–79
Dabin ML, in Institut d'études juridiques européennes (ed), *De l'union douanière à l'union économique: Actes du quatrième colloque sur la fusion des Communautés européennes, organisé à Liège les 23, 24 et 25 avril 1969* (Université de Liège, 1970) 295
Dashwood A, 'External Relations Provisions of the Amsterdam Treaty' in O'Keeffe D and Twomey P (eds), *Legal Issues of the Amsterdam Treaty* (Hart Publishing, 1999) 201–24
——, 'Article 47 TEU and the relationship between first and second pillar competences' in Dashwood A and Maresceau M (eds), *Law and Practice of EU External Relations* (CUP, 2008) 70–103
——, 'The Law and Practice of CFSP Joint Actions' in Cremona M and de Witte B (eds), *EU Foreign Relations Law: Constitutional Fundamentals* (Hart Publishing, 2008) 70–103
——, 'Article 308 EC as the Outer Limit of Expressly Conferred Community Competence' in Barnard C and Odudu O (eds), *The Outer Limits of European Union Law* (Hart Publishing, 2009) 35–44
——, 'EU Acts and Member State Acts in the Negotiation, Conclusion, and Implementation of International Agreements' in Cremona M and Kilpatrick C, *EU Legal Acts: Challenges and Transformations* (OUP, 2018) 185–250
Dederer H-G, 'The Common Commercial Policy Under the Influence of Commission, Council, High Representative and European External Action Service' in Bungenberg M and Herrmann C (eds), *Common Commercial Policy after Lisbon* (Springer, 2013) 87–106
Defalque L and Luff D, 'L'embargo et l'Union européenne' in *L'Embargo, Actes de la journée d'étude du 1er décembre 1995 organisée par l'Association européenne pour le droit bancaire et financier* (Bruylant, 1996) 88–121
de Gregorio Merino A, 'Institutional Report' in Bándi G, Darák P, and Debisso K (eds), *European Banking Union, FIDE Congress Proceedings (Vol 1)* (Kluwer, 2016) 151–98
De Schutter O, 'Transborder provision of services and "social dumping": rights-based mutual trust in the establishment of the Internal Market' in Lianos I and Odudu O (eds), *Regulating Trade in Services in the EU and the WTO: Trust, Distrust and Economic Integration* (CUP, 2012) 349–80
De Visscher P, 'La CECA et les Etats Membres' in Centro Italiano di Studi Giuridici (ed), *Actes officiels du Congrès International d'Etudes sur la Communauté Européenne du Charbon et de l'Acier II* (Giuffrè, 1957) 7–85
de Witte B, 'Non-market values in internal market legislation' in Shiubhne NN (ed), *Regulating the Internal Market* (Edward Elgar Publishing, 2006) 61–86
——, 'The European Union as an international legal experiment' in De Búrca G and Weiler JHH (eds), *The Worlds of European constitutionalism* (CUP, 2012) 19–56

——, 'The Freedom to Provide Services: The Controversial Freedom?' in Garben S and Govaere I (eds), *The Internal Market 2.0* (Hart Publishing, 2020) 137–60
de Witte F, 'The architecture of the EU's social market economy' in Koutrakos P and Snell J (eds), *Research Handbook on the Law of the EU's Internal market* (Edward Elgar, 2017) 117–38
Eeckhout P, 'Constitutional Concepts for Free Trade in Services' in De Búrca G and Scott J (eds), *The EU and the WTO: Legal and Constitutional Issues* (Hart Publishing, 2002)
——, 'The EU's Common Foreign and Security Policy after Lisbon: From Pillar Talk to Constitutionalism' in Biondi A, Eeckhout P, and Ripley S (eds), *EU Law after Lisbon* (OUP, 2012) 265–91
——, 'Exclusive External Competences: Constructing the EU as an International Actor' in Rosas A, Levits E, and Bot Y (eds), *La Cour de Justice et la Construction de l'Europe: Analyses et Perspectives de Soixante Ans de Jurisprudence* (Asser Press, 2013) 613–36
Ehring H, 'Allgemeine und Schlußbestimmungen (Art.235)' in von der Groeben H and von Boeckh H (eds), *Kommentar zum EWG Vertrag II* (Verlag August Lutzeyer, 1958) 445–52
Everling U, in Melchior M (ed), *Les relations extérieures de la communauté européenne unifiée: actes du troisième Colloque sur la fusion des Communautés européennes* (Institut d'études juridiques européennes de la Faculté de droit de l'Université de Liège, 1967) 310
Feenstra S, 'Resolving the Viking/Laval Conundrum' in Vandenbroucke F, Barnard C, and De Baere G (eds), *A European Social Union After the Crisis* (CUP, 2017) 309–43
Ferrari Bravo L and Giardina A, 'Art. 235' in Quadri R, Monaco R, and Trabucchi A (eds), *Trattato istitutivo della comunità economica europea: commentario* (Giuffrè, 1965) 1699–713
Garben S, 'Restating the Problem of Competence Creep, Tackling Harmonisation by Stealth and Reinstating the Legislator' in Garben S and Govaere I (eds), *The Division of Competences between the EU and the Member States: Reflections on the Past, the Present and the Future* (Hart Publishing, 2017) 300–36
——, 'The Principle of Legality and the EU' s Legitimacy as a Constitutional Democracy: A Research Agenda' in Garben S, Govaere I, and Nemitz P (eds), *Critical Reflections on Constitutional Democracy in the European Union* (Hart Publishing, 2019)
Geiger C, 'The construction of intellectual property in the European Union: search for coherence' in Geiger C (ed), *Constructing European Intellectual Property – Achievements and New* Perspectives (Edward Elgar, 2013) 5–23
Gori P, 'Art.95(1)–(2)' in Quadri R, Monaco R, and Trabucchi A (eds), *Trattato istitutivo della CECA: commentario* (Giuffrè, 1970) 1324–45
Grassetti G, 'La Communauté et les Entreprises' in Centro Italiano di Studi Giuridici (ed), *Actes officiels du Congrès International d'Etudes sur la Communauté Européenne du Charbon et de l'Acier IV* (Giuffrè, 1957) 7–95
Hartel I, 'Die Zuständigkeiten der Union' in Niedobitek M (ed), *Europarecht – Grundlagen und Politiken der Union* (De Gruyter Brill, 2020) 447–524
Hatzopoulos V, 'Actively talking to each other: the Court and the political institutions' in Dawson M, de Witte B, and Muir E (eds), *Judicial Activism at the European Court of Justice* (Edward Elgar, 2013) 102–41
Herrmann C, 'Die Gemeinsame Handelspolitik (GHP)' in Streinz R, Ohler C, and Herrmann C (eds), *Der Vertrag von Lissabon zur Reform der EU* (Beck, 2010) 149–54
Hillion C, 'A Powerless Court? The European Court of Justice and the EU Common Foreign and Security Policy' in Thies A and Cremona M (eds), *The European Court of Justice and External Relations Law: Constitutional Challenges* (Hart Publishing, 2014) 47–70
Jackson JH, 'The Evolution of the World Trading System – the Legal and Institutional Context' in Bethlehem D, Van Damme I, McRae D, and Neufeld R (eds), *The Oxford Handbook of International Trade Law* (OUP, 2009) 30–53
Kaddous C, 'The Transformation of the EU Common Commercial Policy' in Eeckhout P and Lopez-Escudero M (eds), *The European Union's External Action in Times of Crisis* (Hart Publishing, 2016) 429–52

Kapteyn GJP, 'Article 235' in Herzog P and Smit H (eds), *The Law of the European Economic Community, A Commentary on the EEC Treaty* (M Bender, 1976) 296–342

Kellerbauer M, 'Articles 114-118' in Kellerbauer M, Klamert M, and Tomkin J (eds), *The EU Treaties and the Charter of Fundamental Rights: A Commentary* (OUP, 2019) 1231–69

Kilpatrick C, 'Internal market architecture and the accommodation of labour rights: As good as it gets?' in Syrpis S (ed), *The Judiciary, the Legislature and the EU Internal Market* (CUP, 2012) 205–42

Klein P, 'Les Compétences et Pouvoirs de l'Organisation Internationale' in Lagrange A and Sorel J-M (eds), *Droit des Organisations Internationales* (LGDJ, 2013) 714–34

Knaak R, 'Trade mark protection and undistorted competition' in Drexl J, Hilty RM, Boy L, Godt C, and Bernard R (eds), *Technologie Et Concurrence – Mélanges en L'honneur de Hanns Ullrich* (Larcier, 2009) 123–38

Konstadinides T, 'The Competences of the Union' in Schütze R and Tridimas T (eds), Oxford *Principles Of European Union Law: The European Union Legal Order: Volume I* (OUP, 2018) 191–220

Korioth S, 'Artikel 30' in Maunz T and Dürig G (eds), *Grundgesetz: Kommentar Band IV* (Beck, 2006) 1–29

Krajewski M, 'New Functions and New Powers for the European Parliament: Assessing the Changes of the Common Commercial Policy from the Perspective of Democratic Legitimacy' in Bungenberg M and Herrmann C (eds), *Common Commercial Policy after Lisbon* (Springer, 2013) 67–86

Krajewski P, 'The European Commission as a Driver of EU Trade Policy: Executive Leadership by Technocratic Means' in Eckes C, Leino-Sandberg P, and Ghavanini AW (eds), *Dynamics of Powers in the European Union* (Hart Publishing, 2024) 97–120

Lagrange M, 'La Cour de justice des Communautés européennes du plan Schuman à l'Union européenne' in Teitgen PH (ed), *Mélanges Fernand Dehousse: La construction européenne* (Nathan, 1979) 127–35

Lauterpacht E, 'Judicial review of the acts of international organisations' in Boisson de Chazournes L and Sands P (eds), *International Law, the International Court of Justice and Nuclear Weapons* (CUP, 1999) 92–102

Lenaerts K and De Smijter E, 'The United Nations and The European Union: Living Apart Together' in Wellens K, *International Law: Theory and Practice: Essays in Honour of Eric Suy* (Nijhoff, 1998) 439–58

Lock T, 'The not so free choice of EU member states in international dispute settlement' in Cremona M, Thies A, and Wessel RA (eds), *The European Union and International Dispute Settlement* (Hart Publishing, 2017) 113–32

Maresceau M, 'The Concept "Common Commercial Policy" and the Difficult Road to Maastricht' in Maresceau M (ed), *The European Community's Commercial Policy after 1992: The Legal Dimension* (Martinus Nijhoff, 1993) 3–19

Matthaiou A and Van Damme I, 'The Administration and Enforcement of EU Sanctions Revisited' in Govaere I, Garben S, and Spaventa E, *The Impact of War (in Ukraine) on the EU* (Hart Publishing, 2025) 185–214

Mengozzi P, 'Trade in Services and Commercial Policy' in Maresceau M (ed), *The European Community's Commercial Policy after 1992: The Legal Dimension* (Martinus Nijhoff, 1993) 223–47

Mischo J, 'The Contribution of the Court of Justice to the Protection of the "Federal Balance" in the European Community' in O'Keeffe D (ed), *Judicial Review in European Union Law – Essays in Honour of Lord Slynn* (Kluwer Law International, 2000) 59–72

Müller-Ibold T, 'Common Commercial Policy After Lisbon: The European Union's Dependence on Secondary Legislation' in Bungenberg M and Herrmann C (eds), *Common Commercial Policy after Lisbon* (Springer, 2013) 145–62

Odermatt J, 'The Principle of Autonomy: An Adolescent Disease of EU External Relations Law?' in Cremona M (ed), *Structural Principles in EU External Relations Law* (Hart Publishing, 2018) 291–316

O'Leary S, 'The Free Movement of Persons and Services' in Craig P and De Búrca G (eds), *The Evolution of EU Law* (OUP, 1999) 377–416

O'Leary S and Sanchez SI, 'Free Movement of Persons and Services' in Craig P and De Burca G (eds), *The Evolution of EU Law* (OUP, 2021) 506–45
Oliver P, 'Introduction' in Oliver P (ed), *Oliver on Free Movement of Goods in the European Union* (Hart Publishing, 2010) 1–13
Olivier G, 'Art. 2' in Quadri R, Monaco R, and Trabucchi A (eds), *Trattato istitutivo della CECA: commentario* (Giuffrè, 1970) 52–77
Ophüls CF, 'Uber die Auslegung der Europäischen Gemeinschaftsverträge' in Greiss F and Meyer FW (eds), *Wirtschaft, Gesellschaft und Kultur. Festgabe für Alfred Müller-Armack zur Vollendung seines sechzigsten Lebensjahres* (Duncker & Humblot, 1961) 279–90
——, 'Staatshoheit und Gemeinschaftshoheit: Wandlungen des Souveränitätsbegriff' in Ule CH (ed), *Recht im Wandel: Beiträge zu Strömungen und Fragen im heutigen Recht: Festschrift hundertfünfzig Jahre Carl Heymanns* (Heymanns Verlag, 1965) 519–91
Oppermann T, in Institut d'études juridiques européennes (ed), *De l'union douanière à l'union économique: Actes du quatrième colloque sur la fusion des Communautés européennes, organisé à Liège les 23, 24 et 25 avril 1969* (Université de Liège, 1970) 295
Pescatore P, 'La Cour en tant que juridiction fédérale et constitutionnelle' in Europäische Arbeitstagung (ed), *Dix ans de jurisprudence de la Cour de justice des communautés européennes* (Heymanns, 1965) 520–58
——, in Institut d'études juridiques européennes (ed), *De l'union douanière à l'union économique: Actes du quatrième colloque sur la fusion des Communautés européennes, organisé à Liège les 23, 24 et 25 avril 1969* (Université de Liège, 1970) 295
——, 'Les objectifs de la Communauté européenne comme principes d'interprétation dans la jurisprudence de la Cour de justice' in Ganshof van der Meersch W (ed), *Miscellanea* (Bruylant, 1972) 325–63
Pila J, 'An Historical Perspective I: The Unitary Patent Package' in Pila J and Wadlow C (eds), *The Unitary EU Patent System* (Hart Publishing, 2015) 9–32
Ramopoulos T, 'The Institutional Structure' in Schütze R and Tridimas T, *Oxford Principles Of European Union Law: The European Union Legal Order: Volume I* (OUP, 2018) 1067–1109
Renda A, 'Single Market 2.0: The European Union as a Platform' in Garben S and Govaere I (eds), *The Internal Market 2.0* (Hart Publishing, 2020) 187–212
Rödl F, 'The Labour Constitution' in von Bogdandy A and Bast J (eds), *Principles of European Constitutional Law* (Hart Publishing, 2010) 623–58
Rosas A, 'Mixity and the Common Commercial Policy after Opinion 2/15' in Hahn M and Van der Loo G, *Law and Practice of the Common Commercial Policy – The First 10 Years After the Treaty of Lisbon* (Brill, 2020) 27–46
Sage-Fuller B, Prinz zur Lippe F, and Ó Conaill S, 'Law and Language(s) at the Heart of the European Project: Educating Different Kinds of Lawyers' in Freeman M and Smith F (eds), *Law and Language* (OUP, 2013) 493–512
Schmitter C, 'Article 228a' in Constantinesco V, Kovar R, and Simon D (eds), *Traité sur l'Union européenne, signé à Maastricht le 7 février 1992 – Commentaire article par article* (Economica, 1995) 757–66
Schuman R, 'Préface' in Reuter P, *La Communauté européenne du charbon et de l'acier* (LGDJ, 1953) 3–8
Schütze R, 'The European Community's Federal Order of Competences – A Retrospective Analysis' in Dougan M and Currie S (eds), *50 Years of the European Treaties: Looking Back and Thinking Forward* (Hart Publishing, 2009) 63–92
Stein E and Henkin L, 'Towards a European Foreign Policy? The European Foreign Affairs System from the Perspective of the United States Constitution' in Cappelletti M, Seccombe M, and Weiler JHH (eds), *Integration Through Law: Europe and the American Federal Experience, vol 1, Book 3* (De Gruyter 1986) 3–82
Syrpis P, 'Should the EU be attempting to harmonise national systems of labour law?' in Andenas M and Andersen CB (eds), *The Theory and Practice of* Harmonisation (Edward Elgar, 2012) 450–73
Taschner H, 'Free movement of students, retired persons and other European citizens – a difficult legislative process' in Schermers HG, Flinterman C, and Kellermann AE (eds), *Free Movement of Persons in Europe: Legal Problems and Experiences* (Asser, 1993) 427–36

Teitgen P-H, in Institut d'études juridiques européennes (ed), *De l'union douanière à l'union économique: Actes du quatrième colloque sur la fusion des Communautés européennes, organisé à Liège les 23, 24 et 25 avril 1969* (Université de Liège, 1970) 295

Timmermans CWA, 'Common Commercial Policy (Article 113 EEC) and International Trade in Services' in Capotorti F, Ehlermann C-D, Frowein J, Jacobs F, Joliet R, Koopmans T, and Kovar R (eds), *Du droit international au droit de l'intégration: Liber amicorum Pierre Pescatore* (Nomos, 1987) 675–89

Tizzano A, 'Art. 8' in Quadri R, Monaco R, and Trabucchi A (eds), *Trattato istitutivo della CECA: commentario* (Giuffrè, 1970) 142–58

——, 'The Powers of the Community' in Commission (ed), *Thirty Years of Community Law* (Office for Official Publications of the EC, 1983) 43–67

Tridimas T, 'The constitutional dimension of Banking Union' in Grundmann S and Micklitz H-W (eds), *The European Banking Union and Constitution: Beacon for Advanced Integration or Death-Knell for Democracy* (Hart Publishing, 2019) 25–48

Usher JA, 'The Gradual Widening of European Community Policy on the Basis of Articles 100 and 235 of the EEC Treaty' in Schermers HG and Schwarze J (eds), *Structure and Dimensions of European Community Policy* (Nomos, 1988) 25–38

Van Gerven W and van den Bossche P, 'Freedom of movement and equal treatment for students in Europe: an emerging principle?' in Schermers HG, Flinterman C, and Kellermann AE (eds), *Free Movement of Persons in Europe: Legal Problems and Experiences* (Asser, 1993) 405–26

von Boeckh H, 'Grundsätze' in von der Groeben H and von Boeckh H (eds), *Kommentar zum EWG Vertrag I* (Verlag August Lutzeyer, 1958) 3–26

von Bogdandy A and Bast J, 'The Federal Order of Competences' in Von Bogdandy A and Bast J (eds), *Principles of European Constitutional Law* (Hart Publishing, 2010) 275–308

Waelbroeck M, in Melchior M (ed), *Les relations extérieures de la communauté européenne unifiée: actes du troisième Colloque sur la fusion des Communautés européennes* (Institut d'études juridiques européennes de la Faculté de droit de l'Université de Liège 1967) 310

Waldron J, 'The Rule of Law and the Importance of Procedure' in JE Fleming (ed), *Getting to the Rule of Law* (NYU Press, 2011) 3–31

Weatherill S, 'European private law – Is there a future after the Tobacco Advertising decision' in Müller-Graff PC (ed), *Europäisches Integrationsrecht im Querschnitt* (Nomos, 2003) 93–103

——, 'Supply of and demand for internal market regulation: strategies, preferences and interpretation' in Shiubhne NN (ed), *Regulating the Internal Market* (Edward Elgar Publishing, 2006) 29–60

——, 'The Competence Catalogue in the Treaty Establishing a Constitution and the Treaty of Lisbon: Improvement, but at a Cost' in Barber NW, Cahill M, and Ekins R (eds), *The Rise and Fall of the European Constitution* (Hart Publishing, 2019) 107–24

Wessel RA, 'General principles in EU common foreign and security policy' in Ziegler KS, Neuvonen PJ, and Moreno-Lax V (eds), *Research Handbook on General Principles in EU Law: Constructing Legal Orders in Europe* (Edward Elgar, 2022) 607–24

Zuleeg M, 'Les répartitions de compétences entre la Communauté et ses Etats membres' in Institut d'études juridiques européennes (ed), *La Communauté et ses Etats membres: Actes du sixième Colloque de l'IEJE sur les Communautés européennes* (Université de Liège, 1973) 23–59

Articles

Amtenbrink F and Appeldoorn JF, 'Is er leven na het Tabaksreclamearrest? De interpretatie van art. 95 EG en de hernieuwde poging van de Commissie inzake de tabaksreclame' (2001) 12 *Tijdschrift voor Europees en economisch recht* 413–20

Andrassy G, 'La souveraineté et la Société des Nations' (1937) 61 *Collected Courses of the Hague Academy of International Law* 375–456

Azoulai L, 'The Court of Justice and the social market economy: The emergence of an ideal and the conditions for its realization' (2008) 45 *Common Market Law Review* 1335–55

Barents R, 'De tabaksrichtlijn in rook opgegaan' (2000) 12 *Nederlands tijdschrift voor Europees recht* 327–31

Barnard C, '*Viking* and *Laval*: An Introduction' (2008) 10 *Cambridge Yearbook of European Legal Studies* 463–92

Barnard C and De Baere G, 'Towards a European Social Union: achievements and possibilities under the current EU constitutional framework' (2014) *Euroforum Seminars on a European Social Union* 1–45

Barrett G, 'Creation's Final Laws: The Impact of the Treaty of Lisbon on the "Final Provisions" of Earlier Treaties' (2008) 27 *Yearbook of European Law* 3–46

Basedow J, 'A Common Contract Law for the Common Market' (1996) 33 *Common Market Law Review* 1169–95

Bebr G, 'The European Coal and Steel Community: a political and legal innovation' (1953) 63 *Yale Law Journal* 1–43

Behrens F, 'Die Umweltpolitik der Europäischen Gemeinschaften und Art. 235 EWGV' (1978) *Deutsches Verwaltungsblatt* 462–69

Berthet A and Devevez B, 'La marque communautaire: intérêt et mode d'emploi' (1997) 15 Legicom 23–31

Bierwagen RW, 'European Communities: Court of Justice Opinion 1/94 Concerning the Competence of the European Community to Conclude International Agreements Concerning Services and the Protection of Intellectual Property – Article 228(6) of the EC Treaty' (1995) 34 *International Legal Materials* 689–717

Boerger A and Rasmussen M, 'Transforming European Law: The Establishment of the Constitutional Discourse from 1950 to 1993' (2014) 10 *European Constitutional Law Review* 199–225

Boerger-De Smedt A, 'Negotiating the Foundations of European Law, 1950–57: The Legal History of the Treaties of Paris and Rome' (2012) 21 *Common European History* 339–56

Bohr S, 'Sanctions by the United Nations Security Council and the European Community' (1993) 4 *European Journal of International Law* 256–68

Bonet B, 'Propriétés intellectuelles. La marque Communautaire: Règlement CEE n°40/94 du Conseil du 20 décembre 1993' (1995) 1 *Revue trimestrielle de droit européen* 31–82

Bossung O, 'A union patent instead of the community patent: Developing the European patent into an EU patent' (2003) 34 *International Review of Intellectual Property and Competition Law* 1–30

Bourgeois JHJ, 'The EC in the WTO and Advisory Opinion 1/94: An Echternach procession' (1995) 32 *Common Market Law Review* 763–87

Bourguignon P, 'De l'entrée en vigueur du traité de Paris à celle des traités de Rome' (1981) 34 *Studia Diplomatica* 293–325

Brok E, 'Die neue Macht des Europäischen Parlaments nach "Lissabon" im Bereich der gemeinsamen Handelspolitik' (2010) 3 *Integration* 209–23

Carstens K, 'Die kleine Revision des Vertrages über die Europäische Gemeinschaft für Kohle und Stahl', (1961) 21 *Zeitschrift für ausländisches öffentliches Recht und Völkerrecht* 1–37

Carter D, 'Equal Pay for Equal Work in the Same Place: Assessing the Revision to the Posted Workers Directive' (2018) 14 *Croatian Yearbook of European Law and Policy* 31–68

Common Market Law Review, 'Editorial comments: Taking (the limits of) competences seriously' (2000) 37 *Common Market Law Review* 1301

Constantinesco V, 'Who's Afraid of Subsidiarity?' (1991) 11 *Yearbook of European Law* 33–39

Craig P, 'The European Union Act 2011: Locks, Limits and Legality' (2011) 48 *Common Market Law Review* 1915–44

Cremona M, 'EC Competence, "Smart Sanctions", and the Kadi Case' (2009) 28 *Yearbook of European Law* 559–92

——, 'Balancing Union and Member State interests: Opinion 1/2008, choice of legal base and the common commercial policy under the Treaty of Lisbon' (2010) 35 *European Law Review* 678–94

Crosby S, 'The single market and the rule of law' (1991) 16 *European Law Review* 451–65

Dashwood A, 'The limits of European Community Powers' (1996) 21 *European Law Review* 113–28

——, 'The Relationship between the Member States and the European Union/European Community' (2004) 41 *Common Market Law Review* 355–81

Davies P, 'The Posted Workers Directive and the EC Treaty' (2002) 31 *Industrial Law Journal* 298–306

Deakin S, 'Regulatory competition after *Laval*' (2008) 10 *Cambridge Yearbook of European Legal Studies* 581–609

De Vos M, 'Free Movement of Workers, Free Movement of Services and the Posted Workers Directive: a Bermuda Triangle for National Labour Standards?' (2006) 7 *ERA Forum* 356–90

Dimopoulos A, 'The Common Commercial Policy after Lisbon: Establishing Parallelism Between Internal and External Economic Relations?' (2008) 4 *Croatian Yearbook of European Law and Policy* 101–31

——, 'The Effects of the Lisbon Treaty on the Principles and Objectives of the Common Commercial Policy' (2010) 15 *European Foreign Affairs Review* 153–70

Easson AJ, 'EEC Directives for the Harmonisation of Laws: Some Problems of Validity, Implementation and Legal Effects' (1981) 1 *Yearbook of European Law* 1–44

Eckes C, 'Controlling the Most Dangerous Branch from Afar: Multilayered Counter-Terrorist Policies and the European Judiciary' (2011) 4 *European Journal of Risk Regulation* 505–22

Egidy S, 'Proportionality and procedure of monetary policy-making' (2021) 19 *International Journal of Constitutional Law* 285–308

Ehlermann C-D, 'Communautés européennes et sanctions internationals – Une réponse à J. Verhoeven' (1984–1985) 1 *Revue Belge de Droit International* 96–112

——, 'The Internal Market following the Single European Act' (1987) 24 *Common Market Law Review* 361–409

Emiliou N, 'Strategic Export Controls, National Security and the Common Commercial Policy' (1996) 1 *European Foreign Affairs Review* 55–78

Engström V, 'How to tame the elusive: Lessons from the Revision of the EU Flexibility Clause' (2010) 7 *International Organizations Law Review* 343–73

Everling U, 'Die allgemeine Ermächtigung der Europäischen Gemeinschaft zur Zielverwirklichung nach Art 235 EWGV' (1976) 11 *Europarecht* 2–26

——, 'The Court of Justice as a Decisionmaking Authority' (1984) 82 *Michigan Law Review* 1294–1310

Evju S, 'Revisiting the Posted Workers Directive: Conflict of Laws and Laws in Contrast' (2010) 12 *Cambridge Yearbook of European Legal Studies* 151–82

Gaja G, 'Opinion 2/94, accession by the Community to the European Convention for the Protection of Human Rights and Fundamental Freedoms' (1996) 33 *Common Market Law Review* 973–89

Gerbet P, 'La genèse du Plan Schuman: des origines à la déclaration du 9 mai 1950' (1956) 3 *Revue française de science politique* 525–53

Giardina A, 'The Rule of Law and Implied Powers in the European Communities' (1975) 1 *Italian Yearbook of International Law* 99–111

Giesen G, 'Posting: Social Protection of Workers vs. Fundamental Freedoms?' (2003) 40 *Common Market Law Review* 143–58

Goormaghtigh J, 'European Coal and Steel Community' (1955) 503 *International Conciliation* 343–408

Grabitz E, 'Die Einheitliche Europäische Akte: Rechtliche Bewertung' (1986) 9 *Integration* 95–100

Guggenheim G, 'Les principes de droit international public' (1952) 80 *Collected Courses of the Hague Academy of International Law* 1–187

Herrmann C, 'Common Commercial Policy after Nice: Sisyphus would have done a better job' (2002) 39 *Common Market Law Review* 7–29

Hervey TK, 'Up in smoke? Community (anti)-tobacco law and policy' (2001) 26 *European Law Review* 101–25

—— '"Adjudicating in the Shadow of the Informal Settlement?": The Court of Justice of the European Union, 'New Governance' and Social Welfare' (2010) 63 *Current Legal Problems* 92–152

Hillion C, 'Tobacco Advertising: If you must, you may' (2001) 60 *The Cambridge Law Journal* 441–92

Jacobs FG, 'The Free Movement of Persons within the EEC' (1977) 30 *Current Legal Problems* 123

Jaeger T, 'The EU Patent: *Cui Bono et Quo Vadit*?' (2010) 47 *Common Market Law Review* 63–115

Jaenicke G, 'Die Europäische Gemeinschaft für Kohle und Stahl (Montan-Union) – Struktur und Funktionen ihrer Organe' (1951) 14 *Zeitschrift für ausländisches öffentliches Recht und Völkerrecht* 727–88

Kaiser JH, 'Grenzen der EG-Zuständigkeit' (1980) 15 *Europarecht* 97–118

Kapteyn PJG, 'The Common Commercial Policy of the European Economic Community: Delimitation of the Community's Power and the European Court of Justice's Opinion of November 11, 1975' (1976) 11 *Texas International Law Journal* 485–504

Kohnstamm M, 'The European Coal and Steel Community' (1956) 90 *Collected Courses of the Hague Academy of International Law* 3–28

Kokott J and Hoffmeister F, 'Opinion 2/94, Accession of the Community to the European Convention for the Protection of Human Rights and Fundamental Freedoms' (1996) 90 *American Journal of International Law* 664–69

Kokott J and Sobotta C, 'The Kadi Case – Constitutional Core Values and International Law – Finding the Balance?' (2012) 23 *European Journal of International Law* 1015–24

Konstadinides T, 'Drawing the line between Circumvention and Gap-Filling: An Exploration of the Conceptual Limits of the Treaty's Flexibility Clause' (2012) 31 *Yearbook of European Law* 227–62

——, 'EU Foreign Policy under the Doctrine of Implied Powers: Codification Drawbacks and Constitutional Limitations' (2014) 39 *European Law Review* 511–30

Korowicz MS, 'Some present aspects of sovereignty in international law' (1961) 102 *Collected Courses of the Hague Academy of International Law* 3–113

Krajewski M, 'External trade law and the Constitution Treaty: Towards a federal and more democratic common commercial policy?' (2005) 44 *Common Market Law Review* 91–127

Kuyper PJ, 'Sanctions against Rhodesia, The EEC and the Implementation of General International Legal Rules' (1975) 12 *Common Market Law Review* 231–44

Lachmann P, 'Some Danish Reflections on the Use of Article 235 of the Rome Treaty' (1981) 18 *Common Market Law Review* 447–61

Lagrange M, 'Les pouvoirs de la Haute Autorité et l'application du Traité de Paris' (1961) 79 Revue du droit public de la science politique 40–58

——, 'L'Europe institutionelle: Réflexions d'un témoin' (1971) 14 *Revue du marché commun* 216–30

Lamblin-Gourdin A-S, 'Politique commerciale commune et protection juridique de l'innovation' (2010) 4 *Revue internationale de droit économique* 441–73

Lang JT, 'The European Community Directive on Bird Conservation' (1982) 22 *Biological Conservation* 11–25

Larik J, 'From speciality to a constitutional sense of purpose: on the changing role of the objectives of the European Union' (2014) 63 *International and Comparative Law Quarterly* 935–62

Lauwaars RH, 'Artikel 235 als Grundlage für die flankierenden Politiken im Rahmen der Wirtschafts und Währungsunion' (1976) 11 *Europarecht* 100–29

Leczykiewicz D, 'Common Commercial Policy: The Expanding Competence of the European Union in the Area of International Trade' (2005) 6 *German Law Journal* 1673–85

Lenaerts K, 'The Kadi Saga and the Rule of Law within the EU' (2014) 67 *SMU Law Review* 707–15

Lenaerts K and van Ypersele P, 'Le principe de subsidiarite et son contexte: étude de l'article 3b du traité CE' (1994) 1–2 *Cahiers de Droit Européen* 3–85

Lenaerts K and De Smijter E, 'The European Community's Treaty-Making Competence' (1996) 16 *Yearbook of European Law* 1–57

Lenaerts K and Desomer M, 'Bricks for a Constitutional Treaty of the European Union: values, objectives and means' (2002) 27 *European Law Review* 377–407

Lesguillons H, 'L'extension des compétences de la Communauté économique européenne par l'article 235 du Traité de Rome' (1974) 20 *Annuaire français de droit international* 886–904

Le Tallec G, 'The Common Commercial Policy of the EEC' (1971) 20 *International and Comparative Law Quarterly* 732–45

Lhernould J-P, 'Directive (EU) 2018/957 of 28 June 2018 amending Directive 96/71/EC concerning the posting of workers in the framework of the provision of services: What will change in 2020?' (2019) 20 *ERA Forum* 249–57

Limpens A, 'Harmonisation des législations dans le cadre du Marché commun' (1967) *Revue internationale de droit comparé* 621–53
Louis J-V, 'Le Fonds européen de coopération monétaire' (1973) 3 *Cahiers de droit européen* 255–97
Lubow A and Schmidt SK, 'A hidden champion? The European Court of Justice as an agenda-setter in the case of posted workers' (2020) *Public Administration* 321–34
Ludwigs M, 'Case C-380/03, Federal Republic of Germany v. European Parliament and Council of the European Union (Tobacco Advertising II)' (2007) 44 *Common Market Law Review* 1159–76
Machnicka AA, 'Territorial Aspects of Community Trademarks – The Single Market's Splendid Sovereignty' (2014) 45 *International Review of Intellectual Property and Competition Law* 915–39
Marenco G, 'Les conditions d'application de l'article 235 du Traité CEE' (1970) 12 *Revue du marché commun* 147–57
Mégret J, 'Le pouvoir de la Communauté économique européenne de conclure des accords internationaux' (1964) 75 *Revue du marché commun* 529–36
Melin P, 'Overview of recent cases before the Court of Justice of the European Union (September 2020–December 2020)' (2021) 23 *European Journal of Social Security* 81–90
Mertens de Wilmars J, 'La contribution des juristes belges à l'intégration européenne' (1981) 34 *Studia Diplomatica* 137–57
Miribung G, 'Changes happen slowly – some comments on geographical indications between the Geneva Act and Regulation 2019/1753' (2020) 1 *European Food and Feed Law Review* 25–34
Monaco R, 'Comparaison et rapprochement des législations dans le Marché commun européen' (1960) 16 *Revue internationale de droit comparé* 61–74
Monnet J, 'A ferment of change' (1963) 1 *Journal of Common Market Studies* 203–11
Mortelmans K, 'The Common Market, the Internal Market, and the Single Market: What's in a Market?' (1998) 35 *Common Market Law Review* 101–36
Mortelmans KJM and Van Ooik RH, 'Het Europese verbod op tabaksreclame: verbetering van de interne markt of bescherming van de volksgezondheid?' (2001) 50 *Ars Aequi* 114–30
Murphy DT, 'The European Union's Common Foreign and Security Policy: It is Not Far From Maastricht to Amsterdam' (1998) 31 *Vanderbilt Journal of Transnational Law* 871–913
Neuwahl NA, 'Joint Participation in International Treaties and the Exercise of Power by the EEC and its Member States: Mixed Agreements' (1991) 28 *Common Market Law Review* 717–40
Nicolaysen G, 'Zur Theorie von den implied powers in den europäischen Gemeinschaften' (1966) 1 *Europarecht* 129–42
Oliver CT, 'Historical development of international law: contemporary problems of treaty law' (1955) 88 *Collected Courses of the Hague Academy of International Law* 419–504
Ophüls CF, 'Das Wirtschaftsrecht des Schumanplans' (1951) 4 *Neue juristische Wochenschrift* 381–84
Peers S, 'Case C-268/94, Portugal v. Council, (development policy)' (1998) 35 *Common Market Law Review* 539–555
——, 'The Constitutional Implications of the EU Patent' (2011) 7 *European Constitutional Law Review* 229–66
Pescatore P, 'Les relations extérieures des communautés européennes: Contribution à la doctrine de la Personnalité des organisations internationales' (1961) 103 *Collected Courses of the Hague Academy of International Law* 3–328
——, 'Les travaux du "groupe juridique" dans la négociation des traités de Rome' (1981) 34 *Studia Diplomatica* 159–78
——, 'Some Critical Remarks on the Single European Act' (1987) 24 *Common Market Law Review* 9–18
——, 'Opinion 1/94 on Conclusion of the WTO Agreement: Is There an Escape from a Programmed Disaster?' (1999) 36 *Common Market Law Review* 387–405
Reuter P, 'Le Plan Schuman' (1953) 81 *Collected Courses of the Hague Academy of International Law* 521–626
——, 'Juridical and Institutional Aspects of the European Regional Communities' (1961) 26 *Law and Contemporary Problems* 381–99
Riphagen W, 'The case law of the European Coal and Steel Community Court of Justice' (1955) 2 *Nederlands Tijdschrift voor Internationaal Recht* 384–408

Rittberger B, 'Which institutions for post-war Europe? Explaining the institutional design of Europe's first community' (2001) 8 *Journal of European Public Policy* 673–708
Rodière P, 'Le droit européen du détachement de travailleurs: fraude ou inapplicabilité?' (2016) 7/8 *Droit Social* 598–608
Roudard I, 'The proposed community design regulation and directive' (1999) 10 *Computer Law & Security Review* 26–31
Schammo P, 'Institutional Change in the Banking Union: The Case of the Single Supervisory Mechanism' (2021) 40 *Yearbook of European Law* 265–309
Schütze R, 'Organized Change towards an "Ever Closer Union": Article 308 EC and the Limits to the Community's Legislative Competence' (2003) 22 *Yearbook of European Law* 79–115
Schwarze J, 'Le principe de subsidiarité dans la perspective du droit constitutionnel allemand' (1993) 370 *Revue du marché commun* 615–19
Segnana O, 'Le contentieux de la base juridique. A propos de l'annulation par la Cour de justice des CE de la directive relative à la publicité pour le tabac' (2001) 75 *Journal des Tribunaux: droit européen* 9–15
Seville C, 'Developments (and Non-Developments) in the Harmonisation of EU Intellectual Property Law' (2009) 11 *Cambridge Yearbook of European Legal Studies* 87–121
Seyerstedt F, 'United Nations Forces – Some Legal Problems' (1961) 37 *British Yearbook of International Law* 351–475
Taylor G, 'Germany: The subsidiarity principle' (2006) 4 *International Journal of Constitutional Law* 115–30
Teasdale AL, 'Subsidiarity in post-Maastricht Europe' (1993) 64 *The Political Quarterly* 187–97
Teitgen PH and Mégret J, 'La fumée de la cigarette dans la "zone grise" des compétences de la C.E.E' (1981) 17 *Revue trimestrielle de droit européen* 68–81
Tizzano A, 'Quelques Observations sur le Développement des Compétences Communautaires' (1998) 48 *Pouvoirs* 81–94
Touscoz J, 'L'action des communautés européennes en matière d'environnement' (1973) 9 *Revue trimestrielle de droit européen* 3–45
Tranholm Mikkelsen J, 'Neo-functionalism: Obstinate or Obsolete? A Reappraisal in the Light of the New Dynamism of the EC' (1991) 20 *Journal of International Studies* 1–22
Tridimas T, 'Terrorism and the ECJ: Empowerment and Democracy in the EC Legal Order' (2009) 34 European Law Review 103–26
Tridimas T and Eeckhout P, 'The External Competence of the Community and the Case-Law of the Court of Justice: Principle versus Pragmatism' (1994) 14 *Yearbook of European Law* 143–77
Vandermeersch D, 'The Single European Act and the Environmental Policy of the European Economic Community' (1987) 12 *European Law Review* 407–29
Van Elsuwege P, 'EU External Action after the Collapse of the Pillar Structure: In search of a New Balance between Delimitation and Consistency' (2010) 47 *Common Market Law Review* 987–1019
van Empel M, 'The EEC Trade Mark Memorandum' (1978) 15 *Common Market Law Review* 57–69
Van Kersbergen K and Verbeek B, 'The Politics of Subsidiarity in the European Union' (1994) 32 *Journal of Common Market Studies* 215–36
Van Reepinghen B, 'Le règlement (CE) n° 40/94 sur la marque communautaire' (1995) 16 *Journal des Tribunaux: droit européen* 25–30
Van Tichelen J, 'Souvenirs de la négociation du Traité de Rome' (1981) 34 *Studia Diplomatica* 327–43
Van Zeben J, 'Subsidiarity in European Environmental Law: a competence allocation approach' (2014) 38 *Harvard Environmental Law Review* 415–64
Verellen T, 'The distortion theory in EU treaty-making: Commission v. Council (Geneva Act)' (2022) 60 *Common Market Law Review* 1705–20
Vernon R, 'The Schuman Plan: Sovereign Powers of the European Coal and Steel Commmunity' (1953) 47 *American Journal of International Law* 183–202
Vogelaar TW, 'The Approximation of the Laws of Member States under the Treaty of Rome' (1975) 12 *Common Market Law Review* 211–30

von Bogdandy A and Bast J, 'The European Union's vertical order of competences: the current law and proposals for its reform' (2002) 39 *Common Market Law Review* 227–68
Vos C, 'De sociale aspecten van de Europese Kolen- en Staalgemeenschap als juridisch vraagstuk' (1957) 4 *Nederlands Tijdschrift voor Internationaal Recht* 37–68
Weatherill S, 'Competence Creep and Competence Control' (2004) 23 *Yearbook of European Law* 1–55
——, 'The Limits of Legislative Harmonization Ten Years after Tobacco Advertising: How the Court's Case Law has become a "Drafting Guide"' (2011) 12 *German Law Journal* 827–64
Wessel RA, 'Resisting Legal Facts: Are CFSP Norms as Soft as They Seem?' (2015) 20 *European Foreign Affairs Review* 123–45
Westhof J, 'L'Union de l'Europe Occidentale avant et après l'élargissement des Communautés Européennes' (1975) 23 *Annuaire Européen* 94–123
Wils WPJ, 'The Birds Directive 15 Years Later: A Survey of the Case Law and a Comparison with the Habitats Directive' (1994) 6 *Journal of Environmental Law* 219–42
Wyatt D, 'The Growing Competence of the European Community' (2005) 16 *European Business Law Review* 483–88
Zahn R, 'Revision of the Posted Workers Directive: A Europeanisation Perspective' (2017) 19 *Cambridge Yearbook of European Legal Studies* 187–210

Doctoral Theses and Papers

Bering Liisberg J, 'The EU Constitutional Treaty and its distinction between legislative and non-legislative acts – Oranges into apples?' (2006) Jean Monnet Working Paper 01/06
Blair A, 'The UK & the Negotiation of the Maastricht Treaty, 1990–1991' (Doctoral thesis, University of Leicester 1997)
Constantinesco V, 'Compétences et pouvoirs dans les communautés européennes: Contribution à l'étude de la nature juridique des Communautés' (Doctoral thesis, Université de Nancy 1974)
Cramp S, *Bird Conservation in Europe* (HMSO 1977)
Gosalbo Bono G, 'The organisation of the external relations of the European Union in the Treaty of Lisbon' in Koutrakos P (ed), *The European Union's external relations a year after Lisbon* (CLEER Working Papers 2011/3) 13–38
Grzimek B, European Commission study entrusted to the Zoologischen Gesellschaft von 1858 (1974)
Peers S and Statewatch, 'EU Constitutional annotation no 2 – Part III, Title V: EU External Policies' (2003)
Weiler JHH, 'Supranational Law and the Supranational System: Legal Structure and Political Process in the European Community' (Doctoral thesis, European University Institute 1982)
WIPO, 'Understanding Industrial Property' (2015)

Blog Posts and Web Articles

Chamon M, 'Commission challenges authorisation granted to Member States to exercise EU exclusive competences' (EU Law Live, 2020), www.eulawlive.com/analysis-commission-challenges-authorisation-granted-to-member-states-to-exercise-eu-exclusive-competences-by-merijn-chamon
——, 'Reinforcing the Community Method – the Commission as a veto player in EU external relations' (EU Law Live, 2022), www.eulawlive.com/op-ed-reinforcing-the-community-method-the-commission-as-a-veto-player-in-eu-external-relations-by-merijn-chamon
Eleftheriadis P, 'Germany's Failing Court' (Verfassungsblog, 2020), verfassungsblog.de/germanys-failing-court/

Khan M, 'Posted Worker Problems' (*Financial Times*, 24 October 2017), www.ft.com/content/6ed52842-b89b-11e7-9bfb-4a9c83ffa852

Kottmann M and Sangi R, 'Gut gemeint, nicht gut gemacht' (Verfassungsblog, 2020), verfassungsblog.de/gut-gemeint-nicht-gut-gemacht/

Maduro M, 'Some Preliminary Remarks on the PSPP Decision of the German Constitutional Court' (Verfassungsblog, 2020), verfassungsblog.de/some-preliminary-remarks-on-the-pspp-decision-of-the-german-constitutional-court/

Sarmiento D and Weiler JHH, 'The EU Judiciary After Weiss: Proposing A New Mixed Chamber of the Court of Justice' (Verfassungsblog, 2020), verfassungsblog.de/the-eu-judiciary-after-weiss/

Szép V and Schaupp L, *'Energy Sanctions Reloaded: Navigating the Trade-Sanctions Divide in the EU's Proposed Gas Ban' (Verfassungsblog 2025)*, verfassungsblog.de/energy-sanctions-russia-eu

'EU plans ban on new Russian gas contracts using trade law' (*Financial Times*, 16 June 2025), www.ft.com/content/8b005c13-2088-47cd-aa47-9163e36efa4a

'Going Posted' (*The Economist*, 7 July 2016), www.economist.com/europe/2016/07/07/going-posted

'Hungary and Slovakia withhold support as EU proposes ban on Russian gas and oil by 2027' (EU Insider, 16 June 2025), www.euinsider.eu/news/hungary-and-slovakia-withhold-support-as-eu-proposes-ban-on-russian-gas-and-oil-by-2027

'Launch of works for the building of a European village in Spiesen' (CVCE), www.cvce.eu/en/obj/launch_of_works_for_the_building_of_a_european_village_in_spiesen_1952-en-ab635d8c-ec6e-4028-9a61-f3f03f91a862.html

'Minimum Wage Statistics' (Eurostat), ec.europa.eu/eurostat/statistics-explained/index.php?title=Minimum_wage_statistics#Minimum_wages_expressed_in_purchasing_power_standards

'What is the difference between a geographical indication and an appellation of origin?' (WIPO), www.wipo.int/geo_indications/en/faq_geographicalindications.html

INDEX

www.ingramcontent.com/pod-product-compliance
Ingram Content Group UK Ltd.
Pitfield, Milton Keynes, MK11 3LW, UK
UKHW020804290926
15470UKWH00003B/943

9 781509 990900